MY GREAT, WIDE, BEAUTIFUL WORLD

THE MACMILLAN COMPANY
NEW YORK · BOSTON · CHICAGO · DALLAS
ATLANTA · SAN FRANCISCO

MACMILLAN & CO., Limited
LONDON · BOMBAY · CALCUTTA
MELBOURNE

THE MACMILLAN COMPANY
OF CANADA, Limited
TORONTO

My Great Wide
Beautiful
WORLD

BY JUANITA HARRISON

Arranged and Prefaced by
MILDRED MORRIS

NEW YORK
THE MACMILLAN COMPANY
1936

SET UP BY BROWN BROTHERS LINOTYPERS
PRINTED IN THE UNITED STATES OF AMERICA
BY THE FERRIS PRINTING COMPANY

TO

MRS. MYRA K. DICKINSON

*Your great kindness to me have made my
traveling much happier if You hadnt been
interested in me I never would have tryed
to explain my trips also your True and
Kindness encourage me and made me more
anxious to tell you the way I spent my time.*

JUANITA HARRISON

'Great, wide, beautiful, wonderful World,
With the wonderful water round you curled,
And the wonderful grass upon your breast,
World, you are beautifully dressed.

"You friendly Earth, how far do you go,
With the wheat-fields that nod and the rivers that
    flow,
With cities and gardens and cliffs and isles,
And the people upon you for thousands of miles?"

W. B. RANDS.

PREFACE

JUANITA HARRISON is an American colored woman who undertook, at the age of thirty-six, to work her way around the world.

Born in Mississippi, she had a few months of schooling before she was ten. Then began an endless round of cooking, washing and ironing in an overburdened household,—labour that might have daunted a grown person.

But the child at work, clothed in a woman's cast-off apparel, stiff basque bodice, long skirt and laced bicycle boots, lived with a bright vision of templed cities in foreign lands which she had seen pictured in the stray pages of a magazine.

Out of the sordid life that colored her early years she distilled a resolution: "I will sail far away to strange places. Around me no one has the life I want. No one is there for me to copy, not even the rich ladies I work for. I have to cut my life out for myself and it won't be like anyone else."

Juanita began her travels when she was sixteen, moving as she found employment, until her journeying extended to Canada and Cuba. Wherever it was possible she attended classes at the Y.W.C.A. or night school and when she had become an accomplished lady's maid, she ambitiously took up the study of Spanish and French.

Because of her yearning to see more of the world, Juanita never remained long in one place, though her employers invariably became her friends and raised her salary in the vain hope of keeping so excellent a servant.

A large part of her weekly earnings she usually managed to save and she had accumulated eight hundred dollars in a bank at Denver where she happened to be working. Soon she felt she would be able to realize her childhood dream. But the bank failed and Juanita lost her small fortune.

Then a happy turning point was reached. She had sufficient money to buy a railroad ticket to California and went to Los Angeles where she secured a position in the home of Mr. and Mrs. George W. Dickinson. How kind these new employers were to her is best told in Juanita's own words: "Mr. and Mrs. Dickinson are like the Picture of Hope sitting up in the world in Their true hearted kindness never useing If." A real estate broker, Mr. Dickinson invested Juanita's monthly salary in mortgages, until he had established an income of about two hundred dollars a year. With this slender security in reserve, Juanita started out in June 1927 to work her way around the world. From that time until 1935 her passports show that she lived in twenty-two different countries.

Juanita spells by ear and knows no rules of grammar,

her writing is artless and vivid, like that of some happy pilgrim of Chaucer. No traveller has given clearer, truer pictures of the people who make up the nations she visited. They are mainly cheerful pictures; her writing sparkles with words that express keen interest and joy; often she reports having spent a "gelourous" day. She is sorry for the tourists who flit hurriedly over the beaten paths.

People, churches, weddings, funerals, bullfights, "circuises," family life, food—above all, good food—caught her attention. Of one notable day of worship and fine music, she wrote, "what topped it off was the clean kitchen on wheels that sold hot fried potatoes!" She showed a genius for making friends. For her, there existed no barriers of class or race; she was interested in all living creatures—men, women, children, cows, dogs, elephants. She believed that every one would like her, and was not disappointed.

Frequently she adopted the garb of the country she visited and was accepted as a native. Her slight form, fresh olive complexion, long hair braided about her head, made her appear younger than her years.

Her first position in France was with my mother, Mrs. Felix Morris, who suggested to Juanita that her written experiences might interest a larger public than her immediate friends. It was then decided that I should arrange her Odyssey for publication when she had travelled more extensively.

In April 1935, having accomplished her ten-year plan to circle the world, she settled down on the Island of Hawaii where central heating is unnecessary and a minimum of work gains abundant food.

Juanita Harrison's story in condensed version first appeared in the 1935 Autumn numbers of the *Atlantic Monthly* and from that fortunate debut she now fully chronicles her travels in the pages of this book.

MILDRED MORRIS.

MY GREAT, WIDE, BEAUTIFUL WORLD

New York City. June 25, 1927.
North German Lloyd Pier.
Hoboken, N. J.

A beautiful June Morning. I arrived at 9 A.M. with my two suit cases the larger one with 2 blue dresses 2 white dresses and one black aprons caps and references. The smaller one with my dress up cloths. and 2 jars of sour cucumber pikles which is so good to keep from being sea sick. Our cabins looked good. I always want a upper berth I dont want anybody making it down on me. I went to the 1st and 2nd Class. Their towels looked more linnen so I took two, the soap smelt sweeter so I took 2 cakes. I went up to the writing room and the paper was the kind you love to touch so I took much and tuked it away in my bunk. We sailed at 1.30 P.M. When I got up on deck it were crouded passangers and friends a German band were playing and all were singing sweet sounding German songs. And the money was flying like rice at a wedding then the Kissing and the goodbyes and the raining of tears. and I was happy that I had no one to cry for me.

June 27th.
On boad S.S. Serra Ventana
Sateroom 657.

The beds are quite hard and so many pilla you feel your sitting up when you are lying down. My cabin mate are a dear German Lady. She worked hard with her Son in Chicago they had a resturant Now she is so happy to be going back. Every morning we are waken by a sweet cornet solo then as each wake up they begin to sing and in a few minutes we have a full chours. Today have been a bit rough. I prize the pikles.

June 28.

There are many lovely goodlooking young men and Ladies on boad
My table mate read the mune for me the food is good. Our waiter is a handsom Boy about 18. this is his first trip so being the green horn we must wait. Herr Paul Huttrig are giving me german lessons I like him because he speak such broken English He is all for America his head reach to my sholders and sure he felt like a very big man when he get his new suit to ware home and choosed by his feeling other than his size because its so much to large for him even his collars is to large in the neck. I am to let him know when I visit there this summer.

July 2.

In the Tourist Third are a Young Student Doctor from a town call "a Way cross Georgia" Ga. and He keep very much to himself. I ask him why and he say he do not care to mix with emigrants. I said these are respectful bisness people going home to visit. He had never been away from his little Georgia Town and read about emigrants at Ellis Island. he has no passport the poor kid is about 19 his greatest ambison is to study medician in Edinburg and he just took a chance.

July 3rd.

I went to Devine Service in the 1st class a Gentleman Preached in English Then another in German I enjoyed that best tho I didnt understand. We had a wounderful dinner each had a stuffed gosslin I dont know if it is spelled right. but it is the geese's babies Our Pleasant but not very hansom Captain name is Gosslin.

July 4th.

Today being the 4th everyone seem to turn American the table all in stars and strips Flags. We came ashore at Plymouth at 8 P.M. It were cold and foggy. A bright fire was burning in the station but in a few minutes they put the gas out so it looked dreary the fire was only to greet us. The taxes to walk out in Plymouth was one dollar so I stayed around the station. Well my little Georgia Doctor did not have a penny They let him come in without a passport and gave him 10 days to get it as he was a studient. He was in the Station when the train left but the Y.M.C.A. will look after him. It was cold riding to London.

London, England.
July 5th.

Arrived at 1 A.M. an ugly woman was cleaning the waiting room and a Pretty Irish girl was expecting her sister on the 3 A.M. train. she taught me how to count the English money. Then she stretched out on one of the comfortable leather couches and I on another. It was a plesant night. When her sister arrive we said goodby she telling me how to go to the Y.W.C.A. Then a nice prim old Lady came in and went out leaving on the table a box I expected to find some food and nicely wrapped in paper was 3 large boiled beef sandwichs, well the cow must have been a capon it was so tender. I went to the Lunch room and had what the English call coffee but what the coffee missed the sandwichs made up also I saved one shilling on my breakfast. The first look at London I liked it. It was a beautiful morning the maids in their neat blue dresses and white caps was cleaning the brass whiting the door steps and scrubing the sidewalks. I promised myself when I Looked For a job not to get in a house with such work but instead a appartment. I went to the Y.W.C.A. at Newton Road Bayswater They were filled up with Students so sent me to several address I enjoyed visiting at each house I had a desire to stay in a Manison so liked best Princess Manison at Rochester Court. I got a nice room with meals 20 shillings I sat at a table of six. one dish of each thing served for two. A young, blond dancer and I shared and I let her have most of it she looked so hungry and I would be on a job where I would have plenty. My room was plesant but on the wall hung two pictures of pretty women weeping at a grave and when I turn off the light

I could not go to sleep so I take them down at night and put them in the closet and hang them back each morning.

July 8th.

Well here are so many jobs you just walk to a corner cards are tacked on the wall of a newspaper place you copy the address and go for an interview. I visited many I just went to see the house and to learn what they paid. I got a job with a South American Lady because I had worked in Cuba and learned Spanish. She has 2 boys in school and a pretty daughter in a convent. They are from Bolivia La Senora is lonely for her country so cry very much. The appartment is nicely furnished but this being my first job since I left the swell apt on West End Ave N. Y. I am disgusted because ever time they want a bath I must make a fire in a little chocked up heater. the Boys go to the Publice bath house La Senora go without I am bathing in a zink bucket.

August 7th.

What a wonderful city London are. I gave up my Spanish place so to take in some cheap rate trips. I had a hard time getting away from La Senora. The traffice are just handled wounderful here you never wait very long. I dont think they does any watering for the grass and flowers it rain so often. I went to "White City" to the Gray Hound race. Visiting the neighborhood first I came to a beautiful tea shack I saw inside a fat Lady and was sure she knew about the races. So as one Kindness deserve another I went in and orded a pot of tea. Never before or after have tea tasted so good it may have been her plesant face. She advised me to play only a shilling and wanted to take me around. but I made an excuse. I never go with a Lady because you must pay her carfare they like to stop and have a cup of tca another stop in the Publice House for a glass of beer and another at the W.C. and the time have pass and your little change. you havent seen a thing when you find the Places alone you enjoy it better. Her Husband was Scotch and She told me about the round trip excursion to Scotland and Saturday would be the last day. I picked a place at the race track in the midst of a bunch of fans. A great croud were out they race with the electricity lights and it were very exciting. I felt happy over the 75 cents I lost I'll be sure to never play again it is a very good sport and one that man cannot cheat you like in horse racing.

August 8th.

I went to Stratford-on-Avon yesterday with a motor party. I crossed the bridge to get a view of the Church just then a heavy shower came. I stood on a poch and talked with a plesent little man with bad teeth. He told me many lovely things about Stratford-on-Avon. He had never been to London. I did not go round the main road to Ann Hawthways Home but cut accrossed the

field like Ann used to do. I went to the Station to en-
quire about the Excursion rates to Scotland and the last
leave London the 13th. I can go to Irland first on their
last excursion and get back at night then leave next
morning at 8.50 A.M. for Scotland so thanks for going to
the beautiful tea shack.

August 10th.
Cork Irland

We arrived at Fishgard Harbour before dark from
the smell of Fish it is true to its name. the boat were
packed soon it seem to me it was going as fast as lightning and a noisy sound just like a churn. A Father was
calling to his son Mick am I dying and Mick answer in
the same voice Yes. The deck was like a skating rink.
I made to a pile of ropes and sitting bent over a fat
woman came and sat on my back I tried to twist her off
but she just sat groaning. anyway she kept me warm
most of the sailors were also sick. the saying limber as
a dish rag sure fitted in well for there were nothing else
on boad. Arrived at Rosslare Harbour island at 4 A.M.
all looking weak.

At 6 A.M. we left for Cork in the compartment were one
man and 3 plesent Ladies the youngest had the luck to
sit on the side with him. I sat tryangle like in the corner
to get a close up on the four and at the same time the
green fields, a turf used to divide each land. The
Gentleman say he never want to go to London again no

one speak so I said I never want to come to Irland again. after that auful trip. then we all brighten up. He began making love to the Miss by his side. Then he said to me he couldnt see what joy I got out of always traveling by myself I said I havent said I was always by myself. Look at you now you are traveling and not by yourself. We had a most plesant trip to Cork. He offred to take me about to the interesting places. I know I could do better alone so I thank him but he told me all about the city.

In my walking I found Pattys market like the low East side in New York only smaller. There was 2 sweet faced little onion girls selling a big bunch of onions. Being quite empty I looked up a place to eat and found "Jacksons Dinning Room" It had just what I wanted the Waitress was an old Girl but a quick steper. at the long table sat several most men. We had fresh boiled hog head and white Cabbag. now no body can cook cabbage to beat the Irish of Cork not even the American Colored Southerners. the old girl was shocked when I had finished up the enourmous dinner and ask her to bring another just like it. then a dish of rice pudding and I felt just right. The Castle are lovely in Cork. I am leaving tomorrow.

In route to Edinburgh.

I left London at 8.30 A.M. I always go early on these excursion trips so I get a good seat in the compartment.

There were two pretty English girls very gay over being off on a holiday their 2 suite cases looked new but they had a funny basket like trunk a man was putting Stickers on the bags I looked up at their basket it looked so dull and the tag so bright I said stick it on that one it will give it a more cheerful look They say Oh yes that poor old basket have been up in the attic.

Then we became a joly three. They say are you going to have a holiday I said yes for about 2 or 3 years. When I told them I was from Los Angeles they thought it just wonderful. They had a bottle of violet toilet water and every second they were washing their hands and faces and powding and each time gave me some. A Bride and Groom got on, she was about 40 and he about 45 right away after the train started he went to sleep. The woman felt very bad to have 6 eyes glood on them, she tried to pull his arm and keep him awake. I wouldn't dare to look at the girls so enjoyed the beautiful English scenery.

108 George Street
Edinburgh, Scotland

The Y.W.C.A. didn't have a room so they sent me to Miss Penn's. her house is 200 years old the only way you can tell that it is old is by the cement stairs steps worn off in the middle. I look out of my window across Princes Garden up to the Grand Old Edinburg Castle. Miss Penn is a short fat Kind Lady She is a dressmaker

and like her dresses the style are betwix and betwine.
This is a Grand Old City it have some wonderful looking old street lanes and archways I just love to slop
around in the rain. They can beat the Londoners cooking.

I had a delightful motor tour to the Trossacks as they
are call We made a stop at a little village Luss I
wanted to have lunch with some of the villagers so went
up a pretty lane and in the front of a cottage all covered with roses were a sign Tea So I went in and a very
fat Scotch Lady got me the nicest dinner a third for
what my friends payed at the Hotel. We stoped again
for tea and I was out looking for a place when I came
around a alley way and saw an auful fight between three
men and a woman over a bag pipe. It was a whole family affair. The two younger men started it and when
they got through the bag pipe wasn't anything but
strings. The wife tried to seperate them and her husband beat her the old father who was sleeping on the
grass got up to help but the son in law nocked the old
man on the head and streched him out like someone had
nocked a cow out. The little boy all dressed up in one
of these Scottish suits was crying he had a very big head
and a cap stuck on it and the little girl was screaming.
I wanted to help the little girl because she loved her
father—she would run up and tried to help him. They
was speaking Scottish and I couldn't understand. Then
the policeman came. I was very mad with the husband

because he beat his wife so I began to interfer. I said
to the policeman That man is a very bad man. When I
got back to the car they had been looking all over for
me. The lady that sat next me were from Fresno Calif.
It wasnt any joy to me though because she had on a little
thin black satin coat I had my heavy new coat that I paid
7 pounds 6d for in London and my rain coat for my
nees. but she looked so cold I had to let her have mine
she were born here but knew less than I did about Scotland I left New York with a ten dollar hat on my head
but it rained so often in London and Scotland that it
have taken all the life out of it I thought of buying
another but for that money I can go into so many grand
old castles and manisons that I can still see beauty in it.
Miss Penn is a very prim Miss and I have notice her
looking at my hat. she said did You make that hat. So
then when I left 3 days early she gave the money back to
me and I am sure its ment for me to buy a hat.

Sept. 18, London
Maida Vale

I spent a week looking for a place and enjoyed it as
much as any of my trips. I knew the English servants
very well I worked in a big house in Iowa with them
and they were selfish and jelious I have often hear it
that they were the heardest of all servants to get along
with I also knew the English ladies I worked for one in
Canada and one in Cuba. They have their servant prob-

lems here. You can always get a place as maid to a
Lady but here are always one or two or more pets to
look after. I was trying to decide if I wanted to be a
maid to a Lady and nurse to her three cats. or a general
maid to a young Japanese couple with 2 children when
I passed an agent and got a place if I had it made to
order it would have been just like this. I am with the
cutest little young widow her husband were a noted flyer
and were kill in the war six months before her little boy
were born. She is an Italian Countess she is my idea of
a real Countess. I look after her beautiful cloths and
she knows how to wear them. I keep the apt. clean and
take care of Polar and Negri being the clevest little
monkey and Negri a Black Chinese lap dog. she is just
like a little Chinese Lady. her little boy is at boading
school. Madam is quite a Flyer herself she is a friend
of all the best Family in London she cannot forget her
husband and never miss going to his grave one day in
each week. Two very fine Gentlemen want to marrie
Her but I dont think she will take either of them.
The foreign people are the best to work for. I am not
getting very much money but I am having an auful lot
of experence. I am glad I didn't buy a winter dress because Madam gave me a lovely one so that means 2 or 3
pounds saved. I am getting quite English you never say
excuse me instead you say I am sorry. The English men
are great lovers and very fond of kissing I think that
they would make poor husbands. so far I have man-

agered to excuse myself before dark altho they are very nice I wouldn't like to be kissed as most of them women and men has bad teeth. It must be from smoking and drinking so much tea and eating sweets.

October 5th.

Today Madam told me she will give me Two pounds more than she paid the other maid because she like me so much better. all of her friends seem to be Ladys and Lords and I like all that I have seen yet. one very Rich Gentleman are so much in love with Her but she only let him come when she have quite a bit of shopping to do and dont want to drive her sporty little car herself. I like him because he ofen gives me a 2 shilling piece at the door.

Nov. 17th.

I am glad I can see even beauty in the fog. A very dear friend of Madam is a member of Parliment and so I went to the House of Commons and heard two debats. Its the warmest house I have found yet in London. I dont know how they can see to read it was so dark in there I went to sleep. We have a Pattys market just five blocks from here where I do most all the shopping all except the fruit and fowels.

The 4 most populer things in London are Fogs bad weather bad colds and chilblains the most rarest thing is the Sun. Madam leaves for Paris in a few days to attend a wedding she will take me with her if I promise

to come back I havent decided yet wether I want to go
under those conditions. Two Ladies ring me up when
they hear Madam are going and said when I had finished with Mme. to come and see them so that means
I can get a place easyer here than in the U.S. I am
rejoicing because I dont expect to ever spend another
winter here. We are having a few sunny hours each
day but cold I think I will go to France and work.

Nov. 27th.
Boulogne-Sur-Mer

It was a rough crossing. When I left London my Lady
knew I was not coming back I thanked her for all her
kindness. Madam left the same day by Newhaven I
promise to be in Paris by Monday to help her to dress
for the Wedding. I went about Boulogne as though
I had lived here all my life and I looked so much like
one of the Fishman wives even the coustom offices refused to look through my baggage. most of the women
have long hair and dress it in two brads as I do all I
laked was ear rings I had 2 pairs in my case Mme.
gave me. Well I put on my correll ear rings and was a
perfect Boulognenesser and for my French I can put
out the words but its the Frenchmans hard luck to get
them round in the proper place. I hope they enjoy it as
much as I do.
This place are famous for bologna sausage so my first
shopping was a penny and half worth a third of a penny

loaf. and 2 large sauces of fresh whipped cream that was my first meal on the French soil and it was joly good. This are like a Cuban Town norrow streets and the women ware black shalws over their heads and the sea front are very much like Havana. I am certonly enjoying the labor and money I put in French lessons the year I took in Cuba and the winter in Los Angeles. I can do some good laying out if I hafter.

Paris, France,
Dec. 4th, 1927

The London Y. had written me a nice letter for the Y.W.C.A. in Paris so I had a very plesant welcome. I went and found a room just as nice and much cheaper than the ones they knew. steam heat good bed clean as a pin and the Lady so nice for 77 francs. Well I know French in a Jewish way and can always Jew them down. then I have a dress and Hat I arrive in and they never trouble taking my suite case or offering a taxi after one look at me I am sure they say she cant afford it. Its just what I want. I get up early and do my shopping. I bring in a long loaf a bottle of milk butter and many little things. all that help me to speak French.
I have been in every corner of the city and all by foot. The men are like the Spanish men great love makers lucky for me the 3 French teachers I had 2 old maids and the other marrid didnt teach me one word of how to flirt anyway I know how to get rid of them I said

something to them and did not know the meaning but it served well. A young Italian boy at the market speak English so I ask him all the silly things I told him what I said to the men. He said it ment Please walk away. Paris is such a beautiful city and clean. I think I love London the best there are something so grand about London. I have called to see Madam at the Hotel but she was out.

Dec. 10th.

I put an add in the New York Herald Paris and received so many answers from French American Spanish and English and they were all good places. This place was just what I wanted. A very nice Lady of New York, Mrs. Morris with Two Grown Daughters. one of the Daughters is a writer and the mother said my travellers should be put into a Book. I told her I would come back after my trip to India and work for nothing if Miss Mildred, the Daughter would help me. I was looking for a place with lots of Francs lots of time off and a little work and I have that Having so much time I de-cided to take German as I may go there this summer. I wanted to know something about the Paris Artists life that I had heard of so went in the naborhood of Ecole des Beau Arts and found the nicest little German artist 24 years. He is a good teacher and I went sevral times to have lessons in his little attic room. He get auful peaved if I haven studied. He knows English quite well have studied in London. Now I have Him to come and give me lessons to my nice big room. He has not charged me anything yet. I have 2 lessons a week.

Dec. 15th.

I get a lot of joy from marketing as each country are diffrent. You go to market with an all over black satin apron and a black oil skin bag. they have delicous chickens ducks and squabs fresh every day. When I go to the open market there is a great pile of cauliflouer greens throwed out I use them to cook with pork and then put a little olive oil and vengar on them the women stand watching me pick over the piles with hands on their hips trying to study what I could do with those big leaves.

The Paris policeman are adorble although they are polite and keep order they can just be human so quick always ready for a nice smile I look at them a second time and they answer with a quick look but they cant foller you so I fool along with them.

I made Mrs. Morris laugh today when I came back from visiting the Cemtery Pere Chase. The caretaker there began smiling at me. I had my Guide book he said Oh would you like to see the monments then I will walk with you. He begain to kiss my hand. there were two women near by weeping he said I have kissed your hand wont you let me kiss you. Oh, I said Here then I broke away from him and ran around the Pyrmid, he was blowing and puffing after me the two women stoped crying and watch us I ran ahead of him and got away. So I said to my Madam Chase is a good name for that Cemtery.

Dec. 28th.

Their Xmas are quite dull to ours you see so few trees. I had some nice presents and we had a perfect jucy tender and brown real American turkey. Going to market I stoped in a Grand old Church to Pray and found the alter thick with cooks their black bags on their arms. I went to the Moulin Rouge at night what the Dancers ware would make Eve with Her Fig leaf feel that she had on a trunk of cloths. I bought a standing place 7 and a half francs you can see the audince better and be on the floor where the cafe and musice are. But the Gayest spot but gay is to dull a name for it is Boulevard Rochechouart where it is never night, and one step you feel in Russia next in Turkey. I read up many good Books on Paris and Visit all the Places. Every book on France are full of Blood and yet they are the most Gayest of all nations they know how to forget. Every Dec. 28 the calender say I am another year old but 1927 found me the same age I was 15 years ago and I expect to be that same age at least 10 years more anyway.

Jan. 15th.

I went up the Seine by tram to Suresnes and was walking around when I saw a arrow pointing toward the

American Cemtery. it was a long climb away up there and so beautiful looking down on Paris the Hundered of White Crosses and a large beautiful American Flag. If only each Boys family could see where he is resting they would not have a sad feeling. I read the names on many and it were one from every state and many from Calif. Then I thought of all those disabeled men in Paris. if they could have a hospital here they could look out on this view. their life would be so much lighter.

Feb. 5th, 1928

I went out to the Garden d'Acclimatation where they are haveing a expostion of Central Afircanes from the French part of Africa. I climbed over the fence and got in the native village where the Plate mouthed women are. a slip is cut just wide enough in the lip to fit around the rim of a wooden plate they can hardly talk with it only the women have the plates there is about ten of them and they took a fancy to me. I think they saw I had some of their blood I couldnt fool them. the yongest wife was during the Cooking as I hung around the Camp fire she offered me some it was good and I would have accepted to save the price of my supper But the spit run out of her mouth on this plate and ofen droped into the pot. When I left I climbed over the fence again so it didnt cost me anything.

There will be Mardi Gras down at Nice soon and an excustion leave for Marseilles. I told Mrs. Morris I felt

I must go now. She want me to come back. I am going to try to. I have had a wonderful time in Paris. I think I love it best of all but I cant help but love the last place best.

> *Feb. 26th.*
>
> *Marseilles, France*

I traveled 3rd class from Paris with Two fine young men one a soldier and the other a sailor I like traveling with the French better then the English who smoke so much and they keep the doors and windows open and you are in a draft all the time. I have a nice warm coat I would not need in the south and I thought how good it would be for one of those Plate mouthed women I was going to throw it over the fence but I didnt have time to go way out there again. Arrived at 10 P.M. the station sits up on a very high hill and a beautiful terrice at night it is as bright as day with lights so I felt very happy. I started out to look for a room. the first was nice but when the man were showing me the room he winked at me I was smart enough to say that I would take it but would go down and registar well I made two steps at a time and did not stop until I was in the street. After looking at three more I saw this Hotel it is two frs. more than I wanted to pay but I heard a child voice so I know it would be just the place the best bed and the Family that run it have a chicken in the patio and the singing of the hens wake me.

I do my marketing in the same street. Everyday I amuse myself keeping count of how many make love to me but the number were to high today I told all to walk away except a very nice colord one a captain or something in the Army. We met in the Museum I saw so many high up offices speak to him I thought this must be some person He were so nice and tried so hard I did not have the heart to tell him to walk away and to I wanted to see how he would act. I had 5 o'clock tea with Him and I never can get enough of the French Pastrys. Then I began to plan how to get away from him, we walked by a Hotel then I said good By with a promise to have breakfast with him at 12. but I feel sure I'll be near Cannes at that hour. When he were out of sight I came out I dont live anywhere near that Hotel. There are many colord soldiers and they ware red turbons. They have string musice on the corners and a girl with a good voice singing the poplar songs.

Mar. 3st.

Nice is such a beautiful place and I enjoy going in those narrow streets some of them are thousands of steps winding up the hills a river runs through where the poorer people live and they do their washing on the rocks by the stream. I always get a comfortable and Home like place to stay for here you never think of your color. I had to sleep in the Bath room for 4 nights waiting for my room I enjoyed it the tub are large and plenty of hot water I had 2 and 3 baths every day. They have very pretty Villars I saw one name Juanita it was the most beautiful of all. I had good luck walking along the Promenade wondering where I could get a fresh bright flower to ware for I wanted to be real dressed up. I had only 2 franc to spend and on the sidewalk a few yards ahead of me I saw the most beautiful velvety red rose. People were passing it but no one pick it up. I ran to it, I got there just as a Lady and Gentleman notice it He was ready to pick it up but I beat him, all I could say when I got it was Oh my darling it did seem so good and funny. It was just as fresh if it had been cut that minute it had a long stem Its the most beautiful rose I have ever seen. I rushed up to put it in water. I put it in the big pitcher and let the water run on it and it was the hot water then I said Oh my darling and let the cold run it was alright.

Mar. 6th.

I had a thrilling day at Monte Carlo. The Laws are different from Nice. In Nice I went several times to play a few Franc in the Casino and on the Ball room floor Dark colord girls in their evening cloths dancing in the Arms of Hansom White Frenchmen. The French are great Love makers being man proof I get a big kick out of them. I even sneeked into the gaming room without paying the entrance fee. But at Monte-C. I found it harder. I had on a little French cap and they thought I had slipped away from the family to gamble. Also you must prove you have money. I couldnt prove that. they said they would let me go in just once to stay only one hour. I ask what if I stay longer he said he may put me in jail. I told him I heard it was a nice jail and I would be glad to see it. Then I laied them all out and they gave me a ticket to quick. I knew I would get in. I just wanted to Know what they would say. I wanted to try the table where they played with the II cards. One of the Guards tryed to tell me. But he looked so big and hansom I didnt remember a word he said. So I lost 20 franc. It was worth it.

Mar. 14th.

Tomorrow ar 2 P.M. the Grand Carnival will begin everything are ready on the Promenade and in the stores the People are buying their white Satan costum I am sure it will be beautiful with the clear blue sea so near. I have picked out a seat so shall have my lunch early. I dont intend to let work of any kind keep me from anything during the Carnival. Why should I work during the gay Carnival. I met an Italian he studied for 4 years at Malin for the opera after he was hit by an auto laied him up for a few years he is over it but still are free of all of his uper front teeth but he is nice looking I have a few sauces of ice cream with him and we go on the Sea away from the croud and he sings to the highest note I tell him diffrent parts of operas that I like best and like a flash he bring out the tune.

Mar. 15. Nice.

The Carnival were very beautiful the girls that rode in the Parad had baskets full of small beauqets of flowers and they throw them at the people that applaud them the most it made it very gay. I no longer own up to be American but are a Cuban. as the American and English drink and gamble so much. the women after men the men though married are after other women those that are not during that are beating up the wife. or she are beating him up the French have not time for them only to make them pay well for everything and I agree with the French.

Cap d'Antibes
March 20th.

I am on a nice job with an English Couple and in a few minutes of Garoupe Beach. My room window looks out on a lovely Pin grove next to the Villa the Orange trees are about 30 years old and the plum trees and persemmons are lovely loaded with blossoms. The Villa were built by French Pheasants some 65 or 70 years ago and so solid and homelike we have electricity to heat also small grates. I have never felt so homelike in a house as I have in this one I sleep with my head to the North its wonderful the other night I had a beautiful dream of the Most Holy Jesus I saw Him in my room under a horbor of ever greens and it was so plain I got up and called out Jesus. The favorite gaiety among the American and English here are Surprise partys the Ladies bring some kind of cooked food and each man bring a bottle of liquire They arrive at 6.30 We had one here and wonderful good food. The Americans raved over my patato salad an Irishman was more American than the others because he call Squash squash where the others say vegetable morrow. Very good for the house its given in You have enough to last for several days they dance and go home about 4 A.M. But not one of Those bliters brought roast Chicken. Everything are pyjmas. My Madame gave me a nice short coat to ware with pyjmas and it fit perfect am rubbin my rabbit foot on a pair of pyjmas. She havent handed them over yet may be it have lost its charm.

April 1st.
Chemin de la Garoupe.

I went to the Dog Show. I cant say which was the most interesting the Ladies that own the dogs or the dogs. They march round and round with the dogs. A dog will be a dog. An English or American juge his eye is for the dog but not a Frenchman thats why I like the French each lady had a chaffer or maid but she would not take a chanct on them the dog may not come up to the mark but if she have a graceful step and smile and

say Oui Monsieur smiling, he'll forget all about that
poor dog. This is the most gelouries of all my life just
the same plesure as when I am traveling. I once heard
a lecture at Cargine Hall in N.Y.C. in 1913 which I
do not agree and have ofen felt sorry for the speaker as
it was on Paradise Lost. its not lost its right here on
earth and I have seen so much of it.

April 15th.

My Couple are going to England for a visit. I must say
she is the brodest minded English persons I have meet
she never say not one thing against Americans always
something nice and he is just the same most Englishmen if they dont say anything unkind about Americans
will not say anything good of course they always talk
to me as a maid and not as an American. I needed
so much a nice sweter and Madame had one just the
right shad she said Neta if you would like it take it.
I like old Antibes in the evenings more than Nice The
people are nearly all working people and ever so family
like. its 8 cafés where they meet dance sing laugh and
talk one of the managers a young Italian French lived
in N.Y. very swell he like for me to come so he can
speak English.
one café has a joly Czechoslavakian Vilionist another
where mostly the nice quiet French Soldiers go and they
furnish the musice. I ofen make the rounds unless you
knew where you would never think any gaiety went on

in those old norrow streets. I have one homelike hang
out its a real Family meeting place from the grandma to
the children thats old enough to prance round on the
floor. I have 3 friends they are the Belles one about
50 white hair stout she ware a red percal dress and a
little black felt hat much the shape as Peter Pan she is
full of smiles and never sit out a dance another 65 she
ware black felt shoes and a tight black bass from the
days of the mutton leg sleves my how both the young
and old men love walzing with her then the other are
about 50 she is at her best during the Italian Phessant
dance When I go out of the little street some say buno
Sera Senerina I like being in a country and yet feel I am
of another at the same time.

I went into one of the Studios at Old Antibes on the top
floor of an old house. There was an everlasting hansom
American all brown from the sea and sun there and four
or five real painters sitting about one very fair in a pair
of brown pyjmas and orange sweter another with slick
black hair in black pyjmas and red sweter I paid no at-
tation to the oil and paint on the walls. I expect he paid
some poor but real artist to do the canvas work. There
are plenty of scandlous durings going on here.

May 2nd.
Juan-les-Pins

My Couple are now in England Visiting her Parents at
Cornwall I took the L'Eclaireur de Nice to enjoy some

interviews and the second one was this place. The unbeleavle thing about the present very rich American I am with is a dear little 14 year old Girl that are not only being disgraced but missed treated as well. my blood boilds. At once I showed my dislike and it is a bit easy on her but such a disgrace and the mother are one of the finnest American Familys and it is carried on with a dark Indian looking poor pennless Russian that have the name to be a writer. and beside she keeping him he beat her up the child lives in terror and ofen go in and help the mother.

this woman is about 40 and most beautiful but adore the very scent of this brute. If it wasnt for the child, I would call him my right hand Buddy because he sure can cook and save me from cooking many meal and he alway leave the kitchen so clean. The Russian are just the size of a broom stick. and about 37 or 38 years. the only thing he keeps the rest of the gang of drunkards away from her so all hate him. He runs away from her but in a few days she comes up there to Paris and bring him back its as bad as that the child only hope is when he runs away the little thing adores her mother and then she takes the mans place but when he is here she is just like a black slave for the two. This woman have a show place in Rhode Island and a winter home at Santa Barbara Calif. Why is it that nature are so unkind that little girl are born by such vile things as this Woman.

She are kind to everybody except this child and every
body like her. but not I I was displeased the other day
over the treatment of the child and the woman like me
and was afraid I was going so told the child if I left she
would send her off the child begged me to stay. I am
making a good number of solod francs packing them
away for some beautiful enjoyable pleasures when I
travel later this summer. I'll start soon. ✗

May 15th.

My family are away for a while so I can go to my
favorite spot one of the Garoupe Points it is so cozy
and private I call it my Villa Pine needles make my
bed and I bring my books to read on my coming tour.
one a short Geography of the World, the other "the
Queen" newspaper Book of Travel it tells you of the
climates what to ware It have every City and Town of
any size in the world. the best time to visit them. it
even tell about the drinking water. I also have a Directory of the Y.W.C.A. a new one comes out every year.
so I feel quite at home everywhere I go. then I alway
love to read Aimee McPherson Angelus Temple Paper.
it is the most snappy Church paper of all. I'll start
roveing again soon I like to stay long enough to flirt in
each country to test the man of each place is what I
like during. ⁄

Its a lot in a light sprit. I was walking down to the big
market place to bring out my lunch I saw a neat greesy

Aimee Semple MacPherson is surrounded by a flock of
doctors in Los Angeles hospital because of a tropical
fever contracted on a Mexican vacation . . . T

8—29—'43

pakage I droped it in my shoping bag hoping it was bacon and when I open it was two large slices of delicious ham and of all the people I was the one to find it thats what a light sprit does for you. I have a perfect little oven made of rocks. when I take my afternoon nap on a bed of fresh gathered Pin branches and enhail the scent and the salt smell from the Sea. with so much kindness and beauty yet if I could die tomorrow and that would be the end of my soul I would be glad to go because I really have nothing else I wish to do in this world nor the next.

May 27th.

I spent the day on a Point with a croud of Campers we had fried fish and the soup fish that are so famous. I wore a red bathing suit a red handkerchief on my head with my hair down and a blue pice of cloth around me for a skirt like an Indian. I made a perfect hit. the men of course had a willing look and when they helped me to the largest fish one of the pretty wives said Holy Marie dont give her the bigest one Jean. I go down every evening and take a peep in to each of the caberets dance café I climb up on a post and have the grandest view Hollywood is the Place of Elegant. I hate to leave here but I must not put off too late getting to Italy I spent half the morning at the Italian Consulate waiting to get my passport vesaid there were so many people. I buy my Tickets from Cook because they are always a bit

cheaper than the American Express but I make my exchange at the Express. I have the Italian money down
to a fine point. I leave in a few days and will stop at
Milan Venice Florence and Rome.

Santa Maria
II Via Balbo
Rome, Italy

The trip was delightful along the Italian Riviera I had
an afternoon until 12 P.M. at Milan didnt like the city
to big and no river nor mountain but I meet a fellow
that lived in the same street I had lived in N.Y. we
had a very joly time He had a sad tale He came to
Italy 15 yrs. ago to visit and try to get His Grandpa
back to N.Y. but could not. He said if Columbus come
back now He would be sorry He discourved America
when they refuse to let them come in. He has two
Brothers there they write him and tell him they would
not take a chance on leaving N.Y. He is a conducter on
the street car I stood outside and when he know I am
from the U.S. he would not let me pay my fare. He
were proud of his English he said to me. Look at me
I am a conducter on this car see how little pay we get
oh, its auful rotten I could be making so much money.
then he introduce me to a man on the platform and said
This is my friend hes perfectly happy here in Italy
because all he like is to eat thats all he think about.
this little friend looked so rosy and fat.

Then I went to the end of the line his work was over and I had supper with him it was a sort of American tea place and I had whipped cream we went round to see all the big buildings he went down to the train with me traveling were very heavy 3 women and 6 men in my compartment the 3 students boys fell in love with a very pretty blond girl about 22 each wanted to sit by her it was so very funny the night passed away in no time I arrived at Venice at 7 A.M. get a nice room in the old part right on the canal every comfort 15 liros a day.

When I started out to look over Venice I came near steping into a canal I went all over by foot then took to the canal by gondola. Venice is so beautiful I could have spent two weeks there but went on as the living are very high there.

I arrived in Florence just in time to see a big procceson around the Cathedral I liked Florence but it is so dusty. The traveling to Rome many people had to stand for a long time but that never happen to me I know how to get about. It was raining and very muddy on arriving just as I liked it the Lady at the Y. were away. Cooks nor American Express do not know anything about good and cheap Hotels. they told me 35 liros would be the cheapest. I only laughed to myself. I found a nice room for 10 liros a day near the third largest Church. Yesterday I told them in the express office where I was staying and what I was paying. they were very much

surprised. I just love Rome I read up the things in a
Guide book I go to the place of interest and waite
until I see a bunch with an English speaking Guide then
I fall in line and get my lecture for nothing\I dont
believe half they say no way. /
I love the old things they look so new. such wonderful
Paintings and my the Churches I am in and out of them
all day because you do not want to miss any. and\I can
never leave without praying I learned that in Cuba./ I
just must do something at night I went to a good
Tradgey play last night. the Spanish make the best
Tradgey actors. the cheapest seat was 6 liros and not
quite 5 cents for taxes there were many swells up there
with me. the Italian are much better cooks than the
French. I take my coffee in a place where they serve it
in a bowl that hold nearly a pint all rich milk and a
little strong coffee you crumble the bread in the coffee.
just once I got stung about ording I saw something on
the list and thought I was getting a dish real Roman.
it was two artichokes we all laughed he said he would
change it I orded again expecting something more
Roman and it was broiled liver. They know me now
and take an interest bring big potions and they dont
want me to tip. the plainest little resturant with oil
cloth on the table always have nice clean table napkins.
I got out and do a little shoping at the street markets
and you can learn so many every day words. The people that I room with are lovely they have a beautiful

Lady daughter with blond hair to her nees. most of the Italians are pretty and what I like best are the modest Girls and not many bobbed heads it is a great change from the American English they are nauty the Scotch very nauty but the French are really bad the worst at Nice I didnt want to believe my eyes. The Italian men are so very gentle and Gentlemen. yet they dont fail to make love to you but in a very nice way. they make good Parents.

Rome, June 14th.

I know every spot about Rome. after I had seen everything I accepted the company of an Italian Proffesor and He took me about. I was studing my Guide book in the Borgese Garden and he began to talk. First he asked me if I were from Spain then he asked me if I would go to lunch with him I said No then he said may I see you at five. and I told him yes then I left to go to lunch and he followed me unbeknownst to me. I had orded my lunch in the little place I go when he came in and sat beside me. I never let any man go to the place I eat and so I were really sorry when I saw him because I had been going so quietly there and they took more interest thinking I were alone. I thought Now this is going to spoil everything. he was disgusted they didnt wait on me sooner it was just the two things I orded when he saw them he said that is nothing and then orded artichokes oranges and cheese. After that I had to change my place of eating. He took me to hear Aida.

Always he would meet me in frount of the church and leave me at the door of the Y. Then Sat. and Sun. another Gentleman that lived in N.Y.C. 25 yrs. took me about. He run a big shoe shop. I went into have heel plates put on my shoes. He took me round But I had seen everything and we went many places he had never seen. I enjoyed the lovely lunch he gave me. I make them think I am living at the Y.W.C.A. and always stop there then come home later.

I spend the whole half day at each Galery and study each picture with two very good Guide books. The Picture I like best is The Crucifixion Reni it was so real it made cold chills run up my back I thought I saw the lips move.

It is the crazest laid out city I was ever in I am always lost and more so when I start home so I never think of turning in that direction until I hafter. The Proffesor wanted to take me to the Catacombs I wouldnt let him because we wouldnt had time to have lunch He had to be at his school at 3.30. It only cost 5 liros return. to go to the Catacombs and a lunch like He gives cost 3 times that. So He took me to lunch instead.

I went through it twice with the Italian bunch and Guide when we came out I told the monk that I didnt understand He laughed and told me to wait for an English Bunch so I did. In the churches the man show

me everything I offer a tip but they wont take it they
say because I am alone but just when I go to step out
the door they kiss me. the same thing has happen in
every Town it is done so quick it make me laugh.
Rome is very dusty its nice you dont hafter shine your
shoes. then when it rains it is very muddy the other
day I went to get on the street car and the conducter
was teasing me and told me not to get on until I got
some of the mud off my shoes.

Via 62, Napoli, Italy.
June 20.

The last day in Rome I was walking through their largest park I notice setting down on one of the lower
Terices a colored nurce about 40 and weigh about 200
lbs. I went and ask her if she spoke English and
laughed when she answered "I say I do" She was a
joly old Girl I spent the rest of the afternoon She think
that the men are the most delightful of all men. She
said it seem like a dream To her to have a Hansom
Italian kissing Her hand. I hadnt give it much thought
but when we got togather we sure did have a good time
talking it over. Then I went home with them and had
supper. the Family are from Albany, N.Y. the Gentleman are in Diplomatic service. they have 4 children
she is so sweet and Gentle with them and they love her
so.

I was down early and got a good seat on the trip

from Rome most of the passagners had their lunch so
it looked like a picnik party all had wine but me. To
be socible I accepted a few swollows from a jug. I
found a large room with a Family it has a nice view
of a big Castle upon a hill. They have a nice clean old
man servant and a boy of 14. am glad to have a rest
from the maids asking me questions. I love the Bay and
Vesuvius look so grand I wish it would spit up a little
fire my love are all for Naples just now. Tomorrow I
will go to all the places that are free on Sun. Its nice
to be in gay Naples after Churchie Rome.

June 30th.

I went up Vesuvius on horseback, it is much cheaper
and more thrilling. We took the train to a town Bosco
Trescasa that were destroyed in 1908 and then a very
old rattling auto up to the white house where we get
the horses. There were some German Ladies but all of
them was poor Hosewoman. I had a dandy little Horse
his name was Spiggitti and I am not saying this to bost,
but I was the best rider of all the woman. I made my
Horse galop as ofen as I could but sufered for it for
3 days. A Friend I met on the train an Italian he looked
German very fair but spoke English. I was really afraid
he made me stand over the edge and the lava was just
boiling and jumping up. The only thing I didnt like
about him he wanted me to eat so much when we stoped
at a town for refreshments.

I had supper with my same Friend at San Martino you get a wonderful view of Naples & the Bay. they had very good musice. I had hiked up there before but did not let on. If I go out without a Hat the Italians do not take any notice of me and always talk right along with me But if I have on a Hat they call me a Chinese or Japenese. You can get along so good if you are not dressed up.

One day at noon time I was in a suburb town I went to a door and ask if there was a resturant they said no the Father ask me if I wanted Spagitti. I said yes. He said come right in and He would cook some He did not look any to clean but he sure did cook clean I watched him. The Son begin to sweep up the floor of the room we was to eat in the Father called one of the Fat Daughters and she got out of a chest a camofar ball smelling napkin. They had 10 loafs of bread for the family and it was hot. I never ate any spagitti that tasted so good. I hate to think of leaving Italy the people are the kind you can live very close to.

July 6, Dijon, France.

I had a delightful trip from Naples on the beautiful steamer to Genor. I was laying down on a roll of ropes on the deck of the 3rd Classe and a Egyptian Gentleman from the Ist Classe came and spoke to me. He was very fine looking and dressed so well I think my nice suite caught his eye. and he said to himself She looks nice. He said wont you come over to our side and pulled out a nice steamer chair for me. He was traveling with a young Sudan Prince as tutor. the Prince wore a beautiful costume. He gave me his address in Egypt and ask me to come and see him. When we left the boat everybody got into buggies but I said to myself I'm not going to be spending my money to smooth it over by taking a carrage so I started right out and truged up the hill with my bag. I had half a day there and a plesant day at beautiful Turin and left with a Ticket to Geneva. A young Italian in my compartment wanted to talk and kept me awake so when I did go to sleep we got to the place I was to change I was so sleepy I couldnt pull myself out the seat was such a comfortable bed I did not wake up until an hour of Dijon.

I had to pay the difference to the conducter and he cheated me changing my swiss money to French franc. I got off at Dijon and was well paid for it is so very Grand looking. they have 3 wonderful old Churches and fine stores. I went to a movie to see Mary Pickford in Sparrow. The girl said the Programs was one Franc. So I did not buy one and she said if that was too much for me I could read it then give it back to Her so I did. just in frount of me sat a French Lady that spoke English they bought candys and gave me some and the time passed very plesant. I found a lovely Hotel and tomorrow I'll leave for Lausanne.

July 29th,
Chamonix, France.

When we get to the bordor of Switzerland I thought
they might make me pay more on my ticket but who
should be at the Bordor but that same old Conducter
who cheated me changing my money on the train, the
moment he see me he looked away. You don't have to
go chasing after people in this life, it may be I got more
off of him than he did of me anyway neither of us was
put to any trouble. I spent a day in Lausanne. It is a
beautiful place a little dearer than France but not so
dear as the U.S. I took the steamer to Genève it make
you think of St. Augustine Fla. they have the buggies
with the Fring Tops and Two rivers run through the
City one are as swift as Naggra falls River. there are
many white Swans. there was a Circuis in Town so I
took a room in a nice little Hotel near the Tent and
went it just pored and hailed every Body was out in
their rubber boots. it was so very different from ours. I
wish I could visit a Circuis in every Country that is a
good way to study the People.

I always get up early and Visit the big market Places
I love to be with the Croud and go into the Cafés where
they take coffee. You can see many things. I have not
seen in my suite case for a week I like it then you feel
just like the birds. I have two pokets in my over coat
Two in my coat suite and two on the enside of my
bloomers and that is enough for all what I need I no

longer wish that I was a man because I can travel with
even less than they and look dressed up.

I found a place where the Lady said she could strech
a cot in the sitting room and give me the same meals as
the others but charge much less I gladly accepted. the
Part I love best about being here. about six in the
evening hundreds of hikers and Guides return in their
ruff cloths and heavy shoes, with their pack on their
backs and ropes. and the non Hikers are all dressed up
to see the Town and everybody walks in the middle of
the street.

8 A.M.

I have just got up and open my Parlor bed room window it has a Piano Victorolor and Kain chairs very
pretty I get a wonderful View of Mont-Blanc White mt.
the Sun are just high enough to make the snow shine.
I havent much desire to hike it is to warm and every
one are as brown as ginger bread. I choose to take the
trips up in comfort and cut out a meal or Two. I look
back to all the hard hiking I did in the Boundries of
Pikes Peak. and are quite contented. I wanted to get
10 dollars exchange before I leave tomorrow. the
Young man had loked the Door to go I peep in and
made signs. He ask me how much I wanted I said 2000
Dollars He said that was worth opening the door.

Lucerne Aug. 10th.

I left Sunday at 8.30 for Interlaken it was a Perfect Day the Cenery from Montreux to Zermatt are just wonderful Sunday are the only rest Day the Smart and and Strudy Swiss have Every man were out with His Wife and Children and Grand Parents they go to other Valley Town to visit. from Montreux to Zermatt are mostly French Swiss. then on to Zurich are German Swiss then there are Italian Swiss—I love them all. For to be a swiss mean you are smart kind and respectfuly I cant say which of the three are the most interesting

In the compartment of the train there was a Swiss man with His Wife and 5 children and His Mother and Farther the Baby was so cute had one tooth and the Grandmama also had one and it bent across the low gums. as I looked at Her I thought how different People are. Americans with all their good teeth and having them pulled out, and how She was holding onto Her one. the Train entered a Tunnel and a Lovely Bird came in through the Window we enjoyed it But it were so frighten. It was a real Family coach they sang so lovely the Swiss songs. It was a bit dusty in Interlaken but it is ever so pretty Place every Poch or winder have vines or bright flowers and everywhere a well keep garden of lovely Vegetables. I went to a Resturant in a Garden and good musice they Danced it being Sunday I was late but the Girl gave me so much I felt misable the rest of the Day.

Aug. 15th. Lucerne.

Ever since the first day in Switzerland I had a desire to sleep on the street somewhere just to see what would happen the Places were so clean and the People so nice that I choosed Lucerne I found a lovely spot the frount of the Beautiful Law Court Building it is away up on the Hill with a wonderful View it have a Pretty Terries at one end a seat made in the corner and lovely trees I thought now this is just the Place I would be out of sight of anyone. I got my Two coats and went up to my respectiful Place it was a Geliouris night I streched out and thought why should I pay to be in a room and shut off from all this beauty. Just below the terrice are the American church and they were having Choir Practing and sang so sweet.

In a few minutes there was a loud clap of thunder and it begain to rain I thought I would go under the Poch then I saw a flash light going in and out of every corner. I knew it was a Policeman He was coming right to the corner where I was. I felt like I had wings on my feet I ran down to the street and was afraid to look back until I got to a tree that would shade me. no doubt he had never paid any atention I left a German evening Paper that I had coping off a Few words. and maybe thats what saved me. It rained hard so I went to the wonderful old covered Bridge I had no desire to give up being out that night. there are only one Bench it is well lit up there also many of the city lights reflects in water make it very bright. I thought it being so light I would be understurbed about 1.30 a nice looking little Fellow Passed and said something He stood a long time and I said to him Passe passe. the Gods will look after me. I thought He had gone. an hour passed when Two more young men came and sat by my side they wanted to know why I were sitting there one a Italian the other Swiss I said in Spanish To go on and mind their own Buisness But they decided they would stay right there with me. I told them I had no fear of them they were like all the Swiss Good and Kind then Two half drunken men passed through I got really frighten but did not show it I ask If they were not going Home they said Yes when I said I would stay there all night the young Swiss throu his Hat and said then they must stay with me. then it lightning and thunder He said it may stunt us but not kill. deep in my Heart I promised never to stay out all night again. Two Fine Looking Policeman passed through and I thought If those Boys leave me I will surely faint then we begain to Talk and we found each other so interesting the Swiss Boy was a studient doctor he said if He could he would vote for Hoover because He were a Protastant and did not approve of drinking. But Smith was a Catholic and aprove of drink. and that He would do as the Pope said. I had to say something for the Italian young man and said I like the Catholic because they Pray every day and the Protastant only pray on Sun. then lock up their church and if you want to see it you must ring a bell and pay.

About 2.30 the Italian begain to get sleepy so He walked down the Bridge and Came back with the one I had said To Passe Passe. He was French Swiss but speak a little English. He said to me in the tone a 28 year old would use to anyone when they are disgusted. Why are you sitting here alone at this hour of the night. I talked up brave but wouldnt tell him why I was out. they spoke German together then he sat down and the other Two tiped their Hats and shuck hands with me and said good night. It was 3 A.M. never did I wish so for the day to come.

the Last one was such a little Gentleman, worked in one of the Hotels and was anxious to learn English. the very large Fish in the Lake made so much noise jumping up. the Policeman came through the Bridge several times but did not say anything. it stop raning and begain to get light we went for a walk until the Resturant open He had smoked up his last cigrette to keep awake When we sat down in the resturant I told the Girl to bring two Boxes of cigretts. they are one Franc. I gave her a 20 franc note and His Two Eyes became like the moon He was so surprise. Then I told Him I had planned to sleep out just to see what would happen and that He proved to be my best Friend. and we would call the Bridge my Parlor and I told him I would have fainted if I had been left alone He was very much pleased. He had to be at work at seven so shook hand at 5 of 7 and ask me to write To Him sometimes.

Zürich.

I am geting a little practis of German Here not so many on the street that speak English. The Y. Lady call up a Plesant Home for Girls as she did not have a single room and when I arrived you would have thought that a Prodical Daughter Had come Home the Lady big and fat German. She is so clean and comb Her hair back so tight that it pains me. The Girls think it is so wonderful I am from far away California and all are so Lovely To me One wanted to take me out but had to work late I was very glad as I would hafter drink Beer I was worried how I could get out of it you can refuse a man but not a woman. I am going to the Curcuis tonight so expect to have a joly time. the Lake are the prettest of all the other Lakes. you can Fish but must not spit or throw any trach in it you do not dig worms to fish but use the little Bugs along the walls that you bate with. those are the things I like to walk about and see. the German Swiss do not like to see you alone so I have lots of fun But I am auful foxie.

München Sept. first.

I love München and enjoy every hour. The beds are a little hard after Switzerland. I go to the Beer Gardens and like everything but the Beer. They do not Dance on Sunday like the French. But their Sin are greater because they sit down and over eat and Drink. Many of the musicians dress in the funny short pants the little brown hat with the green band and a little duster sticken in the back. but every body were Singing right with the musice. They had charcole broilers where they broil the fish and great piles of raw turnips You take as many Turnips as you want the waitress slice them and you eat it with salt cheese and many kind of sausage.

Vienna Sept. 4.

I came to the Lovely Home for Girls the Matron wore a stiff white Cap, blue dress and black silk apron. If we are out after 10 we must pay the Ganitoress 40 Groschen that is just a few pennies. I went to a lovely Opera the Rose of Calvier. I went early as I was going to stand. You can learn so much that way I heard a young man speak English and ask him to tell me the Opera in English. He told it so beautiful then another young man ask me where I was from I said Los Angeles and He said he had lived there near West Lake Park. they have a wonderful market about 10 blocks long but the Austrian are people of few words and that means they are poor Salesmans I see many shoppers go home with their bags only Half full you never see that in France. they have wonderful food wheather in 3rd or 1st class place Hot dogs mustard have the right of way and also Krout. they either have ugly shape teeth or most of them are out I have been looking for a week and just today I saw two People with nice teeth. In this home are about 50 Pretty Girls and not one have perfect Teeth. I have Vienna down to a fine Point so are leaving this noon for Ceskaslovenske I get my Visas at each Place and learn so much none of them speak English but my French serve well.

Brno Sept. 9, 1928.

I have spent 3 days in Czechoslovakia and It have been the greatest of all the trips I have ever had I arrived at 1.30 A.M. and finished the night out in the station. with me were 25 or more woman who were traveling by foot to other Towns. at 5 the country people wer coming in with their wares for the open market and it was the most strange sight I ever saw. the Y. have a beautiful place at the top of a big new building. The first day I spent seeing the wonderful Caves near Brno. Two brothers that went to Cambridge were in the party. so tell me everything in English. they have wonderful sausage in this country and on the way you give your order at the little stands where they broil them. so it will be ready when you come back. I orded 4 the brothers said Do you really want 4? but I wished I had order 6 when I ate them.

The Big Fair are on they formed the Parad under my window at the Y. thousands of people in their native cloths each Valley Town were diffrent and all have their own musice the men were just as gayly dress as the women. on the way to the fair Growns they sang and danced But the Real Bohemian life begain at the Fair Grown. the French cannot tuch them in having a good time. Of course I was not a tourist. I were just one of them.

Inside the Grown everybody were dancing on big wooden floors the girls in their wide wide skirts and they delighted to see how far out their skirts would whirl. A fellow saw me watching he spoke a little English and asked me why I was not dancing. they begain playing a walz and we just walzed and walzed but the big skirts nearly noked me down.

its a great country for dill pikles all over there was little stands with pikles, broiled corn, sausage broiled on coals little broiled steaks. I ate too many dill pikles but the dancing got it down. then I had to leave to get my train but my dancing partner had no time to greeve over a lost sheep there was too many others around. I would like to be here another day but have spent what I had planed to here. I left the Y. this morning and check my suitcase and coats at the station.

Saturday, September 15

I left Brno at 1 P.M. and at 2.30 the train Recked and 26 People were killed I came out with only a big knot over the right eye it is gone now I only have a black eye.

I cannot write about the Reck yet as the thoughts are very sad.

Budapest, Hungary,
Sept. 17.

I have just had a minauil Bath at the new and up to date Bath house the old one I was afraid to go down in to the place the water looked so dark.

I was to leave Brno Sunday night but when I went for my ticket the night express was 130 crowns I spent all the Slovakian crowns but 115 and He could not exchange dollars so I had to waite until the next Day at noon and left on the Express of 10 coches I was in the 6th at 2.30 when we were going by a little station a swich engin was standing wheather the enginnear was asleep or drunk or forgot but He ran into the other engin He and both Fireman and 26 People were killed and many died from inguries.

the first coches were 2nd and 3rd and those were the ones that lost their lives. I got into the coch next the dinner which were the last 3rd class I didnt go forward to the front the way I usualy do, I wanted to go up but my feet wouldnt take me. I was studing the book that means everything to me Bradshaws Continenal Guide all of the sudden I was throwd across the compartment and hit my head. all the others jumped up and begain talking fast I was very dizzy but I thought about nothing but this book and kept calling my book,

my book I was stunted. I found it and then went out
all the phesants came running across the fields. they
looked as clean as pins with white handkerchiefs on
their heads. they was all standing back they was not
allowed to come near until the doctors and offices came.
it was about 10 miles from a Town. it was a hot day
and it happen in a turnip patch we used the turnip tops
to put under the engured ones heads. I stayed with a
German Girl that had been torned into thread from
the waist down She lived a half hour in that half hour
I just loved her she were not more than 21 and had
beautiful great blue eyes. she were well dressed and
had a beautiful engagement ring on I bekon to the
phesant with buckets of water to come at last one took
a chance when no one saw him and brought a bucket.
She kept saying the same thing over and over But I
couldnt understand. I called to a phesant woman for
her to come and thought perhaps she could understand,
the woman came but couldnt stand the sight and ran
away. I had to hold her head up I was praying for her.
The doctors came and said there was no use trying to
do anything for her. I felt terrbly heartbroken to think
they left her. finally she died on my arm. had I been
killed it would have been absolutely nothing compared
to that girl.

there were a man about 30 that was caught under the
wheel in just a few feet of where I was with the Girl
He had his senses for nearly an hour and keep his eyes

right on me as He could not look any other way He
called Wasser, Wasser and I went under the coch and
poured the Water down his throat. I cannot forget Him
and I must keep the light burning all night I am happy
to have such a nice room and a reading lamp by the bed
I think that will pass after a while.

I went around to the other side of the train after the
Girl died where there was many more ingured and dead.
I gave water, shaded their faces from the sun, rub their
hands. I went back to see if I could do anything about
the man and just then the train that was to take us left.
it went off without many of us but my suite case was
on it. and it were put off at the next station. I always
carry my passport and money in my bloomers pocket
with a hook and eye on it so that were safe. the poor
man were dead.

then another train came at 6.30 I had not the heart to
get off at that station so near the reck to get my bag
and coats. so went on to Bratislava and had to spend the
night in the station. My eye was almost closed. I had
on a little white crepe waist and it was very cold but
the station had a beautiful First Class waiting room.
The Next morning I had to go back to Breclan for my
things and reached Budapest Tuesday night. one of
the train men said to me you ought to get something
you got that black eye. So in Budapest I had a doctor
to write up my inguries. Glad I found one that has
Jewish blood because they know what to say the doc-

tor told me You are traveling in that country for plesure they have no right to give you such a black eye as this. they must pay you something. I had to have his writing translated in English and Czechoslovakia. I cannot make them give me anything but the doctors took my name at the reck so I thought I would encourage them. Sunday is the day to see the Hungarians at play I went to a Piknick they dressed like Gipsies and danced Gipsis dances. they think I am Italian and am makeing believe when I say I am American I just leave it to them. I had planned to go to Belgrade by Boat but changed my mind as the whole trip would be at night. I was in a Reck in 1903 on Sept. 1st when I was a little girl also a Monday but it was twice as bad about 100 killed and many wounded I didnt get hurt but many in the coch did so I knew just what to do. I cant bear staying in the hotel room long I feel afraid and imagin the hotel may catch fire and I'd be wraped in flames so I stay out as much as possible.

Sept. 18.

On my trip from Budapest to Belgrade Yugo-Salavia in the compartment are a swell digdfied looking young woman reading a book, a Young mother with a dear 22 month old Baby Boy. When she boaded the train was short of money Her Husband was a Proffosor and most of their wives is short of money. I gave her some Pears and 10 Paras. about 20 cents. She gave me a nice

emboried handkerchief out of Her Hand bag I helped
her to take care of the Baby He was a little Darlin.
I know why the Pretty little Blonde are looking at me
its my Black eye of the Railway Reck. I wish I could
Tell Her about it. The Young Mother left the train at
3 P.M. I was a little tird nurseing as she left Him with
me altogather. Hope to find a Cheerful Room at Belgrade as I am still nevous over the Reck. I know the
money of each country before I get there so can juge
about what I should spend.

September 18, Belgrade.

On my arrival I went to find a Resturant and passed a
Bakery where pigs and Bread are Baked. A Girl came
out with a sukling pig just as Brown as Molasses. and
I said where ever you goth I'll flower it smelled so
good I flowered Her 2 blocks down to a Resturant I
went right behind Her into the Kitchen. and sat down
and when the cook cut it up had a piece with Pikled
Bell peppers. Oh, Mama, How good and at the Resturant was the Best String Orchesters of 5 Pretty Young
woman 3 men they Played and sang I am listing to them
now for I am writing on the table. the musice are a
mixture of Oriental I think I'll love it Here.
I just got a shock a big Turkish looking man with a
Turbon spoke to a Girl at another Table and said in
English He had a head ache. He is looking at me side
ways I think He want me to know He speak English.

He may be sorry for showing off Tomorrow I'll look him up with a list of question as long as my arm This is a second class café where you find them so naturnal. What a place to forget a Reck.

Bucuresti, Roumania,
September 22.

In route to Bucharest I traveled half of the night with a German Lady and Gentleman He knew a little English it took Him from 7 until 10 P.M. before He could get it into His head I was traveling all alone buying my tickets and getting my visas all by myself. But once He understood He said I was the most interesting Peason He had ever meet. He told every one in the coch and everyone that get on after they all wanted to talk with me. It was luck I sat with them because we had to change trains and He helped me on to my train other wise it would have taken a long time to find out the Train men know so little I always ask every one that look like they mite know their name.

The trip the next day through Roumania the train stoped only a few minutes at the largest Towns and we had just time to go to the deep wells with wooden Buckets and get a drink as they have no water on the trains. A Phesant woman got on She sat in frount of me she gave me an apple I was very glad as I felt very hungry in my case I had a warm dress as I know I would not need it farther on she was just my size so I open the case and gave it to her and she took from her bag 8 lovely apples and 4 Pears. for me. I arrived here after 26 hours on the train missed the last street car and was afraid to take a Taxi so checked my suite case and started walking. I took the direction to "The Little King's Palace." It is a pretty neighborhood it was then about 2 A.M. on passing real plesant looking yards with High iron gates all locked I came to one that stood open the moon were shinning and I could see two comfortable looking Rocking Chairs under a pretty Grape-Harber in the side yard and feeling tird after such a long journey before I knew what I was during I went right in and sat in one of the arm chairs. It was not a chilly night I went in so quietly I didnt disturbe a big white and yellow Dog that laid just a few steps from me asleep when he saw me he gave a low groul he was as much surprised as I was. I think he was ashamed to think he was the watch dog and I had slipped in on him. he set back on his hind legs and groul and keep his eyes on me. many times when a dog are barking I speak to it in Spanish he very ofen will stop so I said to him in my softest Spanish a little dog very pretty and sat still. he got very sleepy but never take his eyes off me. the Family were sleeping upstairs just above I could see the windows open. about 3 A.M. two other dogs were in the street in frount of the Gate and my Friend were very anzious to go out the moment I fell to sleep I heard the Gate move and saw him slipping out. then I pulled the Gate tight so when he came back he could not get in. I could see him having a grand time with the other dogs then he tried very hard to open the gate he stood on his hin legs and pulled until he open it enough to stick his nose in and bark at me then I knew I had to leave in a hurry as he might wake his people but I was afraid he would bit me then I got up courage to go out the gate and run down the street I could see him standing there barking after I was a block away. I thought How kind he had been to me and when he run off I locked him out so his kindness must have turned to hate.

It was 4 A.M. and the people was going in one direction I flowered and right to the big market. I asked for coffee and milk in French in a Resturant the waiter did not like that and told me how to say it in Rumania the common class people are funny down Here. then when the Boss learned I was a stranger they was very kind to me.

I would like so much to see the Little Prince. Pork are the main meat for this part of the World in the Resturants at 7 in the morning you can see a man sitting down to a plate of Pork it is the little Pigs that they rost.

After a few days I thought I would look up my Friend the dog after being in and out of several streets I hear barking and walked passed the House there were the two chairs a pretty looking Lady at the window and a

Vegetable man going into the yard the big fiery dog tied to a chain and barking and raning ever so hard to get to the Man \ Then I thought what danger I was in and placed myself with Danial and the Lions den. /
I am going to leave for Sofia, Bulgaria Tuesday. I do not like Monday any more for traveling. I am looking forward to geting a Place to work at Cairo.

September 24, Sofia

I meet an Australian traveling Gentleman He was an American Citizen. He helped me to buy my Ticket change my money. It was lucky I meet Him He bought Fruit for me and orded a seat in the Dinning Car I enjoyed the Supper. We arrived at night. He offord to take me to a Hotel which was kind of Him but I refused. then he shook hands and said good Bye. I like the Bulgarian people I went for a car ride and Visited the City Market. I am leaving at noon for Turkey.

In route from Sofia to Constantinople

The First and second Class are the same the World over but it is the 3rd class that are so interesting. A Couple in Frount of me the wife have on a red quilted dress, yarn stocking and Hair braded in two brads down her back she has a small black shalw tied on her head they are eating dark bread and boiled Chicken gizzards. most of the land are for grazing you can see many Shepards. a Family of Turks got on 4 men and the Grandpa. I wonder where are the Grandma. now there are 2 woman with their faces covered up to their eyes each have a baby and 4 little girls with red hand- kerchiefs on their heads with Flower de percale dresses and many colored bead braclets on their rists. They have much of their Households goods with them. one of the Little Girls are feeling my side. Well I'll hafter nod it through Tonight and give all the space to the Children. The women got off and are having a time Counting their children.

I thought now I'll sleep but a nice Gentleman came in He speak French he bought 2 nice Honey due mellons / for me. I never tasted better. He certainly is a Gentle- man. He is streching out on His seat so I'll do the same on mine. How nice to be away from the Turks and their Thousan Children the women black cloths smelt rancy.

Its 6 A.M. I Had a real good rest. I have washed combed and changed my blous. My friend have also washed He has a nice Towel to dry his face and I have only a handkerchief. so I am the best Traveler. Its nice to travel along side the Water. I wonder if this is part of the Golden Horn.

Constantinople, Pera.
Rue Loli 19, September 30.

I am in the Resturant and have just had a good feed of patatoes smothered lamb. string beans tomatoes and

Orka cooked together I think its lamb, then luttuce cu-cumber tomatoes salad and Bread. all this less than 50 cents. this is a nice place for Buisness men I am the lone woman. I think they enjoy having me stop in. The Kitchen is in the frount right on the sidewalk the same as the Dinning room all the cooks are dressed in white they take off the tops of the caseroles and I point and choose what ever I wish they get a big kick out of me one blond cook cant do his work for peeping through the Head cook trys to make love to me one waiter pull out my chair, another open the door Sometimes I pass by the Resturant pretend I forget the Place they see me and the cooks call Madame Madame and wave and bekon so I know I am welcome. The Owner a nice kind looking old Gentleman have enough space in His pants to put me into He is smoking a Tube attached to a bottle on the floor He's smiling at me He always pat me on the Head and come to see the waiter do not over charge and say come again. I have been praying daily in the many Mosque I like taken off my shoes it rest my feet and the rugs so soft.

I got an auful scoulding from a woman for putting my shoes on enside of the door. Now I waite until I am on the grown. You can see many women yet that ware the vaile I do not like to see them I feel like I are smouthering It must have been very sad Here 20 years ago. now they look like a lot of Ghosts coming through the norrow streets in black with their head and chin

covered. I take a trip on the Golden Horn anytime
through the day I dont ask where the Boat are going I
just get on and pay after.

October 2, In route to Syria.

The minute you leave Constantinople the whole world
is going to change. We traveled all night through the
Desart the moon shine it was nice and cool. Four old
Shephards are in my compartment and one Young He
sings. they are so kind and gentle To me they look like
the Shephards of the Bible times we streched out to
sleep and were very close to one another they had their
long wool Kimono like coats and staffs. At each little
station the Phesant sell mellons Tomatoes red onions
and boiled eggs with a little salt in a Paper and dark
Bread. Here I get the First sight of Camels the Sun are
getting low and they make a beautiful Picture across
the Desart with the red bundles on their backs.

Now we are traveling through cenery like the great
Rocky mountains of Colorado we are at a little Station
High on the rim of a mountain with the level Plains
miles away it is really Grand and the Condoctor a Fine
Young man have just spreaded his beautiful Red rug on
the Grown and took off his shoes and are Praying with
His Face toward the Setting Sun He is on his nees
bowing His Face down to the rug It is beautiful to see
and will live in memories I hope for ever.

The Turkish men are ever so Gentleman to the Women

Passangers and take most of the Care of the Children, they are very soft speaking People. they are your Friend you must know their Buisness and they want to know yours. On the long trips one ofen get without food. When I was without they gave me another time I had plenty and one had only bread so I gave Him. They had watermelon seeds that had been soaked in salt then roasted they were amused watching me try to eat them. A man riding 1st class had several Hundred dollars stolen But I have left change in my coat and went out and never have it been taken.

Hotel Adana.

This is like a little Country Cuban Hotel. Just before the train got in a young man about 27 got on I cant believe that he was Turkish He ask another man if I was French and tryed to hold my hand I got angry and Hit Him in the Face and quick as litning He hit me in the Face another Young man grabed Him then he ask him to tell me if I would Please let him kiss my Hand and forgive him he had been drinking. He held his Hand to his heart I never saw such pleading I said I forgive him but to get out of my sight. I was glad I soon got off the train. that was my first fight. and the only ungentleman man I have meet in Turkey sorry it happen as I had been thinking all day if I had to give a prize to the most respectfuly men it would go to the Turks. the other men felt so sad.

The Hotel is clean and have white mosquitoe netting over the bed kinda romantik looking the Town is a flat flat place in the day these Towns are hopeless dust and so many flies. You see faces of beautiful women in the little norrow windows they stick their heads out and throw back their Vailes for 2 reasons to see you better and for You to see how pretty they are. then this Town that have been so depressing in the day are very gay at night everything come to life and last until 1 or 2 it is a regular Arabic night there are big electric lights little char coal stoves going every one come out in silk kimonos perfumed up. the cafés are always open you look right in the kitchen and the meat broiling and smelling so good you hear stringed musice and in frount of the resturants women during their shoping in the Bazars. I went to an open air like theatre I ask the man for the chepest ticket he gave me a seat upstairs with the women most of them their Head covered 6 Pretty Girls on the stage danced Two men played the musice I was so sleepy I could not stay. the man was dissipointed when I left early after given me such a good seat.

Then I went to my Hotel. I told the maid I wanted to take a bath. She have her Head covered but not her mouth. She gave me a big round zink pan I was glad it was new but I scrubed it out myself I always have laundry soap in my bag and the top of an old stocking so I can clean boul pitcher and stand and throw it away

after. she put it in my room with water and wanted to
stay in and help me but I pushed her out of the door
she ask me If I was a miss I said Yes and she said then
I was ashame. She understand a little French so we get
along fine.

I went to the station early thinking I could go on to
Aleppo but He said the Train did not leave until tonight. the Gentleman in charge sent his servant boy out
for tea right away. He was about 35 with blue eyes
and dressed in Europen style. then I walked to the old
Cemtery and to the Market where the Carvans come in.
When I came back he gave me a seat in His nice cool
office in a big Morris chair where I went to sleep. He
got auful interested no matter where you go You can be
entertained if You are anyways aggreeable. He ask me
if I would like to go over to the Hotel and have lunch
with him. I said no and went across to a resturant
where you eat on the grown under a shelter cool and
nice I went into the Kitchen and choosed and it seemed
like I never ate anything so good. the Gentleman at the
Station sent the boy to see if I was getting everything
I like and if I had enough money. I went over to tell
him what a delicous meal I had He said You must go
for a ride with me. I came out under these lovely trees
so I wouldnt hafter go. Then he had his man get my
ticket put me on the train right by the window then he
waved good Bye. At the station there were women
groaning moaning shaking theirselves all sitting on the

floor I ask what was the matter It was because one of
the Family was going to another town It was like going
to America to them just a nights journey but they might
never see that one again they dont read or write so its
just like a peson was dying no way of getting in touch
with them. The men tried to comfort the women would
bring them sweets.

Baalbec Syria
Ancient Heliopolis
Oct. 7, 1928.

Am sitting on a stone under the portal of the Sun which
have 18 great colums standing this is a great ruin it
puzzles you when looking at these great stones and
how they ever got them here another thing is how the
Earthquack recked and left the ruins great stones are
resting upon a small one and half of a great stone
colum are on 1 or 2 small stones this ruins are more
wonderful than any at Rome At Aleppo they thought
I was Chinese. Here they think I am Aribian I have
no trouble getting into every little nuck and corner I
go into the little Court yards and visit the families after
the day are over at dusk when the Family come in. you
can see in most of the Yards a Camel donkey Sheep and
Chickens or geese and a black goat. I had a pleasant
visit last evening I smelt bread burning while walking
through the narrow walled streets and went into a
Court yard and I hear girls singing. There is always
high walls and a big wooden door to go into the yard.

In a dark corner were 3 Baalbec Girls Baking bread they patted the dough out with their hands one neads and one bakes they roll the bread out very flat and stick it on the side of the big earthen jar to bake it. this jar is for an oven the coals was at the bottom and they stick the round thin dark dough on the inside of the jar and it browned nicely. I had visited the flour mill in the afternoon and thought I would not eat any bread while here. the mill was low down by the stream you have to go down steps to get into this flour factory even with the dusty road the dust is the same shade as the flour and the mill is open an oxen pulls the thing around to grind the wheat men walking around with their kimonos flying open and I thought to myself I dont want no bread in this country. But when the Eldest Girl took one of the thin cakes and gave it to me I had to eat it and found that it tasted ever so good but the little Bakery was so dark and they were sitting there Baking in the dark night and just laughing and Talking. These women are very inquisitive they stay in so much. I could make them understand. They were puzzled that I didnt cover my face and went out in the streets alone.

In their houses is only one room always white washed and that is where I learned the easy way of cooking on the floor on one side there is the cooking the other side shelves for their cloths they put down the bed. a baby is in an old fashioned crib. I spent the night at a large

Hotel with all morden improvements it is a Town of
5000 But do not look it.

I went to a leading cabrat you sit in little stalls just on
the dirt floors the musice is kinda of a mandolin violin
and zither a man always sing while the woman dances
they only have beautiful women they ware nice bead
dresses and the dance is not vulgar it has kind of a little
movement like the Hawaian the ladies smile and talk
to me.

Jerusalem Oct. 18.
Wynham House The Street of the Prophet.
I left my suite case at the Ticket office at Baalbec with
a man that speak French. When I went to leave for
Damascus the agent teased me and said that He had not
seen it and I should have left it with a man in unforme.
The Mayo and His family from Damascus was there
and the wife asked me what was the Trouble. I told
her and said there was no trouble I only felt sorry about
the pictures and Postal cards I had collected and anyway I would not have to bother with a suite case any
more. For while I was standing there I had planned to
get two nice dresses at Damascus and roll them in a
paper. they all was amused and admired me when I
did not seem to worry. the Mayo an Aribian Gentleman spoke perfect English and the beautiful young
Lady wife with their first baby and nurse. Then I asked
for my ticket and the gentleman would not give it to

me and I got angry and told Him I would buy one on the Train. Then he sent a boy to bring the case and the Mayo said He see I am quite cable of taken care of myself. then we all had a good laugh. The 5 studient Boys of the best Familys were leaving on the same train for their college at Beirut. One of them had seen me the day before and laugh at me when he saw me climb up on a high fence to look over into a yard. 3 of them spoke a little English the Youngest of them a Handsome Boy of 14 showed me a scalp wound he got in a auto accident and His father were killed He was a Hundred Had been married twice His eldest son was 65 and His youngest two years. he was active as a 35 year old we found each other very interesting. then on the Train Two nice looking Syrian women one with two little girls got into my compartment and the train started off without the two girls and they ran to get on and I caught the youngest and pulled her on and the other was nocked down by the open door but she got up and we saw her running. Well the mother cried and went on it made me cry she grabe me and hug and Kissed me because I got one in. The condoctor sent a telegram at the next stop. anyway I got to see their pretty but pale faces for they threw back the vail.

We reach Damascus at dark. after visiting 7 Hotels I choosed the eight I wanted one over a stream as that is the Arabic idea of Paradise it was so pleasant and clean I just loved the room and bed and also the view. the

Arabic food are so good and I liked so much the Cabarets the men were such Gentleman the dancing girls tryed to talk to me the dancing are very lady like they served delicious things in small butter plates water melon seed that had been boiled in salt also punkin seeds they laugh at me because I did not know the nack of getting the nut out but I know as well as they do now. at Twelve midnight when I was ready to go a Handsome Policeman went with me. At Damascus are many ruins from the 1925 fighting.

I left the next morning for Afoulah Israel where you get off for Nazareth. An Arabian man got on at a station where He had been to buy Groceries for a village and geting his things on the train cut his finger and it bled ever so much and he did not have anything to stop it I tore my handkerchief in half and gave it to him. I did not have time to get anything to take on the train to eat and the things they sold at the station they had on the groun. they have wonderful large white grapes and they are so sweet the syrup are all on the outside and they are covered with bees. so I offered to buy some tomatoes and grapes from him. He said to the lovely Syrian couple in the compartment the wife spoke Spanish and French that I had tyed up his cut finger so he could not sell me any but gave me so much I could not eat it all. I always have salt and pepper so had a feast. It was late when we arrived at Afoulah so I stayed the night it is a new Village that were open by the American Jewish accocation the River Jordon passes in half a mile of Afoulah. the train stop is called the Jordan Holt the only Hotel were filled. I spoke to a Gentleman he spoke a little English and were the Village Doctor and from Poland. I knew I had found a friend so I left all the worry for him. He was afraid He couldnt find a place for me I told Him not to worry I would be delighted to spend the night sitting on my suite case on the Porch of the Hotel and He wanted to know How I could be so happy when I had no shelter for the night. and would say to himself how interesting I could hear him say it. He asked me if I was hungry. Then I thought how hungry I am. He took me to an elderly German Jewish couple where he have his meals but he had a room in the Hotel. The couple were Two Dears. She gave us soft boiled eggs cheese fresh butter milk and such good bread I keep them buisy bringing bread and butter. I noticed them smiling but I did not think about what they was smiling at until I got filled and I said to the Doctor I cant eat any more. then I said to Him may be the couple would let me sleep in the Dinning room He said I will ask. and the lady said Yes. everything was clean as a pin. She put a couch in the dinning room for the Husabnd and She and I slep in the bed room. All she could say in English was. and It was good. then I would answer that it was good. the next morning she repeated the supper and the Doctor came and we had Breakfast together. I left at 9 A.M.

for Nazareth. She kissed both of my cheeks and gave me a bag of grapes and ask me to write to Her. everybody are very buisy in the little place some have good houses and some just shacks but everything clean.

The Lady who keep the Hotel in Nazareth were born there but her parents are from Germany and built the Hotel many years ago. I went right out and got acquainted with several Nazareth women and went to the home of the prettis one. I meet them at a Bakery the Boy that put the bread on a long poll into the oven spoke a little English. My Friend lived on the side of a hill. She had been married just long enough to have a baby a few months old. Her to rooms were clean and had light and air. In this country are many places that are much like dungons. Like the Japanese they have matresses they take up every morning and place on shelves. the windows have iron bars like Cuba and brick floors. on the floor by the window she had a little chorcoal stove and she sqart down to cook. Her eldest sister live with Her and did the hard work. She dressed like the Nazareth. Her Husband and boy living in Detroit and Her Mother with a brother in Havana so I felt quite near them. She was cooking something that smelt good but I did not stay when she ask me because I had seen the markets and how they let the flies feast on everything. I ate only what I could get that had been wrapped in some Switzerland or French Factory and fruit I would take to my room and wash with soap and water. I thought I would have dinner at the Hotel so tipped into the Kitchen to have a look and saw many flies over what was perparein I left by auto for Jerusalem. in the car were a young Swedish man a Fine looking colored Arabican Gentleman that wore a red turban and a cream colored silk kimono and a long gray overcoat like they use here. He had a thomos bottle with delicious hot tea in it and gave me some the other Gentleman was a Captain in the Worlds war. He pointed out all the interesting things about the Bible times and the war times. He showed me the remains of Herods Temple and where John the Baptist were beheaded also Jacobs well. He and his family had lived many years at Nablous the place of the well and the most prettiest Valley town in Palestine. at Nazareth the night before I had wished it would rain as it was so dusty and a very good shower came the Lady at Hotel said she have never known them to have such a nice shower at that season. so it was delightful next day as the dust was laid.

Jerusalem Oct. 23.
Y.W.C.A.

I have a single room at the Y. it is so lovely here about 4 blocks from the main Gate of the old city. I take my meals at a very nice Jewish Restaurant. it is cheaper than the Y. and I dont hafter wash and pray before I can eat. they cook very much like we do and always

have good icecream. When we are in our own country
we get more Holiness out of the Holy Land than when
we are Here. One have so much to overlook and I have
to think hard to get down to the Days of Our Lord.
Last Friday was the first time I could really live in the
Days of Christ and then there was always something
happen in the streets to make you forget. Every Friday at 3 P.M. from the Armenian Monastery built on
the site of Caiaphas House start the Procession along
the way of the Cross lead by Priests their monks nuns
children from the Convent and Christians the Police
keep the way clear. We went on stoping at each Station
of the Cross but through the winding up and down
covered old streets are many things to take your mind
off. but most of the time I tryed to picture the day of
Our Lord. on the way you meet a donkey loaded with
tins of water or a drove of black goats and there are
the Moslems making noise at their tin making and the
Jews selling their ware. I got the best part inside of
the Church then it were only about 20 in the Procession
and it was 53 when it were over I had a scarf over my
head and looked so nun like.

At the end I felt I would go right home and remember
it as a Holy afternoon but on leaving the Church an
Arabican Friend meet me and insisted that I go to the
Movie and to the Hotel to the Dance. I went to the
Movies but not to the Dance.

I was sitting outside the Holy Sepulcher waiting until

some tourists come so I could fall in line. a young man that speak English said would I like a guide. I said Im a guide myself I've been guiding myself around Europe for over a year. He was so amused at my answer. then he told me he was not a guide but He were born inside the old city and would like to show me about. He had grey eyes and such a nice expression. then he introduce me to his Rich Cousin who has a car. the Cousin had fair curly hair and spoke English like an Oxford gradu-ate. He took me to the Dead Sea I found it different from what you read It was nothing that made it look dead. not near so heavy and salty as Salt Lake. I spent one hour in the water and did not want to come out. 3 Priest that had never had their hair cut nor their beards went in bathing they undressed on the shore and wrapped a white cloth aroun their waist until they got into the water then I thought How nice it must be in that warm sea without a Bathing suite. On the Banks are a refreshment place I was hungry but they only had Libby's corn beef. I was just full of brine and felt just like Lot's wife so I couldnt eat any. Then we went to the River Jordan. on the Banks are a very Cuban like House with a long shelter of polls and a grass covering where you can eat. Hundreds of Turkeys geese chicken and Black goats are there with a few young boy and three dogs. We had a lovely Arabican dinner the man that own the place wares a blue and white striped homespun kimono and a red turban. This young man have met wealthy American women travelling alone but I am the poorest girl that ever travelled alone. I spend a day in a town as though I was going to spend my life there this is for my own consciance and I find men are always willing to treat you nice. I have a very Oriental looking scarf I ware most of the time on my head everyone think I am Arabian but are puzzled to see me with such a short french dress and the first thing they ask my Friend If I am Arabian then when I ware my little French cap they take me for Jewish. I am willing to be what ever I can get the best treatments at being.

I got up early and went down to Joffa Gate to take a Bus to Hebron and was Packed into the Bus like a pea. My Arabian Friend Nizar came up and ask why I wanted to go that way when they would take me in their car. But I was so anxious to be with the People. I knew I could see and learn more than I would with them in their closed car. Well it was a delightful trip about 25 miles and 15 cents one way. next to me sat a Gentelman In Arabican dress. He had spent 10 years in the States. He were a Moslem but in the States were converted and he was a real Christian. I felt happy to have met him. It was from him I learned the faith of the Moslems. I had been very anxious to know something about it but could not learn from my Friends. It is not bad anyway they have a right to believe what they think is right just as we. Around About Hebron are where Girls of 9 and 10 years are married to Grown men. On our return trip the Bus man packed us in I think there were one of every tribe in Palestine and Syria. They ask my Friend If I was frighten of them they talked so much and so loud when he said I enjoyed it they just smiled to me even the women and they have ever so jelous feeling toward a woman.

Yesterday early I went up to the Mount of Olives and then to the Garden of Gethsemane as I wanted so much to visit all the Places alone. a monk that were in the Garden spoke Spanish and gave me a little souviner with an olive leaf.

Friday morning very early I went to Bethleham I have been there 3 times the Birthplace are wonderful to see. the Arminenes were having Service it was 4 young men with Old Rose robes and 6 tiny little Boys 5 with old Rose Robes and one with a Green. It was so beautiful down there in the manger. I love going to Bethlehem. The old City are a real cross word Puzzle. I often get lost in the Jewish quarters and wander around sometimes meet some one I know. I love to be inside the Holy Sepulchre when the Bells ring for the evening Service. There will never be any content here as long as there are Moslems and Jews. They are not really mean to each other as I can see but they have have no love for each other.

It is sad to visit the Wailing Walls with a Jewish Friend. But when you go into the Mosque and a Moslem take you to a window and say look down at the

Jews it made me laugh they did look so funny the men in their long yellow and black striped dresses with round hats and a fur brim and beards and long curls hanging down over each temple and the women in their coloured shawls.

My Moslem friends often ask me if I like the Jews and I tell them I love them last night we went to the Wailing Walls and I walked up and kissed the old stones that have been kissed by the Jews ever since Solomon. my Friend Niza ask me why I did that and when I laugh He was pleased because He thought I did not mean it. When I come again Niza's mother say I must stay with Her I said I would.

It will be a long time yet before the old city will be clean and there are so many flies. I get up early and go out to buy the Grapes and Fresh dates just when they take them out of the boxes from under the leave and before the flies wake up. I love going through the old streets after the Sun sets then the flies and beggars have gone to rest.

Living are quite dear Here I save 50 cents a day by sleeping at the Y. and save 50 cents a day by not eating at the Y. I have 3 places to get good wholesome food. My Arabian Friend often pass just when I am finnishing my meal and He pay for it but He do not like to go into a Jewish resturant because He is Moslem. My stay Here have been just perfect and although I could stay longer just for the Shrines I am willing to leave in the morning for Cairo. where I hope to get a job. The laws are a bit better under the British but the Natives are getting not to fear them as much as in the beginning as they are not so strick I wonder why they Build so many fine Hospital instead of putting up factories so the many idle men can have work to do.

Le Caire Egypte Nov. 2, 1928
12 Sharia El Zumenah, 3rd Apt.

On reaching Kantara East where the Ferry cross the Suez Canal to Kantara West for the Cairo Train the Doctor wanted to keep me for a few days in Quarantine because I had been in Syria. But I told them to give me back the money I spent for the Visas I would go back to Palestine as I did not care a thing about seeing Egypt. It was very amusine they said I could go but they would vaccainate me. After the Doctor had all the things ready I said I would not be vaccainated then He put the things away and I went out and had plenty of time to make my train I got a nice room with a Greek Lady facing the beautiful El Ezoekiyeh Garden. It is good to be in the city again see beautiful trees and not so much dust like Syria and Palestine.

Yesterday I went to Heliopolis. After I had lunched I went to sit in the Park and an Arminin Nurse with a pretty little Girl call to me. She wanted to know if I would go to their house and do some washing and ironing I told her no but she thought I did not understand called to a young man and told him to ask me in French then she knew I understood Her at first. After she had gone I wished I had worked the half day just to see How much they paid and also for the experience Had I meet her before I had lunch I would have gone at once But you could not expect me after a good lunch with Icecream to top. to leave a nice shady Park. and go and do laundry work and it being my first trip to Heliopolis the City of the Sun.

I have been buisy seeing the City the men and Boys look funny in their night shirts under it they ware an under shirt and a cotton vest and a pair of baggy white troussers. and the women the vail and bracelets on their ankles I would like to know what each mark mean on the faces some have little strips cut it must have been painful some are tattooed some have their hair shaved off on the top. in other Europen country they try to grow it and here they shave it off. then some have a round burnt place back of the neck. some one large ear ring in the uper part of the left ear. all this are the men and Boys.

I go to a Greek resturant that have the Best home cooking and resonable but not as resonable as a native resturant so if I am short I go to the Native. I'll be here on a job for some months.

Sat. 7 A.M.

I just open my blinds to look on the Park and the Porter at the Park Gate with His rug on the ground was saying his Prayes a man about 50 dark skin real white hair a red fez and a soldiers suite He as neat as a pin He certainly did pray long and it look so beautiful there in the beautiful Park with His face towards the Sun.

The American Express Co.
Cairo, Nov. 29.

I could fill two or three dozen pages I have had a wonderful Day and come home tird out I went through the Pyramid with about a hundred and fifty School Boys age 7 up to 18. Two of the men Teachers spoke English and told me the funny things the Boys was saying it was dark going up narrow stairs and down the boys began to look after me and help me one would hold a candle in the front they began to strike matches one held on to my hand.

I have a lovely place to work and I had many places to choose the Y.W.C.A. gave me two jobs I had an ad. in the paper and received 6 answers and the Lady at the American Mission school also gave me a place I had a grand time calling on the Ladies I took the one I like best.

I like Cairo so much and have a very interesting young Lady Friend Jewish who has worked in a magazine and Postcard shop and speak 8 languages as well as I speak English. Of course I had to take Her to a few places in Cairo she did not know about altho she has lived here 16 years. She lived with her Mother who died 3 months

ago. They were just like two sisters and so happy together. So Eva are now very lonely she is 27 and thats
old enough. Her mother made a great trunk of Cloths
for wedding whenever the suitable man came along and
one did But he was a Christian and she wants only to
marry a Christian but the Mother would not hear of it
and now she would be pleased to have the money spent
for the chest of underware and linnen.

By making myself so native like with my vail I have
visited many of their feasts. I go to a native wedding
feast nearly every week. I am invited to have dinner at
the Y. at X'mas. I asked the Sectuary if they were going to have Turkey and she said Yes, so I hope it wont
be Chickens.

I have such a good job. I work for a lovely young English couple He fought at Gallipoli and some time get
kind of moody. she say Don't pay any attention to my
husband when he get like that he saw such dreadful
things in the war. She have a lovely little girl who go
to school she is 6 years and a half named Molly. I have
very little to do. I am the first American they have had
and they are so delighted I take Molly to the corner in
the morning for the bus that takes the English children
to school. Then I meet her and we have our tea and go
to the beautiful Club right on the Nile with hockey
grounds and tennis Molly plays with other English
children, we come home about 6 then I give Molly her
bath and supper and that is my work for the day I eat

my supper and go home. I refused several places as
Governess in Egyptian Families because I do not like
Little Girls of either Syria Palestine nor Egypte. I could
not find a place with a little Boy I love little Boys they
are so different from the Girls.

I was thinking of Thanksgiven and wished I had some
Turkey. I went to one of my many eating places and
had native beans and rice tomatoes and young salad. I
felt good. and of all the things in the world Ice cream
only can give me an elegant feeling so I went to Groppi
who make the best icecream after I felt quite pleased
with my Thanksgiven Day.

Dec. 22, 1928.
Cairo Egypte

The Shope Keepers are trying to make their shops look
a bit Xmasie but I dont think much of it. I spend a few
hours each week at the Egyptian Library. the head of
the library is a handsome man—broad shoulders—he
showed me some books they havent cataloged yet and
there I found just what I wanted—he speaks beautiful
English. he kept saying what luck to meet you. I am
learning what each Tattoo mark mean. each ear ring
the Bracelets and many other things that had puzzled
me. The King arrived several days ago for the winter
here. the City was beautiful at night and I enjoyed his
welcome. He is a quiet looking Gentleman about 45
but a bit over feed. My young Jewish Friend Eva asked

me to stay with Her. I wanted to be at the Y. but felt
sorry for Her so I went to stay but it seemed so quiet in
the short narrow street I came back to the Y. that night.
Then I thought how lonely it must be for Her and worried so I could not sleep so the next morning I moved
to her house. I pay Eva $2. a week. a little more than
the Y. to help her. It is in the old part near the street
that leads to all the famous Bazaars. to get to Her
house we go through a long passage and must have
flash lights as it is 8 or 9 oclock when we reach Home
and the shops are closed and everything are very lonely.
once inside you are all right. She had a dear little Pup
that was given to her Mother. the Owner who lived on
the top floor gave him chicken bones and when we
arrived home found him dead well she was so sad I was
glad I was with Her. but I never felt so much like running away. I put him on the dust pan she did not want
to take Him from the house so quick but I told Her it
had to be done. We made a Procession. I in the front
and she behind with a candle down the stairs through
the passage and in the street when I got back I felt so
creepy I was afraid of my own shadow. Now I have
been with Her Two weeks and feel quite at home and
She are much happier. the owner of the House are a
very Fine and Good Gentleman about 45 and well to do
they are Christian Egyptians. He live with his Mother.
for several nights when he would hear us coming up
the stairs He could not see us but would ask if it is was

us and If we had any one with us He was afraid that a
man would folower us Home and we would need Him
to send Him away. Eva got angry and asked Him if He
didnt have any confidence in Her. so now He never do
that any more.

The neighbors are mostly Greeks one Turkish man married to an Egyptian. He is Her second Husband and so
kind she said she like Him better than the First. Eva
dont know much about the Jewish releigon she spent
two years in an English Boarding School in Constantinople. But she had to learn many of their coustums after
Her Mother die. One of them is If the Mother Father
or sister or Brother Pass away for 8 days they must sit
on the Floor without shoes and have some one other
than a kin to cook their food and serve it to them they
must put dirt in their shoes so to be as though they was
on the ground. When Eva tell me all the funny things
that passed during the 8 days she sat on the floor I
laugh until I cry.

Cairo. Egypte.
New Year 1929.

I had a enjoyable Xmas. I was out every Day window
shoping. Molly hung up one of Her Mother's long
white stocking and a pillow case. and awoke at 4 A.M.
From her Mother I rec'd a small clock. From my Friend
Eva a oil Painting of The Pyramids and from myself
two bottles of Scott's Emulsion cod liver oil. I enjoyed
the Christmas Dinner but did not get enough Turkey so

had to make it up on roast Pork. and there was no dressing and the gravy was like water. and all the while I was wishing my feet was under some American Table. I went to a native sweet shop and finished up on sweets. I spent the afternoon with my Library Friend Mohomed Laki Hassan. It was like something pleasant and yet not sweet. It was like mint—our after noon on the Banks of the Nile River.

In the afternoon today an Egyptian Studient took me to the Courthouse where many of the Prisiners were set free. in frount of the Court House natives sat beating the Tom Tom singing and dancing while waiting to greet a relative or Friend the Studient told me many things they said and one of the songs they sang was My God will set you free. They repeated this over and over. while a native Girl bet the drum. Then when the Policemen would bring some one out they would hug and Kiss them it was a joy to see it. The name of the Gentleman I went with was Tenefik Mahamod Omar.

I moved from my friend Eva I spent 25 nights a few nights ago just as I was going in the Passage Two big rats was having a fight so they brought my visit to a quick close. I found a lovely French Family to stay with I did not go back to the Y. as I could not have a room alone. I enjoy the names of the streets. Eva's was Sekket Darb El Barabra 4. I am now at Charch El Cherefein 5.

Cairo Egypte Feb. 19.

I have some new Coptic Egyptian Friends. as they are still proveing to be interesting I dislike leaving them before it wares off. I gave up my place. Mrs. C. hopes to have me back in Two weeks Nothing are so nice as to get a job when you want it and nothing are so nice as loafing when you want to. I have always enjoyed each of the two just when I wanted to.

the Mohommonds are having their great fasting month they eat at 4 A.M. and 6 P.M. between that time do not smoke nor drink water the fast will last until the next new moon then they will feast for four days and keep all the Doctors buisy. I hear the Mosque cannon fired every morning a half hour before it is time to begin the days fast. anyway its the men that does the most praying while the women are asleep.

Sunday I took the train to the little village of Bedra-sheen and from there the Sheak gave me a nice Boy and donkey I had the roads all by myself it being early I made friend with an Arabic Girl. After we had gone about half a mile I gave her 5 cents at first she did not want to take it but after she said she wanted more I took it out of her hand and told her she would have nothing. after another half mile the Donkey Boy beg me to give it back to her. being tird of her company I gave it back. When we got to Sakkarah I layed on the sand near the tombs of the Sacred Bulls buy the time I had a good rest a German couple came with a guide so

I fell in line. I returned to Bedrasheen on foot alone just as I got down the hill when I see a man coming I would wrappe my head and face in my scarf and they were very puzzel but went their way then I had to pass a bunch of boys the eldest about 20 with a blue strip mother hubbard wanted to see who I was and ran to catch up with me but being quite a good runner gave him a real race he had give it up he was blouing so then he caught up again I stepped up to him and knocked him on the head with my fist and that was the last of the Arabic. I have got 140 lbs on since I came to Cairo and was glad to work a bit off.

then I came to a bridge where are a little lake and a few huts so before reaching there I covered my face the men and children were waiting for me and asked me why I covered my face an old man was sitting on the bridge I said good day to him then he gave them a good scolding and made the 8 or 10 children get in the house. I got back to Memphis and there were about 140 Tourist American French German I don't blame the native for staring at them they looked just like a circus with those auful ugly white hats breches and legons one man had on a red and yellow head dress that hung down to his waist. when I got back and begain to tell my Friends about returning from Sakkarah alone they were frighten.

for Two days I have been to every store looking for a dress one that was stylish that the sun could not fade which would not need to be cleaned or washed and one that I could pack in my case and not need to be press I found one for 750 francs its a little french model and look swell on me. I expect to leave in the morning for Upper Egypt I wrote to the Railway Co. about the Reck and my black eye at Brno Czechoslavakia and asked for Two hundred maybe they will give one third of that. anyway I am not lossing any sleep over it. Calcutta India may be the next Place I stop to work.

Luxor Upper Egypte
Hotel Karnak Feb. 25.

I just could not go straight on to Luxor so I got off at Assioun. A few minutes after arriving I meet a Mr. John Awad Christian that went to school at the American Mission I had 5 oclock Tea with him and then we visited the Bazaar and went over the Town. Had a good dinner and the Egyptian coffee. He took me to the Station at 9 P.M. and told the Station Housé men to make a bright light in the first class waiting room altho I bought a 3rd class Ticket and to see me on the Train at 1 A.M. He gave me a small green scrabe ring and His servant Boy walked behind us to the Station with a package when he said good bye he gave it to me it was a box of sweets and a Bottle of Palestine Wine it was just the thing as the night grew cold and that warmed me up.

I arrived at Luxor at 7 A.M. and went off to see the

Town and look for John Awads Brother Benjamin who own an amber and ivory place and to Find a room and saw a Hotel setting back in a big yard right on the edge of the Nile. I told the manager I wanted to stay right on the Nile and could pay only 40 cents a day. He let me have it for 50 cents. the Musicians of the Palace Hotel have rooms here and some of them have their wifes. never have I sleep in such a wonderful bed with linnen sheets and white blankets and Towels from the Winter Palace. I wont let the Boys come in my room and do the cleaning myself they look very sad about it but I dont want them messing around hitting a lick here and there. Then the next thing was my food the two restaurants are high I have a canned Heat which I cook 3 eggs for breakfast with bread butter and a cup of hot condensed milk. then I go to the market to shop for my dinner and supper yesterday I had 2 lovely fat swuabs of 25 cents 2½ cents of potatoes a head of lettuce 1½ cents and large tomatoe given to me. I brought it to my room and cleaned it with butter and took it to the Bakery shop where they put it in a nice covered pan and Bake it in the Bread oven it takes 2 hours and it is done so lovely and jucy they charge 2½ cents to Bake it. at Present I am so full I can not set up straight. today I had lamb I bought 27 cents of lamb a 5 cent cabbage and a penny's worth of new white onions I washed and seasoned it put it in a towel and took it to the Bakery they have wonderful Lamb it being the Arabians meat. I have a nice Friend at the Market that speak English and He help me to buy the best and cheap. You should see the crowd that stands around me when I am marketing. It makes me laugh But my market Friend scould them and tell them to go away but they only get thicker.

The next thing was getting a pass for the Temples and Tombs. I called at the Chief Inspector's Home and he was just getting on His motorcycle I told Him I was working in Cairo and could not pay to go in. He was a very Handsome young Egyptian. He said the Tombs would be open the next morning and for me to go there and ring Him up at His office and He would speak to the Guards. Well the next hard job was to learn to say His name as I Had to speak with Him over the Phone. I found a Turkish Gentleman that have a Buisness near my home and spent about 10 minutes going over it and he teach me How to say Tewfile Boulas Bey. this Gentleman that help me was the owner of all the Donkeys and Carriages. and said I may have number 72 Boy and donkey. When I got there the others did not know the Bosses order and I thought the 25 of them was going to have a real fight about who should take me. by the time I arrived with the help of Joseph the Donkey man could say Tewfik Boulas Bey well. They have a little Boaded up Tele. Booth and by the time you get connection to Luxor you forget what you want to say. after about 30 minutes I spoke to Him and

a great load left me when I got through Tewfile Boulas
Bey. He spoke to the Guard and such wonderful
Smiles. they gave me. I visited all the Wonderful
Tombs It took the whole Day and it all cost me 90
cents. I had to laugh at two American Gentlemen I was
going over the Temple built by Queen Hatshepset when
the Guide pointed out the Queen on one of Her war
boats disguised as a man with beard he said she was a
man by day and a woman by night one of the Gentleman said those Dames know what to do back in those
days. When the Native Girls ask me for money I answer them in Aribic that I am poor then I walk up to
them and take hold of one of their ankle bracelet and
say if they give me one I will give them something.
then we have a good laugh.

I have Tea with Two young Jewish Egyptian that have
a Perfume place they have lived here for six winters
and know nothing about living so good as I do they
have a lovely big house and Two servants. they gave
me a small bottol of very fine perfume and a brown
scrabe. I call one of the Brothers the Yankee Egyptian
He went to Harvard. Yesterday evening we went for
a sail along the Nile the moon being full many Boats
were out and you could hear lovely singing.

I was to leave in the morning but I am living so good
and cheap I'll hang around a while longer I can get
a job Here if I want to but there are no tips to it and
soon it will be warm so I'll not settle Here for any

time. I had a delightful Tea with the Twins served with Amber Past but I dont relish it. I will stop at Assouan and go to see John Awad Brother. He has a store there and I can get all information I need from Him.

Assouan Upper Egypte.
Khedival Hotel Room 10.
Mar. 3, 1929.

I am the only Women in this Hotel which pleases me a Friend at Luxor sent me here 50 cents a day. it is so clean and every one are so nice. The Nile are much pretty here than at Luxor. I left early this morning and walked along the Nile over the rocks I stoped in many Villiages twice lost my way but each time a native would go a little way with me. I arrived at the Neighborhood of the Dam where the Government have Lovely Bounglows for the Families of the Engineers. I asked a Lady for a drink of water and She gave me a nice tray of Tea and home made Cookies then I stayed an hour. When I was ready to go She went into the chicken house and got 4 eggs and one turkey egg and from the garden 4 large tomatoes and gave me some cookies to take with me. Her next door Neighbour a refined young Egyptian couple that have a beautiful Baby asked me if I would like to have a place with them they would pay me well I told her no. then I croosed the Barrage and Viewed the Island of Philoe. It is a beautiful sight to see after crossing the

Dam I took off my shoes and bathed my feet in the lake and washed my stockings and dryed them on the rocks. and had a nap at the rest house then I crossed the Dam and took the Bus back to the Town for 7 cents. I have fun Visiting the Bazaars. I am leaving tomorrow for Cairo and then to Port Said where I expect to take the Steamer to Bombay.

Port-Said Mar. 6.
Hotel Monopole Room 219.

The nights ride down from Assouan passed off very pleasant on the Train were two People that I had meet on my way up I was so pleased to meet them. We ate Sugar Cane most of the night the next morning the coach looked like a cane field. I had time at Cairo to go to a Friends house to wash up and have breakfast then it was train time. most of the way here was so dusty you could hardly see.

I spent most of the day trying to find the Steamship companys and the cheapest way to Colombo. I got tird at 7 P.M. and found a large room and a balcon open over a nice flower garden and just a block to the water frount it is very gay with the steamers coming all the time. last night I slept like sleeping beauty. the boy did not clean to suit me so I had a grand time Sunning the mathresses and blankets scrubing the floor and washing the mirrows and draws the boy did not know what to think. most of the People are Greek one Lady speak

English and I let Her do that in the Hall or on the stairs as I dont want neither man women nor child in my room when I am in I am always buisy. I have great joy going to the market and have delicious food for less then 40 cents the whole day.

I got a passage on the Orient Line on a lovely boat and they say the 3rd Class are as good as the second on the other lines. I gave my likes and dislikes a Cabin without children and uper berth. and will be ready to fight to get what I want once on boad so no one need piety me.

I am in just a block of a beautiful Greek Church so pray daily. I thought that all of Port-said was modern until I got out to the Native quarters there the streets are filled with children billy goats kids chickens ducks cats and flies the children sit on the side walks their backs covered with flies and the chickens jump up and pick the flies. I started through the quarters with my hat on but found I was out of place so went back and got my Vail then everything went lovely.

Sunday I see a beautiful enfaints Funnel at the Church and had tea with a Friend if you want a nasty tast put lemon and amber past in your tea.

I had planned to take the Sudan Government steamer up the Nile to Halfa. then a two day trip to Khartoun then a 5 day trip to Abyssinia then to Bombay and Calcutta and later go down to Colombo. it would have been a little hard to travel through 2 deserts but what would I care as long as I was getting my moneys worth.

I could have got across the three countries for the same money I am paying to Colombo. but when I went to the Railway He told me I must have a permit from the Sudan Government at Cairo and to send my passport back to Cairo to have it sign of course I would not part from my Passport for anything so I decided to come to Port-Said and Sail.

last night was the last fasting day of the Mohamonds so Today are the beginning of the 4 day feast. It was really a pleasure to go to the native quarters everything was so gay all the dirty children were washed hair comb their little red Fez blocked and redder than ever all the Boys had new and clean night shirts on and the Girls Pink green and orange colored dresses with hands red with Henna even the flies had gone.

I went to a circuis at 10. A.M. then another at 3 it was 5 cents to go in and 5 for a box seat I being a guest they gave me a box seat free I did enjoy seeing the way they run their circuis the greatest trouble was keeping the ring free of the Kids it was just like the Old Woman that lived in the Shoe. The actors are usually a family. they had a fire eater he also walked on sharp nails. but the real joy to me was to see how the children had the way of the tent. most of them stood up they gave me a nice chair but it served for me and several children. there was real Harem boxes with the Curtain to draw. we ate Spnge cake and penut candy most of the time there was the man with his stove near the ring making tea the smoky kettle looked so funny.

Well I hate to give up my home the Greek man that
have a room next to me say his prayers so lovely every
night and morning then he sing. I met an Egyptian
that have a lovely shop and gave me a little box of
amber past—it is very expensive. He invited me to dinner and he said I will have my cook to cook a nice
English chicken and rice and after we will go to a nice
apartment of a friend of mine and have an auful good
time. I went without eating food all day so to enjoy
it. he had it served in his shop with all the little things
that go with it, radishes, olives, my heels was just smiling, how I was going to get out of going to the apartment after. That day I went to the church and prayed
I wanted proction. while we sit there he say, "You are
not the cold English type," and I think to myself I'm
going to make a grand fool out of you. When the time
came to go I said, "We'd better not go together, you
are so well known here. I'll come behind," and he said,
"You're quite right. a wise little girl." so he started
ahead through the dark streets and when he came to the
place he went up to the apartment and I disappeared
I went down to the Y. and left the next day.

Orient Line England and Australia
S.S. Orana Mar. 13.

Well the Orana are a Queen. I went straight to see
about my cabin as I intended to get off if I didnt get
what I asked for. the Purser said I wanted all jam.
he gave me an uper Berth in the quiet foot of the Ship

with Two lovely modist young Greek Girls one are
going To Sydney to be married Her skin are so fair
she have never used Powder the other are a very modist
Flapper we keep the Cabin neat and all retire at the
same hour so everything are peasful in that line. I went
over to the First Class to see the Slighter hand entertain
the bigest joke are on the Passangers they play their
tricks with the Guests own money with a promise to
return it but have a clever way of keeping it with the
concent of the owner.

On boad are Hundered of English going to Australia
at the expence of the Government young couples with
their children and single young men and Girls from 17
to 22 and they are certainly a bright healthy handsome
ship load.

the Third class are lovely large wide decks a swiming
pool everything like a pin then a large laundry with
soft water and ironing boads. at night most of the Girls
sleep on deck since it became warm they use the First
Deck and the Boys the Second. we had chicken only
one day and that day I was sleeping under a life boat
and did not hear the bell I did not care but the others
felt sorry for me.

On Boad the S.S.Orana
Mar. 21.

the time have gone so fast I feel like asking for my
money. It would have been more enjoyable to me to
have been traveling third class on train through the

Sudan and Abysscina half starved thirsty and dusty
then I would have had something to remember.

the young people are just to amuseing the Boys are
under the care of a very refine minister and the Girls
are under two or more Elderly Ladies. the Boys going
as farm hands the Girls as maids some have Friends
that went Two years ago and like it so much have en-
couraged others. we dont really need the Ship Band the
youngster furnish all the singing. they have dancing
every night except Sunday. the best dancer are an India
Boy about 20 and a dark haired English Girl a real
flapper but are modist She never dance with any one
but him and He only with she. the Girls look cute in
their little sleveless dresses some with stockings and
some without. but everything Fit in lovely. the Boys
are not allowed on the side of the deck when the Girls
are swiming but some of them sneak over and hide the
girls Kimonos so they will have to go to their Cabins
in their suits and they stand off and watch for them.
they had a baby show its about 75 babies on boad so I
did the right thing when I was looking out for my
Cabin, somebody must be in with them.

Colombo. Palm Sunday
March 24.

The Salvation Army Hostel.
We arrived at 6 A.M. yesterday and I found so much to
attract my atation I went nearly all over Colombo before I found a Place to stay they have a lovely Y. but

they are to dear for me so I came here a beautiful and
pleasant house just a few block from the sea with big
growns cocoanuts banana and other fruit trees and many
beautiful Girls they have long black hair some of them
in the Costumes like they ware here. its lucky I like
Currie powder and red pepper but tonight I am sorry to
say I felt myself filling up on it I trust I can hold out for
a week. most of the Girls eat with their right hand
useing all the fingers Of course I like to see them do
that all of them are refine and speak English. last night
I walked down to the Sea and the women go barefooted
and ware short white tight waists with their stomach
out they were in wading so I took off my shoes and went
in walked back Home barefooted. it was a real joy.
When I started off to the sea tonight my friend a beautiful English Girl told me not to go as they would think
I was not high class I told her I would not miss being
with the women and a good wade for a little thing like
that.

I can get a Place if I want to but I will take a few trips
first. I feel like I have been in Colombo a long time.

April 7. 7 P.M.
Room 23. 2nd floor
Salvation Army Women's Hostel

I found Colombo at Its very best Holy Week. every
body were out in their best cloths those that did not
ware any had their lovely long black hair combed neat
and their little cloth nice and clean. I was buisy going

from one church to the other the different People were
so interesting in their cloths the high and low Singalese
the high and low caste Indians. It was at St. Lucia's
Cathedral I always got my fill. Thursday of Holy Week
in all the Catholic Churches they had washing of the
feet. the Priest washed the feet of a few poor and kissed
them. After Good Friday I felt I could not go to church
until after a whole afternoon rest so I Took the bus.
to Mt. Lavinia Hotel and had a wonderful time in Bathing. on the beach I meet an old Fisherman that owned
many out riggers and when the men brought them in I
went with Him to look at the fishes I had no time to be
lonely.

the Hotel are enlargen and I saw some women carry-
ing motors in pans on their heads so I asked the Boss
how much they got a day he said 18 cents so I asked
him If I could get a job. He was so surprise it made
me laugh then He said he did not think they would let
me work. then I walked through the Villiage and to get
to talk to the Natives I would stop and buy a cocoanut
in a half minute it would be many around me.

I was surprised Easter morning when I got to the Cathedral of St. Michael and all Angels the better class that
had been there during the week had given it over to the
poor class it were filled. Some had big holes in their
ears with 3 ear screws in the uper part a screw in each
nose bracelets on each leg and two toes with rings. and
such bright colors. Easter night the Archbishop of

Colombo passed away he was much loved for 24 years. So it was a great contrast when I went to the Funeral. every one tried in some way to be in mourning many of the native that used only a short piece of cloth wore a black belt.

Well my Friend gave up trying to make a high class Sinhalese out of me She thought I got worse and worse every day I went to the Circuis and sat where men only sat just to see if the men could be trusted the man at my left had very long hair he bought 3 leaf of Betel and gave me one it is a green leaf with a nut like nutmeg and a pink dab of past like tooth past and two pieces of tobacco leaves. I chewed the Betel then when I got home with a red mouth they wanted to know where I got it and when I told them they were shocked. it sweetens your breath but it made the inside of my mouth sore and when I begain to eat my dinner with red pepper I jumped out of the Chair so I have had my fill of Betel.

I have learned that the high castes would like very much to walk and save their Rickshaus fare like I do but of course their caste wont allow it.

I enjoy teaseing the Girls and ask if they Wish to be free like me to go out in the street at any hour I told them if any one were bad it was the Girls the men were always nice to me. Now they wish to be like me. For a change I went into a native Hotel they were surprised to see me a lone woman coming in I had such a Wonderful Sinhalese dinner a big saucer of rice then eight other side dishes when I would empty one the boy would rush to refill it and all for 18 cents.

When I feel tird I go to the Library I have read some very good books on Ceylon and the Buddishism which I knew very little.

the Girls all make their dresses I made my Easter dress that cost $1.26 and a pretty fugih silk dress for $1.08 neither sun nor rain will hurt it. Colombo are much dearer than Cairo and the Egyptians are a much more polished race than you find here yet I am not finding fault ever one are kind to me. but here are so many Crows that roost in the cocanut trees in the Yard and Graphones with those big horns they play all day until late in the night I get very little sleep. the Crows are perched on my windows all the time and when I speak to them they are just like human beans. There will be a big meeting Wed. to celebrate the Berth Day of General Booth. For years in N.Y. I was a love of the Army so feel at Home.

I went to see the funeral of a very Rich Person and the next day out to see how the body had burned the logs was red hot and only a few bones could be seen a watchman keep the fire going on my way a Hindoo funeral were going there a poor class they have no Prest. they get quite drunk the nearest kin and friends are the drunkest then they dance sing and play music along at the grave the Son was given a water jar full

He stagared around the casket with it on his head and the water would fall on the body of his mother. Then his drunken friends break the water jar at the Head of the grave and he sit on the ground a barber shave off his hair and put it in the casket all the time they are making a loud noise. I was the only woman at the grave and it was pouring rain after it was over I went to the Chapel out of the rain and meet a polite Buddish Gentleman who told me the mening of everything that I had seen. He wanted to know what I thought of the different relegions—I said the Hindoos had the same right to think they were right as the Buddish and as we—how did we know any one were right. He said he had never met any one like me before. They are puzzled with the Christian relegion When you get it all added up I would have been just as well pleased to be a Hindu. Well after all that last night I felt so creepy I could not sleep and was glad to hear the graphone playing. Every evening at about 5 it rains for an hour or two. the mornings are breezy and the nights are starie sometimes a light spread over you.

> *Kuwara Eliiza.*
> *April 17.*
> *The Sinhalese Palace Hotel.*

I had a wonderful trip up the Mountains through the rubber plantations then through the tea fields I wish it had been tea Picking time it would have been fun to pick tea for a few days. When you change for the norrow gauge train the trip up are very much like going up Mt. Lowe. on reaching Kuwara after looking over the Village I went in a little Chapel on the Mountain Side to Pray.

This is a very nice Hotel but they dont object sleeping on the same sheets after each other so I had to make them understand I wanted clean ones the Egyptians are the same. also I had to fight for Two sheets. it is very beautiful up here the mountains so green but I'll be ready to leave in the morning.

Thursday 18.

I took the train for Kandy and shared my lunch of cucumber cheese and chocolate bars with an old couple I sat with they was eating dry bread. they sang and had musice so I did not like leaving them. the City was looking its best with red carpets spreaded in many places that the Highness the Prince was to be. He is a big fine looking 28 year old Chap. it being the Sinhalese New Year it was most gay all the Hindoos have new cloths on they will not allow you in their temples.

I had a pleasant Visit by train to a interesting fishing Village Negombo Ceylon. two Sinhalese Ladies wanted to go with me but they being so high casted would not cared to go whare I would go. So I just told them I never had a traveling Companion and If I just had to

have one it would be a man and of all things not a
Woman.

Kandy Ceylon
April 22.

Kandy is such a Fairy like Place. I have a pleasant
room but like Cuba I often see a nice little lizzard running on the walls. the whole Town are covered with
Trees mangoes bread fruit trees they say if they eat
very much bread fruit it will close their eyes. This noon
I went to an English Wedding about 20 pretty little
Choir Boys in their red and white robes with Buster
Brown Collars. I was thinking how Perfect it all was
but when the Bride came down the isle she smiled at
some friends and her teeth were to long for her thin
Face.

I am leaving tomorrow for Madura which have the finest Temple In India. I hope to take a place to work at
Bombay. I went to the relegous Feast at The Sacred
Temple of the Tooth it being the second day of full
moon it was interesting to see the many different dressed
people bringing fragrent flowers to offer to Buddur.

April 23.

I took the afternoon Train so to reach the Plains when
the afternoon showers make it so pleasant then I saw
Anuradhapura by moon light the Train were filled with
Indians that had been in Ceylon working on The Tea
Plantations and were returning to Madura for the Fes-

tavel. When I got on every place was fill the men and children sleeping on the seats and the women on the floor so I turned up my case by a window and narded the rest of the night. the moon was bright and the whole trip was through the jungles took the Ferry at 7 A.M. it is 22 miles across to India. in the train were two Tamil women and a little unkept Indian Girl about 7. I thought she were with the women but learned she ware a wise little Hobo. She took a fancy to me after some time I took out some change to count it and she begin to beg me for some. I offared to buy her pop but she refused after we had traveled a while and she knew I wouldnt give her money she took from around her waist a little white bag and before my eyes begain to count all the time looking at me sideways Then we had a good laugh she had as much as Two dollars. She had a great respect for me because She did not fool me. when we arrived at a station she hid under the seat and told me not to say anything to the Condoctor.

We arrived at Madura and the Railway own a traveller's Bonglow. It is comfortable built with poach all around. in each room in the top of the sealing is a wide thing with a rope that pass through a hole in the wall on to the poach and a coolie sits on the poach to pull it and fan you.

Last night I went to the Great Temple about 7 P.M. it are wonderful and takes up about four blocks and did not take off my shoes I walked up the steps to the shrine of the Goddess Minakshi. a half dozen got behind me and told me to get out of there and not in a pleasant voice. Many were crowded around me all naked with exception of a thin white cloth about their loins and their bodys marked with yellow paint a red and yellow mark on the forehead and their hair shaved off except a long pigtail on the top. a young boy told me that Europeans were not allowed in that sacred place not even without shoes and that I was fined 3 rupees about a dollar I told him I did not have any rupees. I must admit I came off those stairs on wings. Early this morning I went back but took off my shoes and stockings and hid them in my umberella so meet them all again they wanted to know where my shoes was I told them I did not have any I started in another sacred place but they told me to go the other way.

The people are polite and never stare at you I like them better than in Ceylon but the Sinehaleses women are more stylish and beautiful than in this part of India. I followed behind a rich Hindy family when I visited the grand Tirumala's Palace. they were as interesting as the palace. The women with diamonds in each side of their nose and great diamond ear rings but bare feet the girls with nose rings and the man almost naked with marks on his body and long hair they came in a swell auto.

I want to visit 3 or four other small places in the Home

rule state but could not get any money exchanged except at Madras and had planned not to Visit there as
it is British but will have to go there before I can reach
Bombay. anyway I have 20 rupees and will go hungry
a few times so to Visit an extra Town.

Madura Sat. 29.

You get so much of the Hindu life here. I enjoyed
going to the Great Temple at 6 P.M. when the Elephants
was brought in for the night and given their bath then
they are chain in the stalls. But the one thing I would
like to be is a Mrs. Cow they are the ones that have the
right away then I would know my Children would get
the best of care on every poach are a nice bed of straw
for the calf but the Children sit on the floor. every one
seem to be leading a Cow in the Streets. Two Hindu
Women were pleased with me when I stoped at their
door and Kissed their pretty new born Calf. A Hindu
never pass a cow he do not kiss his hand and touch the
cow as much to say you dear old Holy Saint.

In route to Madras
April 29.

I am in a coche for women and Children they look
so interesting in their red with a little Yellow micture
in the goods their dresses are about 8 or 10 yards draped
about them most of the time their breast are free but
they have an extra two yards or so over their sholders to

cover it and their head when needed. Here are many different cast some ware a short waist but everyone have jewelry next me are a young wife with her first baby and a nurse am sure she is high cast on each arm are 11 bracelets and in each ear 10 ear rings the ear flaps over with the weight of the rings then she have a large gold collar and many gold necklace. and 3 heavy silver ankle bracelets She has a head dress to cover her face. I like to be in their coche they bath and ware so few cloth they never have an order. I did not like traveling with the Egyptian or Turkish women because of their black robes.

At the second stop when the train started off a man fell under my coach Everybody got excited and I was sure of an unplesant trip but the train going slow he managed to roll from side to side and keep out of the way of the fictures under the coches and he was alright so that made everyone happy.

Madras India,
General Station second Class Waiting Room
the trip was lovely and cool and at most of the Stations when the train stoped a monkey would jump in every window they were so pretty and fat if you be eating they would slip up and take it out of Your hands. I had a few hours at Trichinopoly and visited the Hindu Temple then left for Madras at 5 PM. the Women were a better class most of them were to be on alnight

everybody were trying to save a space many qualls took place but not without merriment I had a good snug place so sat back and enjoyed the fun. Once an Indian woman got in and wanted me to get out—she thought I was low cast—I have a red shawl and bare feet looking auful casty—about as low cast as a European can look—plenty of high class Indian women ride in the 3rd they dont want to mix with the Europeans or with classes—then they say to a low cast on a bench you get down there and lay down—when I didnt get down she sat and looked at me with a puzzled face. I dont mind being a high cast but I want to be a low cast too.

One of the most pleasant thing In India is that all but the smallest Stations in the 2nd and 1st Waiting rooms are large bath rooms and a nice loungering room it was great to go in and take a cool bath and change your cloths. the maid told me if I were going to spend only one night to go to the Surpentender of the Station and tell him I am a Stranger and could I stay in the waiting room it wouldnt cost me anything. I thought to wait until the last train arrive and they lock up then He couldnt refuse me I went to the wonderful beach on the Bay of Bengal and got back at 8 P.M. the maid was excited as I was so late the supt. had gone home but I told the assistant if He refused me I was going to the Beach and sleep in one of those large fishing boats and that frighten him so he said I may stay. I locked the door on the inside and washed my cloths they have nice

cloths Horse. it was cool and quiet. the Maid had Her
sister to Cook my meal and brought it to the Station and
I had a real feast. you see very few horses and Bullocks
doing the halling in Madras it is done by men great
wagon loads drawn by five or six thin but strong coolies.
many of the Public buildings look like castals. /

The porter told me to wait for an 8.30 Passanger train
in the mornin it would be cheaper I had more time then
Rupees also a cheaper train would be more interesting
people. so I waited.

In route to Bombay

The Condoctor felt I being a European should ride in
one of the compartments of only 3 or 4 people but I
refused Two of the Women when they saw him want-
ing to help me tryed to pour water on me He scoulded
them it was a plesant bunch a girl about 16 very pretty
begain to sing and made both her eyes and hands sing.
Its wonderful how little luggueg they have. they go
into the Lavitory and take a bath and wash out those
yards of cloth and put on the other then hold one end
let the other blow out of the train window 10 or 12
yards of red cloth blowing until it drys. /

I like the women even the lowest cast are jolly and
broad minded every one mind their on buisiness and ask
few questions for 20 minutes we traveled through heat
and the wind was just like a blaze then we had a good
shower when each one want a place to sleep I gave my
share to a woman and climbed up to the baggage rack

it is as wide as a lot I had a great time looking down
on the others the woman I gave my seat to qualled over
it with another most of the night. I was glad I gave it
up it was such fun. In my red shawl and black vail on
my head no one would think I had seen Broadway.

Y.W.C.A. Bombay India
June 5.

The Y. have two big buildings in the best part of the
City Each room have a name, my room is the "Sir Sas-
son David" and the one next to me "The Sir Shapurji
Broach". It is good to become a Member of the
Y.W.C.A. when you start out traveling. I had 3 Y.
Cards when I dont know the language my Bible and
cards speak for me. Sometime some one ask me—Why
do you carry such a big Bible—I always find room for
this Bible. Then if you have your Y.W.C.A. Directory
you always have an adress to go to. Even if you dont
stay at the Y. you can come in and get news and there
are plenty of girls to talk to.

It cost 90 cents a day but that is far too much for me.
all men servants everything are served beautiful beautiful plates changed at each course. a tray in our room
at 7.30 tea bread butter fruit then breakfast in the
Dinning room at 9 then a lunch of 3 courses at 1 P.M.
dinner at 8 and afternoon tea in our room at 4 P.M.
one week will be enough of that for me You can see
that a Christian home will soon empty your pockets.

A missinory must have a pretty hard task trying to teach

Christianity in India where the people know more about it than themselves. a buisness man leaves his office to worship.

I know a Gentleman that own a Indian sweet meat shop when I want to know anything I go by and always he give me two small packages of sweets. I dont like them much they use a flavoring that tast like medican.

I go often at the foot of Malabar Hill to the bathing beach they cook many things on the beach potatoe cakes fried brown then half it and put in a very good tarty sauce everything are served on leaves after a day going about samplein the dishes first thing the next morning I take a good dose of Epsom salt.

Rioton was very bad last week and I payed so little atention. Sat. walked right into the dangerous neighborhood. When I meet an English Gentleman and He told me to go home as they were expecting an attack then the troops were everywhere and I walking about sight seeing. Sunday at 8 P.M. I was sitting so peaceful on the Beach when a nice young studient Doctor told me it was curfew. and all the cars and buses had stop so he took me home otherwise I dont know how I would have got back as it is across the city. He is going to Paris next summer to study I told him where to stop so he felt well paid for his service.

I never pay to have my dresses press I walk about until I see a Tailor shop and the iron in use then I go in and ask them to let me press and it is something new to them so they will never take pay. I will go to the Times

office to see if I got an answer from my add that I put
in Monday if not will put another one in the morning
paper. if I dont get work will look up some american
Family and offer my service for a room. food I can get
cheap enough. good wholesome meals in a little resturant for 9 cents noon dinner and 6 cent supper.

if I dont get something to do then I will visit Delhi
Agru Benares and to Calcutta for it is cheaper traveling
than boading.

I go swimming every eve at six I dress in my suit and
put a dress over it so my baths do not cost me 18 cents
as it would if I went into the bath house. a card was
tacked up at the Y. that at Christ Church would be a
jumble sale so I went and got 7 pairs of silk stockings
without a brake for 60 cents a good voil dress the sun
cannot fade for 70 cents and a beautiful silk dress for a
dollar I wanted two nice white silk ones but was afraid
to spend more.

> Situations wanted—
> Experienced woman desires
> place as Nurse or Housework
> Box 1495.
> The Times of India 11918

Mary Lodge
Hornby Vellard
Worli Point
June 10, 29.

Dear Madame:
    Having read your advertisement today in the Times of
India, please come to interview me at the above address at

5 o'clock any evening. There is post vacant of a nurse companion to me, open for a European lady only.

Yours Truly

(Miss) B. A. C. . . .

This was the most promising place for me but she said
I had to share her room and right there I said no. She
is a wealthy Parsee Lady of a very fine family some days
she is with feaver 103 but look the picture of health.
Warlie Point run right out into the Sea and there is
a small but beautiful mosque thats built upon a high
rock at the frount of her apartment. She told me to
wait and her car would take me but I walked to the car.
well for 4 days I thought of riding about in Her car
so I went back and told her I would try it for a week
she said she decide not to take a nurse at present but
if she changed would write to me. I enjoyed the second
Visit I had time to visit two other places of interest
near there.

Watson's Annex Room 126
Apollo Bunder
Bombay June 14

Yesterday so bright and early. the pleasant Postman
with his bright red clothed covered Head knocked at
my door at the same time the Broadcasting Station next
building to me was sending out some good musice after
opening the long envelope It would have put Madame
Pavlova to shame with the graceful steps I made about

the Room. Altho I asked for it I never expected to get the money from the R.R.co. for the black eye I got in the train reck and they took me at my word and sent just what I asked for. Well I am glad the first letter I written them came back as I forgot to put all the little ups and downs over the letters. in that one I asked for 150 dollars but when I wrote the second one I added another 50 dollars. never have I got something for nothing before and I dont feel I can use it for Globe-trotten.

The rainy season begin the first of June and everything look so fresh and green the children had their holidays Mar. April and May and now the Schools open last week and it is much gayer to see them going to school in many different dress and Caps.

the shops are full of rain coats rubbers and covers for the Topees, the European stores have out the jersey suits for the cool days but what I would like is to be like the Native in their White or red cloths and a short coat with their shirt tails out and walking along in the rain in their bare feet the cloth can be pulled up to the Waist.

11.30 A.M.

Well I feel just right now I had a nicely cooked tendor beefsteak fried onions a native vegetable boiled potatoes two slices of bread and a side dish of relish which cost me 5 cents in our money that are 3 annas then I have a good Dairy where I buy a pot of fresh butter 1¾ cents and a loaf of bread also 1¾ cents to have on my return from swimming I always have such an apetite.

Here in India people that live in one or two rooms have dinner pails with 5 or six pans that they send to the resturant for their meals by the month. I dont think there is another such good resturant in Bombay—I just will find those Places. It is run by a young Christian native and his wife I am the only woman that go there and they are so kind to me.

I had a grand time intervewing the answers from my Advertisement besides finding the Places which took me in every Corner of the City I would look in the neighborhood to see the rooms for rent just to pass away the time. Think what a turist miss not to do such things. Then some would call to see me they would turn out to be a Widower with Children looking for a Housekeeper. but that kind of job I could never take. One Hindu Gentleman came to intervew me He brought an enterpter He had on a nice shirt and several yards of white draped about his loins a black silk coat that came to the knees a black turban nice black low shoes and no stockinugs when He sat in the Chair in frount of me I was afraid the folds would fall apart but he Keep them in place. that call was worth the price of the add. I sent an Indian Girl to see Him. Some of them have the nerve to ask you to send a Snapshot with the promise of returning it. I was sorry I did not answer

one such and send a picture with that Egyptian water
jug on my head just for the fun of it. Its always the
Husband that write and ask you to call.

I visited a most beautiful Home of a rich Mohammend
Family His Wife a young fat fine looking brown mama
with diamonds in her nose I sent an English woman to
see her.

I didnt get suited in a place but I found a room with
a very nice Widow Christian Lady for 9 dollars a month
but the first night I saw a big rat. altho I had paid her
she gave it back to me She thought I was stranded I
moved the next day to this pleasant place I had it in
View. It is a handsome building that was the leading
hotel 60 years ago and have several hundred one room
apartments. I have a most pleasant room with an Indian bath white not quite knee high in one corner where
my heart rest.

I think it just wonderful to live like this, my stretcher
cost $1.80 which is 5 rupees. a old rose spread which
answers for sheet at night cost 36 cents. a zink water
pail for 12 cents. a yard and half of pink cotton crape
for the Hall window 12 cents. My coat and underware
make a good Pillow the suit case made a nice table
for my Bible and clock. I have a thick piece of brown
paper with a nice handkerchief on it where I keep the
7 or 8 good books I get from the Y. most of them on
India and the rest of around the world the best I have
found at the Y. are by American authors. the prettiest

thing I have three cocnuts shells with the bottoms cut to
sit on the side of the bath and I keep them filled with
fresh Vines that have white blossoms that smell so
sweet I also have a tin of canned heat for making
coca or coffee and a little pan for stewing eggs frying
bacon the pan is a present.

the next best thing are my neighbors on one side of
me a Christian Indian Young Student at the University
to my left a Young Turkish Jew His Father sent him to
do buisness Hes in love with a Girl at his home when
He feel love sick I tease Him so I think he is getting
over it He has three chairs and try hard to get one off
on me but I told him I had always sat in chairs. now
I wanted something different I liked to sit on my clean
floor.

Across the Hall are a Parsee Young man also a Studient
He say to me the English is nice but oh. I get so chilly
when they come near—then he say youre not English
are you? I told him No. I am american. He said when
you come I feel like smiling. they are all so quiet and
gentleman and never out late at night. there is a pretty
Anglo-Indian Girl and Her brother near me. He is 5
months behind his rent there is a summons tacked on his
door. everybody stay in their own back yard.

altho they have only one room each have a servent they
felt so sorry for me the smartest looking servent boy
came to me and said Mem Sahib which mean Lady I
feel so sorry for you because you have no servent I will

do what ever you ask me without any pay but the next day when he saw me on my knees with a brush scrubing my floor I am sure He changed his mind. I pay 11 dollars a month for my room and the light is extra but I never use it. If I want to read at night I take my book and sit on the sea front at Apollo Bunder better known as the Gateway of India. In just a block of here a great crowd stands every evening at the Taj Mahal Hotel under the ExKing of Afganistan Window until He comes and speak to them.

Watson's Annex Apollo Bunder
Bombay June 28, 1929.

I had a nurse job with an old Lady that was a little quare. but I gave it up I got tird of getting up at 2 A.M. to write out dying remarks. The husband of the old Lady I was taking care of was so extremly a gentleman. He dressed in white duck suites he would never sit in the company of his wife and myself without his coat. His parents was Scotch but he had never been out of India. She was English and came to India to teach school. She'd say at first, "the Lord Has sent her to us —Now husband you pray" she say, then we close our eyes and fold our hands and pray. After I guess she thought the devil sent me. She was terrbly gelious thats how we fell out. She would call out from the bed "Oh, Frank you are not there talking to that young woman I wont stand anything like that"—and she

would throw pillers. then I threw pillers and she would
say "Come here, Frank, I'm afraid of her She has a
temper," and he would say, "Well so have you a temper." She was very particular had lots of old lace and
must have been a very pretty and briliant woman. I
have soft print and blue dresses I always keep them
fresh. I wear them with a big black belt and she would
say "You keep all pumped up and so nice and I am ill."

Bombay July 10th.

I have another job in the Bath de Luxe it is a real joke.
a 22 year old Hindu doctor of a wealthy Papa. So he
do not trouble hisself nor the 3 Girls and Boy He hire
and everything goes along lovely. The two Portuguese
Girls are good and nice and the Doctor a High intelli-
gent Hindu he speak German English French I was
haveing a gelouries time practising massageing on the
two nurses but on the third day the Doctor told me to
go in and give a coustomer a massage I told him I just
could not do it. if I had to beg the next minute we had
a great laugh after. Well we have a nice tray of tea at
4 P.M. then at 7 a good Hindu dinner we have a joly
time He is the Hindoo faith and we Christians He will
Kiss our Christian lips freely but he would not let our
Christian hands Touch nothing that He eat. When He
bring the dinner altho we have a table we never think of
useing it each have a piece of paper on the floor he
Take out his dinner and he never take any more after

we have touched the rest. The Hindoos have real good food but rich.

He has such nice white soft cloth for his loins about 10 yards to each the most delicate finest stuff I wanted to learn how To drape it on Him so he let me do it 3 or 4 times it is quite an art. When there are no more coustomers we spend the time danceing the Girls are engaged. their sweethearts call for about 10 minutes every eve. This is a very high class bath place and only high class men come here. they just like nice brown mamas rubbing them up but the Doctor is always around to see every thing is Alright. the Bath fee are 4 rupees if the Custumer doesnt look very rich If he look rich the Girls say 7 rupees.

I could stay right here at the bath and have my room rent free but I dont want anyone fooling with my room rent. my room is my personal self they can give me my food or little presents but I dont want any one to be able to come to my room.

Bombay in the Train at Colaba Station
July 1.

I wanted to leave for my trip through the north as the rain are not so heavy and on to Calcutta but when I told the apartment house manager He told me I must pay a months rent as I failed to give Them a months notice. While teaching a little Boy 13 years from The Annex how to float in the sea I was telling Him He said if you want to give up your room do so. they just want the rent money. I took his advice. So I left this morning at 4.30 A.M. it had been pouring most of the night I was up watching the time as I wanted to slip out before the manager awake. I took the Street Car and all the while I felt the Coolie Servent that slept in the Lobby would rush up and tell the Manager. When I got to the Station I meet a Gentleman I knew and He ask the Guard at the Gate if I may take my seat in the Train I thought I had better get in for fear the Manager may come down. thats why I am sitting hid away in the Coch.

It will be a sweet memorie my stay at the Annex the sweet musice from the Broad casting Station across the narrow court yard the delightful Bathing at Back Bay and the Kind young Christian native and his wife that run the resturant where I took my meals. The train is pulling out in a heavy rain we will travel along by the Sea for a while. I am the only one in the woman's coche. I have just changed my black silk dress French cap and old shoes for my pale pink cotton dress I always ware when traveling and each night I wash it out and the next morning fold it and put it under the suit case to press. then my black voile for the head and black sandles without stockings.

I have a big lunch of steak sandwiches I have a large cup so paid 3 cents for the delicious tea and milk you can get at all times in any part of India.

Well I wasnt alone long here the coch filled up with lovely looking Jains and Parsees. I like the way the Janiser Ware their covering just like the Virgin Mother. One Himlain Lady have a nose ring with pearls it touches her chin. the coch look just like a rain bow. I am always happier on the road. All the refine looking Parsee Lady next to me could say was I cannot speak English I was glad I like best to make signs. It would be better if people didnt talk so much. they could live through signs.

We have just crossed an inlet of the sea and the Parsees had offorances to throw in of sweet smelling flowers and a handfull of something that look like salt peter. I wished a piece had droped by me so I would know what it was.

First stop I bought 1½ cents the best shelled and parched peanuts in a pan that keep them hot and with something yellow on them and dry chilli They can teach us how to serve nuts. next stop I bought 1½ cents of native fruit next a cup of tea and a mango the size of a mellon sweet as sugar. 3 cents. There are many sheep and Goats through Here but are different like in other countries.

Surat India. This is where we loose our best dressed Parsees and Jaines The Coach are filling up with Mohamedans a young mother with a little boy she has barefoote Pretty little feet not a corn mark. Well she isnt Moh. But Parsee I mis judge the tatoo mark we passed a river not having the offerense of flowers she threw in money. and seem sad because it fell on the tressel we are crossing. When She leave she wanted to say goodbye and pat my arm and said good evening. Each sect try hard to sit together they prefer to be uncomfortable all crowded on one seat than to be comfortable sitting with one of the other sect. an elderly Mohamedan got on She have a tight fitting waist to hold Her anousmas bust and the stomack a great roll of fat are free to the air. one woman legs are covered with brass bands 1½ inches from their knee to the instep arms from the elbor to the rist. the first I have seen in any parts. Most of the women are rich I can tell by their Jewlry and long pants many of them use a black tooth paste.

Miyagam. each Town seem like a different Country up here they have much farm and but few people. different from the South of Bombay more people than Land. another Family of Four girls have on little motherhubbards green old rose head cloth The colors alone will make you gay. some have real red gums and jet black teeth. and a piece of net over the mouth and eyes it is made of changeable silk.

5 P.M. Baroda Chip munks are running all about the station and there is a large gray bird black wing with orange eyes and bill. They have flies up here Mohamedans worship them. all the People carry their brass water jugs polished so you can use it for a mirrow. The white oxen take the place of mules and Horses.

the Water Buffalow are the milk Cow you see many in the rivers with just their head out. We have just pass a little Town Wasad and the only Christian Church I have seen since I left Bombay.

Anand. This is a Hindoo Town. They wont have any other but Hindoos in their resturant altho my Christian feet have been in several But they would stretch out their arm between me and the table or pan they use for frying. A Salvation Army must be here I see a young Indian in a red coat and orange skirt.

Nadiad. Here are many morden Homes and also grass huts everything look open and free.

Mehmanabad. Here I see the first Camels and many Donkeys on this trip I can just judge how the country changes. I see a drove of Peacock in the twilight.

Ahmedabad. 8 P.M. on the Bombay Baroda Central Line. The first Thing I notice You could not hear the Train noise for the Chirping of The Thousand of Birds That roost in the Station I went out to find the Grand Hotel I meet a nice gray bearded Gentleman. a Doctor He was waiting for His cart and Ponie so he took me to the Hotel. He also offored to take me to His Wife as He said She would be pleased to have me stay for a few days. Thanked Him and refused. The Hotel was full but if it hadnt been I wouldnt have paid 9 rupees a night. No true rover would do such a Thing in the Summer in a Country like this where most of the People Sleep on the side walks. I came back to the

Station 1½ miles. They allowed me to sleep in the clean Waiting Room. But the Birds Chirped so I was awake most of the night.

July 2. I got up early Bathed in the large Tiled Bath Room and went sightseeing. I visited several Bazaars and beautiful Mosques. Then I climbed on top of the old ancien Walls. A large but very unatracted City many Mills. the People in their different dress make me feel I am at a Carnival. The streets are very bad. I am not allowed to spend another night in the Waiting Room so I am sitting on one of the small truks they use for moving trunks. The Town are full of Peigons goats cows a few camels and many white donkeys that carry dirt for the building. The cows and goats are just the same as the People.

Ahmedabad Station. July 3. Well I pass a better night last night than If I had been in a palace bed room. The night Policeman have a nice corner on the Platform He made is so comfortable for me. he have a long desk I put my over coat on it and slept so good I had to open my umberella over my head as there were thousand of Birds. many people were sleeping on the floor of the station and on the grown under the trees. This is the Land where every body take up their bed and walk They always ask me where is my bed I tell them it is in my case. About 10 lovely fat milk cows also sleep in the Station yard maybe they dont care to walk up the 3 steps to the platform.

The Young Policeman layed his bed just outside of His corner and the eldely one layed His in just a few feet from me. At 12 the Birds got a little quiet and we were having a sound sleep when several dogs begin fighting and two came right over the old man it woke us up and we had a good laugh. In Honor of me They keep a big light right over my Head the Umberella keep it out of my eyes. I got up had a wash and walked a few minutes between the Cows.

8.30 A.M. We left on the mail Train and Now I see why they select the City all the rich Indians Own Villas out from the City in front of some of the homes stands a Porter all dressed up in a red suit.

There are droves of those lovely light gray monkeys with black face just like children all around the first Town we stop at. The assistant engineare are a nice looking White Boy He is furnishing fun by throwing pails of water on the Phesant women that are walking along the track when they look up I wave at them and They also laugh.

District Rajpitana. Ajmer July 3. Arrived here at 9.15 P.M. I like the Maid in the Waiting room four toes on each foot are covered with clusters of silver grapes toe rings She have a Silver Chain from one ear to the other to hold back the ear with its many silver ear rings. I told Her I would sleep There and she called the Girl of lower Cast to dust up. I walked about a few minutes and found a place to eat The owner was so nice

to me and had the Boy to stand and fan me while
I ate.

Ajmer. I went out early this morning. This is a Valley
Town many streets with arches and the green Hills are
lovely. the Best of all are the Lake with its beautiful
White Pavilons. I layed down in one and had a Wonderful Three hours sleep. and the little Chip munks
made a bridge of my legs. I like the People they are
Happy looking even the Young Women under their
load of jewels they cover their Faces more than in Turkey. They peep out at me with one eye I know just
how to sulute them and we smile and try to talk. I
visited some old mosques They are different from the
Turkish ones. I had a peep in a big private Home.

July 4th. When I returned to the Waiting Room two
Indian Gentleman and their familys just arrive Five
large fat Ladies and six Young Girls a few small Children and a few Servents they filled the front room and
also the Bath room they had those tent like covers with
a square piece to throw back from their faces and a
small patch of net to fit over one eye. When I came in
the high Lady showed her face and ask if I was a
Tourist then the rest also uncovered their faces. We
smiled and made signs. Then the Gentleman call the
coaches to take them Home Three Brown Stage coches
with blinds. they fill each stage coch shut all the blinds
tight I gave a sigh. the High Lady with a Satin tent
cover refused to ride in any other but the long green

Box 4 coolies carried on their sholders by long polls.
Then they closed the box tight They all tuched their
foreheads to me and I did the same but forgot and
turned the back of my hand instead the palm.

Jaipur. July 4th. I took a mix coch from Ajmer I hadnt
traveled with the men in this District and wanted to
know them. A nice looking young man that spoke English I could see before the Train left wanted to talk
with me He worked for the Company and was well
dressed in a White Duck suit just before the train
started He jumped in and got a seat in front of me
and wouldnt let the others crowd me. Then He wanted
to know where I was going I said to Jaipur as short as
I could then He ask where I was From and I said
Ajmer. I didnt care to talk as one word bring another
and I was going to Jaipur with the hope of being a Guest
of the company. He offored me Tea and tried very hard
to be nice and I disliked not being the same. At 4 P.M.
He left my coch. It begin to rain and pour in the coch
I took off my sandles and remained bare footed and put
my case on the seat and sat on the end for the rest of
their amusemient. A eldly Mohamdedan man tryed
to keep me from sitting there as it was near time for
the Sun to set and He wanted the space to pray and no
doubt didnt want a Christian near his Praying place
Two nice young Hindu men begin to talk and the eldly
Mohamedan got another to sit between me and His
Praying space then he begain to pray and the young

Hindus touched me to look but I didnt. I thought He
may pray for me knowing I was angry with Him. They
wanted to know Why I didnt ware anklets and bracelets
instead of gold in my mouth.

Arrived at Jaipur at 8 P.M. A nice Mohamedan man
managed The Railway Resturant I had fried fish bread
butter and tea. They gave me the first class Waiting
Room. I let the fan go through the night. the next
morning my washing was dry. I went to the City early
it have a High pink wall all the Buildings are Pink the
houses on side streets are white with elefants painted a
bright color on each side the front door or a God or
Godness some houses are a pail green. The Wide
Streets look like a carnival many different carts drawn
by white Bullocks Camels and Elefants with two bells
that swing and tinkle as it step. I didnt see not one
Eurpean Person. I meet a nice Hindoo Studient who
took me through the Maharaja's Palace and the Elefant
stable and the place where they keep those carriages
that are carried on poles. which the Young Maharaja
wouldnt think of useing in the day of autos. the Studient had to go so I meet the nicest little Boy about 13
he went with me to the great Observatory and when I
offored to give him something He said I will not accept
anything.

When it was cool I went back to the City wall for the
afternoon Bazaars. A marriage procession passed a
Band then in a little high two wheel cart with two white

Bullock sat the Young Couple dressed in red silk and gold their backs together the Bride's face covered and the Groom smiling and talking the women of the Family flowered singing. I had lunch of cantlops sitting in a woman's Fruit stall but there were 5 cows trying to take each piece out of my hands the Woman would run them away but they would come right back. They have loads of mellons but they are tastless.

Agra Fort July 6. I arrived at 8 P.M. I could not have the Waiting room but an Englishman nice looking told me I may spend the night in a First Class Compartment Coch that was standing on the track in front of the Waiting room but I must be out by 4 A.M. as a engine would take it off. That was the best luck It was just like a living room with leather couches lights fans and lavatory I undress bathed had a good rest and just out in time in the morning.

I got much sightseen over before 8 A.M. I went in to mass in the Girl Orphand Home of St. Francs. the Girls looked so pretty in white dresses and white net over their Heads of long slick Black hair. I found a Good Hotel for $1.44 per day and no end of servients. to think an old waiter that served me had spent several years at London Nice and Italy in the service of Her most Highness Queen Victoria I felt so small to have him serving me. But He did it well. I had a bath and my Breakfast served in my room then a good sleep after I walked 2 miles to the Taj Mahal. on the way I meet

a nice Englishman that was riding his bike I asked him
how far it was and he said a long way. I wanted to get
there just as the sun went down and thought it was
houses all along the way so didnt think about going
alone. He went on then he stoped got of his bike
looked back at me and then rode back and caught up
with me. and went the other 1½ miles with me though
he had to be back at his Barracks at a certain hour. He
was so polite and told me all the details of the Taj.
we arrived just at dusk and it was the time to see that
wonderful monument for the first time. it thrilled me
through as the beauty cannot be painted. it came to me
that this beautiful thing was built through love, from
the love of a man for a woman so it was much nicer to
see it with a gentleman and such a nice one who ex-
plained it all to me in such a cultured way.
As we left he asked me how it impressed me. the night
was getting dark the dew was falling heavy and I said
"I would just like to put a glass over it I feel I must
cover it over." He said, "That's beautiful." I was
pleased to have company as the road was very lonely
returning. The Englishman just had time to get back
to the Barracks that are near this Hotel I returned tird
and altho I told the Waiter to put my dinner on the
table in my room there He was sleeping by the door
waiting to give it to me nice and Hot.
Monday 8 I got up early and walked the two miles
again to the Taj I arrived just at Sun rise removed my

sandles washed my feet and had a nap on the green grass under the shadow of the Taj so Big White Grand and Beautiful the well kep green lawns and trees and the great red Mosques make it more whiter and Grand. it cannot be described eyes must see it. I took my time and walked from room to room in the vault to see the tombs of the Emperor Shah Jehan and Queen Mumloz Mahal. Then a restful Climb up the many winding steps of one of its beautiful Minarets and altho. a Big Grand building You feel that You could lift it up and put it away in a china closet. at the top I sat down and talked with a Plesant Hindu Gentleman that had long promised his little boy a trip up.

I returned at the Hotel Hungry and tird had a four courst breakfast and a good sleep then I went To the Fort All wonderful Palaces How Wonderful it must have been to see the Emperor sitting upon His open air Throne with Indias gay colours. then I went in the old city to the Bazaar and watched the real Oriental Crowd. then to the most interesting Hindoo musical Show a good Bombay Company the manager gave me a good seat Free. it begin at 9.30 P.M. and end at 2 PM. I left at 11 but the acting singing dancing was so good I could have stayed to the end.

July 9.

I had planned to leave for Delhi but did not feel I wanted the trip after I had seen the Fort. so I left for

the Emperor Akbar's Deserted City 23 miles from Agra.
12 cents round trip 3rd Class it is a beautiful Palace.
I bought fruit cucmbers Bread and butter for my trip
to Benares. The train left a 2 A.M. I made a misteak
and got in the Second Class night coch for women and
had a wonderful night rest only 4 other women one of
them had only a platform ticket she picked up and had
rode all night. when we reached Cawnpore at 7.30 in
the morning a woman comes to the Coch and look at
the tickets they took Her off But did not tell me I was
in the wrong Coch. at the next stop another woman
told me I would have to pay the different I told Her it
wasnt my fault the Coolie put me in that Coch but I
didnt have no Coolie I carried my suitcase my self.

The Holy City Benares July 10.
Arrived at 4 P.M. and walked 1½ miles to the city
through the long crowded and noisy leading street true
Oriental I went to the only Hotel right in the City
very nice but realy I never heard such noise. The Cart
drivers elefants auto and Hindoos in their stage Coch
like carriages with two footmen in blue livelry and two
half naked coolies sticking on behind and the drivers
yelling to clear the way and then the musice from the
Theatres and bands leading processions the Hotel have
a wide poach over the Side Walk to look down on all
of it but I had walked up and down in the mist of it.
always on reaching your room 3 or four half naked

coolies stands at the door to be at your service but I felt tird and cross and sent them all away I told the manager I came to the room because I was tird of looking at naked men and I didn't want them near me.

I slept through the noise and was up early at the River watching the Hundreds of men and women washing away their sins I asked a Priest if I may come in and he said take off my shoes then I left them off because everywhere are sacred grownd. I climbed up the steap steps to go in and out the narrow street of Thousands of Temples it was fun walking through the muddy streets and it squshing through my toes. I went to one of the Great Temples where the women worshiped I Heard the Singing and drums it took me sometime to find the enterence. about 3 hundred of them dressed in orange sitting on the floor some with drums others had Brass plates in each hand. hiting together I touched my forehead the younger ones smiled a head Lady in White said to me to stand on the side where I could see the gold alter and Godness Imiage I thought she said come in I stept but as quick she made me step back some of the Girls laughed. then I talked with some but not with my feet inside.

The River is very yellow but the water clean. I took a Boat of a Kind naked Coolie and sat in a comfortable Chair and had a pleasant trip passing many Ghats The boat cost 18 cents after my bargain. I saw one Pyre on

fire and a male and female corps wrapped in bright red
waiting to go on I got out and went back to witness the
whole thing. It is not at all horrod to look at anyway
I am quite a Hindu now. Then I thought of the millions of wives that have been burned alive in the same
spot only a few years back.

A Holy Man was sitting like a Buddha statue under an
umberella near the Funeral Pyres and I stood around
looking at him to see if I could get his eye there was a
Hindu nearby not quite as holy as he was so he began
to flirt with me asked me why I was all alone and said
I look- different. A good Flirtation was just the thing
after the Funeral Pyres. on the way to the Station I
stoped to buy Fruit and meet a Wealthy Family they
offored me a nurse place. I felt like kicking myself
after I left them. I should have took it if only for a
week as long as they spoke to me first.

I bought a 3rd Class ticket for Calcutta When the train
leave Benares crossing over the long iron bridge the
people throw money in the river and there is rows of
People standing along the brige waiting to get the
money that doesnt go in the river.

I am getting ever so native dont care much if I have a
ticket or not. as it was crowded I got in the second
Class sleeper. it was empty and I planned to get out
at daylight and go to the 3rd. But was so comfortable
I rode right in to Calcutta. I felt uneasy when two of
the train Conductors stands at the gate to take the

tickets they had seen me on the train at the right of the Gate was an Anglo-Indian and the left an Indian I stood off and looked over their faces the White one He was surprised and said you have a 3rd Class ticket I said Yes. He said alright go on I went as fast as I could go through the Station to the street then after a few minutes I came back to the First Class waiting room had a good Bath for nothing.

July 18.
Y.W.C.A. Calcutta.

I am in the new and beautiful Y. most of the Girls are Anglo-Indians work in offices nice Girls dress simple but they are not many prety ones and age quick. Calcutta is not near so Oriental as Bombay and I feel so happy I visited Bombay first. You dont see the lovely Parsee dresses the shopes are keep by Burmases. the City have wide streets and a great beautiful place for Races foot Ball golf. I wont stay here long.

Darjeeling to see Mount Everest. I take my suitcase to the Station at 6 A.M. before the High casts or the Coolies awake. This is the Rainy season so most of the trip was rainy once in a while it would brighten and I could see what a wonderful trip it was but couldnt see Mt. Everest. the mountain People made me feel in another fareoff Country they look like Eskimoes at every station there are women girls and boys and men with a rope they put around a trunk or suitcase and put it on

their Back and forehead to carry it up the mountain side
to where the Passanger wish.

I went with a Eskimo Looking boy to the Y. I have a
room in the Cottage that hangs over a cliff. I am praying for just a few minutes of Sun light. the Coolie came
with a dinner of hot beef broth rost lamb potatoes
boiled cucumbers and later desert. Then I had a good
night I like one of the Guest a Lady from Burma. and
are working her way about India but are afraid to take
a chance on going to Europe.

July 19. It cleared up and it was such a beautiful sight
the mountain sides of tea plants the red roofs and the
Valleys were a floor of white clouds. it didnt clear
enough to see the Snow covered mountains. But I feel
I will get my wish of a sunny day. I had a wonderful
hike and like here better than Switzerland. Here you
are always above the clouds and natual nature beauty.
everyone tell me it will not be clear. But I have faith.

July 21. Darjeeling.

I did not sleep much last night because I was up many
times going to look out at the weather each time I went
back to bed happier when I woke at 5 it was very bright
and the Sey quite free of cloud then I knew my Prayer
had been heard. I dresses and went right out in the
direction of the mountains in front of a native Shrine
where they were having a strange like service. in 3
minutes the Sun came out and the Clouds settled in the

Valleys and there were Mount Everest and others in all their Beauty then I felt well paid for my Chance trip up here. in half an hour they were out of sight. the People here are different from any I have seen. and it is good to get a rest from beggars of the Plains. here they never beg. I feel so happy to finnish my trip In India with a few days up here.

My last night at This wonderful Place. Darjeeling Bengal 7,000 ft. I have packed my suit case and are ready for bed but I cannot because the secnery are to wonderful. and I must stay up and go to the door to let my eyes feast on it. the Moon is bright and the houses on the many mountains seem to be touching the sky the snow covered mountains are like pearl just below my cottage are a floor of white Clouds. the darkness of the tall fir trees and tea plants on the mountain sides beside the snow white clouds far below are to wonderful. up and down are the thousand of light as this is a City above and below mountains and clouds the lights seem to mix with the stars I have just had my last look for Tonight. I have been treated so sweet and kind here and I love every one and every foot of ground.

I went into a big postal card shop and meet an Anglo-Indian. He gave me a lovely Painted View of Darjeeling. I went in his shop 2 or three times and he wanted me to go on a horseback trip I didnt want to go the road is all cement. He gave me another picture of the scenic Railway and told me how the Englishman that

built it was assisted by His Wife. My friend is fair
born and reared in Portugal of Portuguese descent.

I wish that all the ones I love and all the ones I hate
could see This Wonderful Place Darjeeling. a man
serven with long whiskers he have them combed and
parted and rolled back to each side of his Cheeks. He
cleans the bath room and sweep and dust my room another one with white mustach serves my tea in the
morning another bring the Hot water when I leave tomorrow the 3 will be in line for me to give them something one Rupee 36 cents will be devided between the 3.
11.50 P.M. In route to Calcutta. A Burma Lady said to
me at Darjeeling you are just betwixt and between. one
minute you have a fine time with the lowest cast next
minute with the highest Hindoo. one minute you wear
a blue suit next minute a dress of 2 cent a yard crape
then a little velvet dress with diamond ear rings how
can we tell. one minute you stay in a hotel at $5.00 a
day then go to a resturant and have a 5 cent meal. youre
betwixt and between.

I expect to go to Rangoon Burma so to see that end of
India then I will be in Burma until the next French
Steamer leave for Marseilles France. I think that will
be about the 20th of Aug. I hope to return at that time
as it is the last Boat of the low Summer rates. I will
have to go from Rangoon a four days trip by water to
Madras the nearest place of sailing.

The head of the Y. and the Burma Lady come to the

cottage to see me off at Darjeeling. I am to find a Husband for the Brumser. she is a great treasure for some
man. They enjoyed so much hearing of my durings and
say it have been a treat to have me. They got such a
big kick out of the lesser things I did not go into the
more Thrilling.

July 26. Arrived at 6 A.M. and left Calcutta the same
day. This is Goalundo Passanger Ghat a buisy little
native place on the River Puja the Huts are made of
Kane. and are built over the water. I had my Breakfast sitting on my suit case in the Kane made waiting
room. on the Banks there are many River steamers
that leave from here It was interesting to see the
coolies load. the Women have their faces tatooed with
a square like design which must have been painful. but
where they suffered a few days from that we suffer
for life from corns made by Tight shoes. 12 P.M. I came
aboad and had decliously curried chicken and rice and
string beans. 36 cents tip included. Two other trains have
arrived and we have more than 2,000 on boad. We
left at 1 P.M. and the trip on the River Puja have
been Wonderful I saw great big aligators swimming
with their mouths wide open. It is a wide body of water
and quite choppy on nearing each Village along side
are Thousand of quaint little black pointed sailing
boats with a woven kane cover and sailes of many colours orange brown and pale Blue being the favorite
colours the Venice Cannal are not so beautiful. one

place we stopped there are no Warf the banks crumbled away so it was a long time before they could find a solid place for the plank they were to cross on I was expecting to see a bunch fall into the water but nothing nice happen.

we arrived at 7 P.M. at Campur Kalipuri the Trains were there and I got a good place to sleep this being my third night on train.

July 26. traveling through Land of water covered with green rice fields. Chittagong July 27. I went to the Dak Bongalow owned by the Railway Co. always nice and cheap I payed $1.08 Chicken is the meat down here and they serve so nice you pay 6 cents for the use of the lamp at night. the mattrews are covered with a white slip. and at the door are wide green creton curtins so no one can see in. I asked for another curtin to go to the side door and keep it to use for a covering as they do not furnish pillous nor sheets or blankets every one travel with their bedding but me I have been lucky in always getting some. On the train I use my good and servable gray coat I bought in Paris and it was a Wise buy.

I went to the Market this morning took some crackers butter and salt bought a Cucumber and bananas stoped in a clean dirt floor tea Hut and had my breakfast with good Hot tea. the People were nice but so amused they could not speak I laughed so then they laughed.

I was walking through a narrow lane and heard musice

and knew it was well played so stuck my head in the door and a sweet face Lady asked me in the Hut on each side a platform are made for the bed and they have kane and woden stools it was clean as a pin. the Husband a Handsome Gentleman with a nice piece about his loins spoke English he is a proffesor of many Insterments He was beating the drums and a pretty Girl with a red betel mouth played the little Organ she sang lovely. They offered me Cigaretts which I never take. and invited me back at 6 P.M. I walked 2 and a half miles to the Bay to see the steamer it arrived yesterday. I dont think there will be much of a crowd so may sleep in the second if it get cool. the weather doun here are ideal the sun and a shower in between. there are many European homes up on the Hills about the Town. The women dress with one sholder bare the older ones with their brest free. the men look gay in Their shirt and Scarlet Skirt.

I had a hard time learning about this way to Rangoon no tourist ever travell this way but direct from Calcutta but they miss so much. My train and steamer fare are just $4.68. from Calcutta to Rangoon 2 nights half day on the steamer and another day and half train to Rangoon. I just returned from The Home of The nice Hindoo family where they had 4 musicians and a Pretty Girl with slick black hair doun to Her knees. one man played the Violian another two drums and sang the Girl danced very graceful with 50 small bells on each

ankle another man played the small organ and a little
Girl beat two silver bells togather. The Lady owner of
the 4 Huts took doun a matting for the Girl to dance
on. Before they began each one made their sign of the
Cross and the Girl Touched each player each insterment
and Her feet Then She begain to Dance and danced and
sang for two hours I could have looked and listen for
several hours Their whole Hearts were in it. many
things passed while I sat there. the Lady took down a
Brass bowl with holy water from over the door and
with Her hand rubbed it across the door sill. It was
near time for my Dinner so I had to leave. I had grilled
chicken little potatoes nice and brown cooked in a
covered pot and string beans. last night they gave me
meat balls but I refused to have anything today but
chicken.

My how powerful rich one can feel in India with just
a few pounds or Dollars but it take so much to get
there. Tomorow I will have a great time paying off the
5 or six men servents one cook for me another bring my
meals another heat water, another bring up cold water
for the bathroom another take out the night glass as
they have no toilet another clean the room. one Rupee
devided between them are quite enough. They serve
you so quiet and faithfully it seem a shame to give so
little that's why when I am travelling I carry my suit-
case so to save and give a little more to them. This is
one country where the servent problem never worry

them at Bombay I did not have a Pillow to sleep on yet I had a boy servent. at Agra most of the nurse maids are young men or Boys they look nice in their nurse cloths.

July 28. We are traveling on the Bay of Bengal from Chittigong to Rangoon. I must get back to Europe as my checks are getting very low. I have stretched them out wonderful. and feel very happy and pleased with all that I have seen and enjoyed out of it.

On Boad the R.M.S. Chakdara. they have many hundred 3rd Class on boad at one end of the Boat are a Hindoo resturant and a Mohammed one Both very clean I had dinner from the Mohammed. Chicken curry with Rice The curry doesnt tast nothing like the dryed curry powder we get. Here they use the fresh Curry. I ate so much and to fast so with the Sea became seasick and felt wonderful after. When I came on boad they said that European women were not allowed to travelle as Deck Passanges. I answered I had my ticket and I couldnt pay any more and if they didnt like it they must pay the differents. everything is going lovely now. Akyob. I went ashore first visiting the big market I bought two Grape fruits there a stall keeper gave me some sugar. The men were so very nice if they would stand to look at me as they do in India another would make them go on. now I am beginning to see and smell the Chinese. The men ware bright coloured skirts and a piece of silk on their head pink is the most used. The Women ware bright yards of cloth wrapped around them and a thin short Shirt waist their hair high on their head then put flowers in it. The colours are Wonderful. I had lunch at the only Hotel. the Soup was Chinese the Chicken Indian.

July 31. KyouKgyu I went to see the little jungle village an English Gentleman that are in the Freight office gave me the use of his Car to go to the Market. Cucumbers are half an arm length very cheap I bought 3 and bannas I enjoyed one cucumber but the other Two was taken by some hungry man. For that a Gentleman gave me another and two good Oranges. in the jungles have been many death from colo. The fishmen of this Shore have their limbs tatooed from the waist to the knees.

On Boad the Chakdara. Aug. 1.

I meet 2 very nice Burma Gentlemen One are looking after my comforts. He is a merchant in Upper Burma and have given me a list of the interesting places in Upper Burma and how to make the tour. another Gentleman a Very smart Professor and a strong Buddish He talked for 2 hours to me on that faith and I was so thankful it was just what I wanted to hear I sat very quiet and took it all in he spoke about it said I was a good listner as most Christians argue. He has long black hair twisted in a knot on top of his Head and with his dress I had to keep my mind and eyes on his mustache to remind me that He's a man. He is a fighter for Home rule. India are very anxious for Home rule.

Rangoon Harbor. I have all my meals and tea from the Mohomedan Resturant because they have things I like chicken. They have been very good to me I was surprise when they invited me in the Kitchen to peep in each pot and point out what I wanted They didnt speak English but of course I knew better than to touch any thing with my Christian Hands. Sometimes I'd tease them and start to touch it. I took notice that my plates was always set off on a side to be scrubed by itself.

That remind me while Visiting the Deserted City of Folchpur-Sikri I was resting in the Office of a Hindu Gentleman I asked for some water He gave me His drinking Cup after I had finnished He told the Coolie to Scrub it the Coolie took it out and sat on the ground and scoured it with sand when he came in the gentleman ask him if he did it well. I wanted another drink but I didnt ask it put them to much trouble.

I smile when I think of the many times my Christian hands and feet have trespassed on the Hindus and Mahomedans. I would step in on them so quick and give them such a surprise that they would forget themselves. They have been most kind.

Rangoon Burma Aug. 5. Y.W.C.A. When I came ashore I walked just as straight to the Y. as though I Put up the Building the male maid got my room ready had a good rest it has been three nights since I slept in a bed. I went to an Indian Theatre I bought a half Rupee Seat but the door keeper gave me a 2 Rupee seat I have the same luck every place.

I am surprised to find Rangoon such an interesting City what a joy to see the wide streets and the Women enjoying so much Freedom. and The Burma Women with their High Crown of black hair. I do not like their big cigars that are stuck in many of their mouths but they say inside is as harmless as corn silk. I went to the lovely church of St. Anthony's this is St. Philomence week of Feast I had a dear Friend in Cuba of the Saint's name. I put an advertisement in "The Rangoon Times" for a situation. I went to the Free Library and found good books on Burma. I like the weather a little rain then a little sun shine.

Aug. 5.
To Mrs. Myra K. Dickinson,
423 South Lafayette Park Place,
Los Angeles, California.

Dear Mrs. Dickinson:
I went to Cooks & Son. and got the Happiest shock when I open your letter and saw the Photo. Just think what joy it gave me arriving here just about the Same hour that I arrive. The Photo. looks swell on my walnut dresser. and each One in it have their own beauty. I feel highly horned. Please feel happy over sending It

because it have given me great joy when I sat on the seat by the red hankerchief head of Cooks Porter and open it he looked once then the second look he stood up and looked I just passed the joy over to him he was pleased then I hurried out before he asked me any questions.

I am just beginning to feel a bit tird of this Part of the World and I am pleased to find that the People here ware more cloths I was getting tird of India and so many naked men.

Write me at Marseilles and if you have a little interest money will you send it if not kindly stick in a love offering I'll keep an account and return it. I'll probably leave India Sept. 15 and will need it when I arrive at Marseilles.

I havent visited the interesting Temple yet having a cold it is to damp to walk on the stone floor bare footed.

Yours Truly J.V.H.*

Aug. 7. They had a fair at the Y. to make money to buy crokery for the Dinning room. the large sitting rooms were decerated beautiful in flags ferns and flowers tea and cakes were served on tables with pretty white tea cloths. and musice by some of the Talent Girls. It was a beautiful picture a few fair Europeans the Anglo Burmases girls in their cool short frocks some fair some light and some dark. the Burmases Ladies in their

* A letter to Juanita's employer who befriended her in Los Angeles.

bright silk cloth wrapped around their suple bodys then
short white waist bracelets of gold bare feet in sandles
their black hair slick as an eil and like a black crown
on their heads and their soft yellow skin. made it wonderful it was like a reception instead of a fair they made
more than a Hundred dollars. I bought a box of powder which I needed for 6 annas cheaper than I would
have had to pay and to bunches of yarnd flowers. 75
cents in all. The Burmases had fresh flowers tucked in
the side of their hair. The Young Ladie that I liked so
much at the Y. was of Dutch French and Burma blood
I thought she was about 21 instead she is 32.

British India Steam Navigation Co., Ltd.
S.S.Ethiopia. Aug. 11.

On Boad this pleasant ship in rout to Madras.
I didnt wait about the add. I put in the paper but leave
for Madras my Cabin is furnished beautiful and so
clean all by myself I have the run of the ship. The
Ship Library have many good books. an Indian Doctor
and I are the Faithful Two havent missed a meal.

Dear Old Madras the Home of Kindness
Aug. 21. Quarter of The Anglo-Indias.
Y.W.C.A. Poonamallee Road Vepery

I am glad to spend my last days in the South and to be
in Madras. I went to see my Friends of April. They
said I was thinner but had such a good color so that

mean I was better looking. I had a cold and they told me not to think of giving my rupees to a Dr. to go to the General Hospital it is the finest in India. They gave me some very good and tasty medician. each one must bring their bottles it was great fun going there. Then I went to see a Prof. Dandoo a high caste Hindu and a Perfect gentleman as most of the Hindus are he sent one of his many servents for cold drinks I was thirsty. the first time I stoped in to see him He kissed the palm of my hand I liked it only because it was not the back as had been done by the French an Itailians Then he kiss the rim of my glass and ask me to kiss the rim of his. I laughed when he said he shouldnt have done that as he is a Brahaman He say "I am not supposed to touch a Christian because I am a 'twice born' they are very high they come before a Priest.

He called at the Y. that evening in his car with two the chauffer and another half naked foot-man. He wore a white piece around his middle. His shirt tail out and over it a white coat. He had a ring on his toe and lovely Ruby ear rings in his ears. He came to take me for a drive and brought me some Hindu Sacred pictures. But being in the Anglo-Indian Y. I knew it was best to refuse as they do not go with the Hindus nor the Hindus with them their faith will not allow it. I was sorry I had to refuse.

They have big grouns with a small lake and wonderful trees and seats all about and the Girls have a jolly good

time spooning on the grouns with their sweeties. the
Guest houses and large buildings are all built with big
alround poches white and green with the ever red tiling
roofs. They have a butler with a clean white piece
around his loins and a white head dress and his skin a
clean shining chocolate color. The food are served on
big platers and the Girls all eat very dainty with their 5
fingers after they finnish they keep the hand in the plate
until all are ready then they go on a side poch to the
fosit to wash their hand. They have Indian food plenty
of it and little style. But the Anglos have plenty of service and just a dainty bit to eat so the Girls are of course
like the Europeans thin and stylish.

Miss O. the Treasure are a lovely young Anglo-India.
She has a nice Irish terrie name mike and have brought
him up a real Christian dog. He walk around from
table to table in the dinning room and very softly touch
your arm sit up and shake his to paws but no one must
never fed him. Then He comes in to the pray service
and lay down in the front after he has turned around
a few times.

Most of the Anglo-Indian Girls are ladylike but a bit
reserved. They are not as good looking down here as in
Bombay and Calcutta. at Calcutta they dress good and
pretty have the cleanest teeth and finger nails Bombay
come next. Rangoon they have more pleasure and are
lovely but not as good dressers and you can see a
little trace of that Burma-Chinese blood so are not as

good looking as the Indians Anglos. I have had much joy noticing the difference. The Girls were very much amused when I told them my impression of the Holy Land where the East and West meet where you neednt to sit out a dance and You have such a short time to snach a pray you feel like a thief.

Sunday morning I left by Bus for the sacred place of St. Thomas Mount. I stoped at the Bazaar and bought a big lunch wrapped it in brown paper and tie it around with a bright scarf to give myself a native touch. I went a mile out of my way through a Village and there found a big Hindoo feast to Kali the Godness they sacifice goats to her. the women were cooking rice and other things in their earthen jars over fires of cow dung inside a big yard with walls painted white and red stripes the smoke was so thick I couldnt keep my eyes open hundreds of pots on the fire. and outside of the yard the men were cutting the head off many goats and hanging them to a limb of a tree skinning it. the women and men which were to offer the sacrifice for themselfs were at a big well drawing up water and bathing in it then they striped themselfs and tired the branches of a sacred tree about them and marched behind the musicians to the shrines with a Priest in lead. Other had committed some heavy sin they bathed themself and with only a red cloth and much agoney on their faces was throwing themself flat down in the dirt in the procession all the way until they made the round of all the shrines. It

sure was hard work. To this Godeness they also offer
sacrifices for proctions from snake bites. I was going
along in the procession to the Shrines with my shoes in
side my umberella when a Hindu man told me to get
out. I gave him one unpleasant look and that settled it
when I got back to the Shrine he ask me my name and
smiled the Hindus are not a bad sort.

I started off again to find St. Thomas Mount. I had fun
running after a little 12 year old Hindu girl she had had
her bath and of course didnt want my Christian Hands
to touch her. Then Two Native Christian girls scold
her because she didnt want me to touch her. I got so
much joy out of it all. then I gave them 8 annas. which
surprised them but make them very happy they said they
would pray for me every day. I was just about to turn
in the wrong road when I got a view of the Mt. through
the trees. The Great Saint Thomas Mount is the most
interesting place in or near Madras. in the central alter
of the church is a big Stone with a Cross Carved and
other writing. tell of while the apostle Kneeling at
Prayer a Braham transfixed him with a lance. I went
To the side poch of the Church and had a wonderful
nap. at the foot of the hill is another Church Where
the apostle are surposed to have staggard and died.

I had planned to go back to the Hindu Feast about
4 P.M. when the goats was cooked but over slep. and
when I got down to get a Bus found them Crowded.
with the People returning to the city after the Festivale.

I thought I was tird of curry rice but it was because I
didnt like the way they cook it in Burma. every town
cook it a little different. it have been interesting to me.
Yet I'll be pleased to give it up when the time come.
and shall welcome the Country where I can have good
green Salads again.

In the Y.W. Yard are so many birds some with long
bright tails but make unpleasant noise. I always feel
afraid at night on the ground floor when I hear the
least sound I think something will be crawling in my
windows which is a few inches from the groun so shall
be glad for that reason to leave. on the walls are such
beautiful fat pink lizzards with bright black eyes. I
always feel they will drop down my back and every
night in the Bath room are such nice neat gray todd
frogs. I feel so creepy.

My Steamer is due Aug. 23 and Sail the same day. the
Messageries Maritime French Mail Steamer Chantilly.
I hate to travel the same way over again but the world
are not so big. I shall be pleased to be in Port Said
and hope to get another bottle of perfum from my
Friend that own a shop and gave me such a delicious
dinner.

I havent been able to read Miss Mayo's Book on Mother
India. I didnt care to spend 5 Rupees on it but what
ever it is she have many enmies a Hindu said that he
would go to America and write one of all the Black
sides of America and call it Mother America I told him

thats a good idea. All the Y Girls ride to their work on
Bicycles.

Aug. 25.

I went to a Garden Party. The People sat in the Yard
under the big trees Two Pretty Indian Girls one played
the Veena to play it you must sit on the floor the insterment are much pretty to look at than the musice It
give the Other Girl sang you must always sing with
the Veena. I know a Hindu Girl that play the Veena
and I have heard her play to her Sweetheart Sitting on
the floor tailor fashion and he sitting the same but
far apart then she was always at her best. there was a
play taken from Mary and Martha of the Bible the
poch of the lovely house was used for the stage with
ferns and flowers but just at the end of the first act a
heavy shower came and we had to run in the house. the
Indian dresses were just the cloths to go with the play.

S.S.Chantilly. Aug. 27.

I had spent as mush as I cared to spend and still had
one Rupee and 8 annas to buy books you can find good
ones on the groun in the Bazaars for 2 or 3 cents. I
bought several. then I had enough to buy oranges and
lemon drops to bring on boad. I have a nice cabin all
to myself. the Waiters and cabin Boys are Chinese
which I like. Its good to be with the French again and
get a change of Food. most of the Passangers are

French. an English Lady an her young Lady Daughter sit by me at table they have lived down here 5 years but know nothing about India. they eat as though they havent had anything for several days. 5 are served together so I let the Mother and Daughter Know there was some limit to each dish. we have lovely food wine fruit salad and other proper dishes for the sea. If the English Ships would take lessons from the French what to serve on boad. we have lovely red flowered Table cloth and very large Table napkins. the Indian Passangers sit togather as they have their food curry and such. I feel quite sure I'll never want any more curried food.

A very sad accident happen just before we sail a young Indian man a passanger He was standing by my deck chair with his Parrot teasing a little French Girl. then he walked away and fell from the top Deck to the hull where they were loading bales of cotton he hit the third deck in the fall. If he live he will always be hepless they took him to the Hospital. When I looked down and saw the dead Parrot I was shocked for then I knew it was the young man that a half minute ago was so happy.

It was beautiful to see what tender care the coolies with their red strip around their loins and a piece on their head handled the young man. there are no roughness in the Indians and still less in the Hindus even the lowest cast seem to be the most kindest. I was

amused when they started off with the Boy on the
stretcher one of the coolies put the dead Parrot by the
Boy's side and the English Doctor threw it out But
one of them Picked it up maybe they built a funeral
Pyre.

I thought I wouldnt care for tea after that then I felt
happy that he was in a Hospital in Madras where he
would get good treatment then I enjoyed my tea.

S.S.Chantilly. Sept. 6.

We arrived at Colombo at 9 P.M. The next morning I
went to see my Friends they was surprised and I enjoyed seeing them again. We sailed at 6 P.M. Yesterday I had to use my coat it being our first rough sea
and while most of them was nurseing their sea sickness
I to keep it off scrub my Cabin floor washed the mirrows
port hole and the seat that run across the wall. The
Boy had let it go for two days. I found his brush and
soap and felt fine altho the boat was jumping up and
down at each end. I am the first woman on deck each
morning I enjoy seeing the Sun come up out of the Sea
I was pleased it was rough yesterday it was the first time
we had roost chicken plain lettuce salad and icecream.
My Friends in Colombo thought I looked fine and said
if I keep up travelling when I am 90 will look the same.
To me they looked liked they had aged so much since
I left Colombo in April. the Secutary of the Y that had
just come back from a year stay at her home in England

and was so fat and pink looked thin pale and old. If
I had to choose a home down here it would be in Bombay and the next Madras.

Djibouti Gulf of Aden.
Sept. 9.

A few Passangers went ashore in the mortor larnch but
I choosed a native row boat so to be out of style. It
was more pleasanter. This would be the hottest Place
but the Sea are on every side and always a cooling wind.
I felt much at home on reaching the American Concel
Building the Stars and Strips waving a welcome to
me. I looked over the Town and at the same time was
looking for a place to take my afternoon nap. a native
had just been arrested so that made it quite lively I
went to the Police Station just to get a look at the Style
of the men. The Town is quite new and must be very
healthy the very soil are salt. many little deers are
running about the streets and quite tame. I could see
the Tennis Court in a little Park I felt sleepy so went
over there and a native boy that helps on the court gave
me a Kane settee but it being to short I stretched out
on the floor of the Band Stand and had a good nap.
with the Sea Breez blowing over me. Then I went
over to the Coolies quarters and on reaching there several women and Girls came out and begin to dance. I
suluted them in the Proper way and having a black Vail
head dress very much like the married women ware they

fell to me. a little girl put out her hand to me for a
tip I gave it a gentle shake and kissed it and the
women laughed so over it. She was cute although her
hair was black the sun had turned it brownish on the
top of her head was a long piece of hair and around
that a round space shaved then a row cut to an inch
then another space shaved. When they are older they
let it grow and braid it in hundred of small plats. I
saw a tribe in Upper Egypt something like them the
older women shave their hair clean across the front
of the head here are a mixture of Indian and Afri-
cians.

there are thousands of huts made of straw matting and
sticks and gunner bags but they are very different from
the Arabs of Egypt for here they are ever so clean the
narrow passage ways between the huts are as clean as a
floor and no flies. I stoped at the Open Air Bazaar
where they are hundreds of camels and in just a few
seconds after suluting a few women I had swams around
me first they thought I came from Greece after a while
they decide I was Chinese as many as could get to me
I had to shake hand it was very pleasant. then a woman
came up to beg and another let her know she were not
to beg me. Then I said goodbye with hand shakes and
touching the forehead. I would look down each street
and if I see women I would go down that street. It
being Sunday they were in their best. Only a few ware
ear rings nor anklets and few have their face cut with

cast marks like you see in Egypt. Their orments are a
long string of good beads and a bracelet on each arm
above the elbores and a gold bead collor the women
are all slender in the bunch at the fountain were a little
Flapper. They said I took special notice of her because
She had her hair bobbed and one felt my head to see if
I had mine bobbed.

I meet a young woman in her finery and went along
with her until we came to a house I could tell by the
singing it was a new Bride's house when she went in
I tryed to slip in with her but She wouldnt let me and
shut the gate to the high walled yard of course I was
expecting that a Christian would be a bad luck to the
house.

Djibouti is French so in the evening there was many side
walk Cafés. I had a most pleasant time and at 9 P.M.
was walking along the road to the Pier when 3 Boys
cought up with me two of them begain to be fresh as
quick as a flash with my fist I landed a upper cut under
his chin then I turned to do the same to the other but
he was running for life the other was holding his jaw
the third one tryed to be nice and said I did right I could
see that he felt uneasy walking by my side he took off
his white emboried cap and said Bon Soir Madame. In
a few minutes two others came up one got fresh I
landed one somewhere near his eyes such a groan and
holding his face. On reaching the Pier I told a man
about it and He spreaded the news. So at the end of a

perfect day I was so tird I could hardly climb up the steamer ladder.

8 A.M. The water are very clear and it was very interesting to watch the men with ropes for a line fish out fishes longer than my arm and very wide you can see dozens of them swimming about.

We expect to reach Port Said Saturday. I hope my Friend that own a Perfum Store will give me another box of Amber past it cost five dollars I have the one He gave me.

Sept. 13. We are on the Red Sea and the mountains on each side look grand the weather are ideal the moon so bright and the Sea just nice. all the Passangers must have a Doctors certific that they have been vaccinated not more than a year passed I was vaccinated Tuesday but it didnt take but anyway I have the Certifice and when I get to Port-Said will ware a dress with long sleves and just show my certfice.

for the little Breakfast the men all come to the dinning room in their pajamas most of them have bright flowered ones. I keep auful neat I wash my dresses and fold them very careful and put it between a thick brown paper under my suite case and it is pressed perfect. long ago I have taken my suite case as a companion it often serve as a chair pillow and do most of my pressing.

We are still having good food but my English Mother and Daughter are not filled up yet. I have never seen

any thing like them. For the first five days I drank
the ice cold wine then I turned against it I felt like it
made me bilious. Yesterday I took a little and the
Gentleman that sit at my left was so happy because
then he could put ice in my glass fill it with wine or add
water but when I dont take it is nothing for him to
do for me. But I cannot like it any more and I am
very glad water are much better and cheaper.

It is ever so home like on this Steamer everybody do just
as they wish. the French, Germans and Itilians are so
much nicer to travel with than the English and yet the
English are lovely in their country.

Port Said Sept. 14.

I went ashore and in just a few minutes while walking
up the main street meet my friend one of the Son of
the Amber paste King of Egypt. He gave me such a
look. I said quickly "What happened to you?" But it
was a sore question. he wouldnt speak of it. He would
not give me another box of amber paste but made me
a present to take on the steamer a fine cake of soap
and a box of amber cigaretts I was glad of the soap as
I had to buy some for my face and laundry soap so had
only to buy the laundry kind the cigaretts I give to or
three sometimes in place of a money tip.

It was a real joy to be in Port-Said it is so bright at
night and musice everywhere and the cafes are filled
with family Party the People seem to be such a decient

sort and the men are nice on the streets. I met a young fellow that owned a big shawl store and we had a dance togather. he bought me some fruit and came aboad to bring my magazines He is a fine looking fair Egyptian and such a Gentleman. all the Passangers were giving him an extra look. Because I have not spoken to any of the men passangers French nor those that speak English only the Frenchman that try to serve me at the table and then only at meal times that was the best way. I am the only woman traveling alone and there are many men. and I have a cabin by myself. My friend wanted to kiss me but I was all packed up with this fruit and things. he was not going to force himself so he kissed my hand. bowed his head to the ground, real Japanese bow and said "Goodby Madame." that was a little bit curt for me I was ready to do a little wrestling with him but didnt get to do any.

There is one French Wife I sized her up when I came on at Madras and knew she had a clock pendel for a tongue and have found it true and are so happy I choosed to be silent to all the men when they try to speak to me I walk away and never say a word. then the voyage are to long a one to have friends. So everything are just right. We sail about 1 A.M. for Marseilles. I did not want to finish up my around the world trip from India as I wanted to be in Europe for the Passion Play next summer.

Marseilles France
Sept. 24.
Hotel Mossilia. Room 22.

I being the first one off and through the coustom I took the tram down to my same little home of a year ago and told the Lady I would be back. Then to the Express and received nine beautiful letters. When it is a long time since you have received a letter you say a little prayer in Your heart that the letters will be of happiness only. so when you find them so a heavness are lifted off of your mind. So of the nine each had beautiful news. Two from Mrs. M. I worked for in Paris one forward from Bombay She always enclose a new dollar bill I always kiss bills the minute I draw them out I saw several People looking at me in the Express Office.

It was a very high wind and plenty of white dust it whiped you so I could hardly stay on my feet. everything is bright gay and beautiful the maid are different at the hotel the other one were a great talker I dont give this one a chance. a few doors down have been built the Salvation Armys pretty little Hall Sat. evening they had a Fruit feast a good musical programme a very big and portly gentleman a proffeur no doubt sang a solo he had a powerful voice and by keeping my eyes off of his beard covered face it sounded wonderful. he turned his sheet of music about as if he were mad with it. all the Girls though young in the Army Uniforms

had lovely long hair here I will say that mine are almost *strange*
to my waist. Some people came dressed up others from
their shops in their aprons the French are very proud
of their aprons shopping bags and carpet or felt slippers but all had a smiling face. the next block are the
fruit stalls bakers and cafés. a little noisy for here are a
mixture of French and Algeria but just in frount in the
same street are a grand old Church so when they look
up at it will always keep them from being to noisy.

When I was here before in the yard a chicken and a
black singing hen woke me early. But the Hotel have
not lost any of its family life across the alcove on the
floor below me are an artist family if You could see
the room he paint in I wonder how he can put so much
beauty in the picture that he is working on. he sit with
his side to the Window and on the sill are a large red
painted Cage with 4 lovely canaries one setting they sing
just enough they own also a big police dog. in the next
room on that landing the couple have two sweet little
Children and when I came in from the Salvation Hall
Sat. night and was ready for bed sitting reading my
Bible next door the Father were teaching one of the
children their prayers.

then the Young Husband to the wife next room to me
came home and gave her such a good and quick spanking I was so angry with him and think she must have a
heavy heart having a Husband living in one room and
getting a spanking on top of it. and in a few minutes

such pretty laughter came from that same wife. I just turned over and went to sleep.

Sunday I went for the 18 mile trip to Aix. the trip through the towns were interesting many orchards of blue grapes. Then when I got back at 3 I spent until 7 looking for a pair of shoes had given it up and started home with a heavy heart on the way found just what I wanted for 3 dollars. I also wanted a dress up dress but couldnt find one for 5 dollars so may make one here they ware their dresses to show their knees.

The first thing I do on entering my room is to cover the key hole its human nature to use them other than insert the key the mother with the lovely children are washing the landen when she got to my door she stoped so I went and peeped into a beautiful big black eye.

the world over!

Barcelona Spain
Sept. 30.

I had a pleasant trip from Marseilles. My Guide book gave the names of some of the leading Hotels I came to the one with the cheapest rates in a clean and home like street with the resturant dairys and such places where I can buy a centimos worth the entrance of the House have large palms and the sheets P cases and towels are put on fresh every day. the maids wash them and dry on the roof and are ironed like from the Laundry. my room have runing water and large window and I pay 35 cents a day. I had to choose a room near to the top and back from the street so to be from the much played Painos and Huddy Guddy's any way I like to be up high.

The City are clean and beautiful and the People are more cleaner than the French all the shop markets and such ware clean all over white aprons everybody go without a hat it is quite dusty altho they use the sprinkler freely like Rome there are beautiful fountains and taps everywhere. But the water is not so good as Rome's here it is a little hard.

I went to the Exposition it is on a mountain and the buildings beautiful but it is the great fountains and Water falls and the changing colour light that are so beautiful. on my way out I found two peseta the price I paid to go in so will visit all another afternoon.

The City look grand with Flags of every colour and the Spanish Balconey red velvet drap and like all Spanish Countrys Sunday is the biggest day. I went to the Monument Arena. I had a 15 cent seat the cheapest and good when the last Bull is turn in You can go to any part I went down to the groun seat to get a close up on the Face of the Fighters. Well of all the excitement nothing can come up to it. Between the Killing of the first and second one I did not know which side I would lean to but at the third I was as much Spanish as the rest. but I enjoy it best when the bull are let in the ring for a while he has it all to himself. the Band playes and the men look very pretty in their gold suits. the first fighter did not kill his bull it took him a long time. They called him fool, drunkard, ass, they were so disgusted with him. The next two were very cleaver and drove their soward in up to its handle in the left sholder. more excitement and hundreds of hats and caps thrown in the ring. One hurt his hand driving the soward in so he could hardly use it. But the Crowd did not care about his injuries. At the end little anxious to be bull fighters jump in the ring with a red cloth and a long stick under it in place of the soward and tease the bull. they are only 15 or 16 yrs in a second the bull had one of them in the seat of his pants on its left horn and droped him on the groun the men with their capes stood in frount I screamed for I was sure he were killed If one had been killed as often as I surposed it would have been several corps. he got up without any hurt except a big hole in his pants with all of his shirt tail hanging out the Police took him out. I been wondering if I want to go again. Every house shop and Church door are closed when there is a Bull fight so maybe I'll go again. each evening going to mass the Churches are so packed and everybody rushing to get there so they like to pray as well as fight. another thing at the bull rings there are always a little fight going on between men. Today is Monday the Spanish day for Weddings so I'll get near some church. 9 P.M. or 10 are the hour. The living are cheaper here than in France. I expect to

take the day trip to Monserrat and when it get cold go
to Seville for the Winter.

Barcelone Oct. 7.
Calle San Ramon

After looking over this nice little city I felt I would like
to stay a while. So I looked up the news Paper Offices
and this afternoon will have an add put in. Sunday the
King Queen and Two Preincesses were here and there
was a grand Parade along the Beautiful Ramble de
Gruerer where the Roylaty had a place with a Canop.
first it begain with the Priest. then the Soldiers of the
King in their blue and white with silver helment and
white feathers then the rest in blue red and yellow the
King looked Capable nice size and bout 35. He is 43.
when the regement would pass in frount the King He
would sulute them. I liked to see them sulute the
Spanish Flag. He lowed his head then raised it straight
very quick and the Queen and Princesses and another
young Lady in black that stood with them would give
a very stiff and quick curtsey the King and Queen stood
at one side and the Princesses a little apart from them.
The Queen were in a simple black crape de chein. and
the Daughters in simple white with plain wide white
hats. The Queen is still quite medeum fair and good
looking the Princesses look much like twins and not fat
but good strong looking Girls. I was at the very head

of the Ramble when the Procession turned in the King
and Queen in a carriage.

Afterward I went down and hung on the back of a bus
that was standing right in frount of the Viewing Stand
I look at them until I lost use of my arm and Today it
hurt. I remembed that in London I waited to see them
and got chill balms on my feet but that will never happen in lovely Barcelona.

at 3.30 I went to the Bull Fight there were two very
clever fighter one teased the beast when a hat would
come in the ring he would hang it on one of its horns
and then He killed it quick. one bull cleared them all
out when he jumped right behind the Fighter in the
safety ring a young man hurt himself very bad getting
over the wall in a hurry. after the fifth bull have been
drug out I go down to the first class place to pick up
a Sunday paper and magazines I had two papers and 4
magazines on my arm and on the way home I passed a
big dancing Hall and thought I would stop and look
on when I got to the door the Porter told me newspapers sellers were not alowed to go in and sell papers.
that gave me an idea if I cant get a job I'll sell papers.
It is ever so gay here cafés everywhere they have musice
in the side walks they dance formed in a ring some time
as many as 20 joined hands and as many as 10 rings
on the side walk and in the street. it is very pretty and
child like.

I made a round of many dancing halls cafés and cabrats

I started at the high Class then at 10.30 came back changed my dress for the second and third class. where some were in their aprons bed room like slippers which they use so much here and the men in black shirts velvet trouses and a red sash everybody enjoying themselves exciting but orderly.

I have a favarite one at the end of Calle del Conde near to me they have a very good program you pay for a five cent cup of coffee an spend from 9.30 to 12.30 it is a Family like place seat about 300 and is crowded mothers papas little babys and all sizes the Parents walk between the table quieting the babys nearly every body in a gingum apron but clean I have a special table.

I went to the Fair again and meet several Bombay Ceylon and the English Gentleman that mananges the Oriental Theatre of 7 Ceylon dancers and a good Snake Charmer I went in Free. I laughed so when the Ceylon dancer that look so much like a Girl told me how a Spanard tryed hard to make love to him and he had such a hard time to make him believe he was a man all of them have the long black hair done in a knot.

I can get everything in two blocks of my street from a good plate of Itialian spaggetti to a Turkish bath. I have just found the number of an employment office in the paper I picked up at the Bull ring so will first go there before I put out an add. as I can learn much by listen to the girls talk. I hope to get something as I would like to stay here. it is so gay I missed Indias gay colours the days I was in Marseilles the people in dark cloths made me feel lonely. but I made a good move when I choosed Spain at this time of the Exposition.

Barcelona, Spain, October 13, 1929.
The Instituto.

I went to the employment Office and was offered a place in a Home for Feelable minded children. It sounded interesting and new. so I took it. My reference of the Lady I worked for in Cuba sure did come in handy. When the Lady had talked with me at the Instituto I knew the job was mine for as long as I cared to keep it.

It is on a high mountain overlooking the City and far out to sea. At night the City lights and Exposition are wonderful. It is in a Privat Home for about 15 Wealthy Foolish mined children it is runed and own by Young and lovely Dr. Cordoba His young wife they have a baby boy laugh whenever he see me. The pretty Blond sister are the Housekeeper. They have plenty of help for the children.

it is just like a big family and every body are kind to each other. I take care of the sitting hall Chappel and waite on table. they like me because my name are Familer to them. 3 boys and one little Girl are quite ensane and eat different food in a private dinning room. The Doctor get home about 10 and they sit down to dinner one very rich boy wait to eat with the Family.

first they will have a dish of patatoes and a vegetable like spinnish then fish egg ormelit chicken bread cheese apples and grapes then bouls of sower milk with sugar and then will send word to the cook to make another ormelit. after seeing them eat like they do at 12 at night I have sized them all up to be crazy. why will the Dr. let the rich little boy sit up so late and go to bed with a stomakfull of all that food. Yet he is the Picture of health.

I dont know what the cook get yet but it is not more than 15 dollars the rest about 10 dollars a month. They ask me why I did not take a place in a wealthy Family I could not tell them I am here just for the interest. I can teach a Spanish maid more in a minute than she can teach me in a week as far as the work goes but she can teach me manners if I would learn it. One of my favorite little boys about 7 He hate to drink out of a cup and He always say give me a drink of water and whisper in your ear, in a glass. he is the pet of the whole bunch and can do the Spanish dance well Sunday they go with their caretakers down to a church they dress in their nice suites and look each others cloths over.

October 18.

I have caused some changes the Family eat early and quicker and I did not like the pot the soup was served out of so a nice new one came today. they are amused at me I get through with my work so quick and it is done so well and sometimes I am in the garden gathern flowers or in the sowing room mending or visiting in the class rooms. they are afraid I will quit. but giving up this job is my least study.

they have many old ways of during things the Spaniards are like the Indians their coustoms are to old The laundress get 12 cents an hour and wash sheets in cold water. and all cloths with a brush the piece laid on the seament side of the tub.

when the Children does something wrong they are sent up to the dinning room of the 4 ensane children to have a meal. its not the children they mine but eating on a table with out a cloth in white granit plates and drinking from tin cups.

The Doctor is like a Father to each child, that is the beauty of the Doctor. He sits with the craziest child and seem like he would say all of these are my beautiful children.

October 26.

One of the boys about 15 a Fatty He felt I was afraid of him and I was He would walk up to me so quick I always felt he would bit me. today when I passed him on the stairs He jumped at me, now I am not afraid any more. the ensane have a lot of sense. I was also afraid of the only Lady in the Instituto she is a Blond and about 40 nice looking she talks to herself very loud. Yesterday she came into the dinning room and saw the

Fresh Flowers I was putting in the Vases. I was so afraid I smiled and she came to me and ask where I was from and I said the U.S.A. and she said it over and over in Spanish put her arms around me and Kissed me many times. Now I am not afraid of her any more.

October 30.

The first week I could not eat a thing they cook everything even to frying eggs in olive oil it taste so strong now I use more oil than any one else. and the Girls notice the change how full my face is getting I am looseing most of my Egypt and Indian brown I was a dark chocolate when I arrived back in Europe. I have to hide my soap and clean cloths from the Cook the only safe place was in my room under the mattrews. The Doctor is the pick of the whole lot. He always bring in something good to eat and the only words He can say in English is And this is for you. They always give me some of whatever they have extra.

November 4.

I went down yesterday to the employment office and a Lady in there was looking for a girl she said she would like to have me and ask me how many days before my month was up. I told her it was up the next day. I thought it was better to do what Shakspear say never put off for tomorrow what you can do today. I went back and told them I was leaving the next night. everybody were surprised and very much upset. They said I was the best waitress and all the rest could leave but they wanted me to never leave. because I was always smiling. one of the Teachers wanted to come and see me and I told her I never have Lady Friends because I dont like any one in my room. The men friends I entertain on the street or theatre but not in my room. You can work one month and it seem like a 100 years. but when you loafing one year seem like one week.

Nov. 1st.

I was so happy to get to my little buisy neighborhood on a corner a good string band playing the latest Spanish songs I turned up my suit-case and sat for an hour. you can walk through the streets with your suite case on your sholder and no one ever notice you. I went to a good Play in a 15 cents seat and had plenty of company the Theatres are out at 1.30 then everybody stop at the milk daries and have a plate of whipped cream and rolls or rice custard. A man told me I spoke spanish just like a Cuban.

Molina del Rey Spain
Nov. 10 1929

The eldest daughter of Senora Planas the Lady I interviewed in the office came for me we went to a big store and she bought two house dresses for me. I did not ask any questions about the Villige they live in I wanted it to be a surprise. In half an hour we arrived and I looked all about for the molins not one in the Town. I asked the Young Lady why the name molins and She said they were made here many years ago The name in English mean The Windmills of the King.

It is a pretty little place mountains everywhere. this part is called Catalana and the language are a little different I cant say anything about the Catalanaians until I live with the Spanish, then I'll size the Two up. one thing they are known to be serious and not much for smiling. every Peason that I meet say to me. Juanita I am not Catalania I from another Part where the People are much nicer. but every body has been kind to me. so I forget there was no smiles.

Nov. 14. I miss understood the sound on the last letter in Daughters I thought the Lady said she had four sons hijos but it was four hijas when I arrived at the house the mother said welcome Juanita I hope you will stay many years and I looked over Her sholders and saw 3 Girls fat and beautiful 12, 11 and 10. I felt just like turning Back to Barcelona. But they are the most perfect taught Girls I have ever seen in any home She certainly is a mother for Girls. La Sra. were born in this house Built 85 years ago it is a beautiful Place the Brother is a Priest at Montserrat. Her husband were Born in the same Town and went to Lima Perue when a young man and became very rich and he came back after he lost his first wife and married this Lady and she

gave him a child every year for eight years four boys
which died and four girls all the children were born in
S. America they came to Molins del Rey 6 years ago to
put the girls in School and the Father died 3 years ago.
The eldest Girl finnished her educate in Paris and play
the Paino wonderful but eight children will destroy
Satan. The mother is the same age I am and look so
mother like when she ask me my age I took off 7 years
and did not feel a bit guilty. She is the Good Samari-
tain of this Village at this very minute she is at the bed
side of a maid that worked for her six years. her husband came Right away to tell Her she have been twice
since Sunday and the Daughter once. and everybody in
the Villiage bring their troubles and sit and blow their
nose in Her face and tell Her everything every day 4 or
5 come in for to beg. Tomorrow is Friday the Day set
aside for beggars they begin coming at 7 A.M. in the
Hall on the table are a little basket of pennies each one
get a penny and if there are no penny pieces only two
penny piece the beggars must go and get it changed and
bring back the other penny. they tell me the beggars
do not belong to this Villiage and I never see any on the
street but they come from somewhere.

I told her if she put two or 3 to work in the garden she
would get rid of them. when they come other days and
tell a sad tail La Sra. doesnt give them money but if
they want food or medicine she will write a note to the
store.

This is a real Villiage the people look quaint every body get up early and sprinkle water in their half of the street and sweep it scrape up the horse dung with a shovel seem like the horses wait until they are in frount of my door and do what they want to on my half of the street. donkeys bring in the vegetables and milk and the milk maids come at 7 A.M. with the milk in a cooler. everybody wares an apron the old women ware wide skirts and black or brown silk handkerchiefs on their head tired under their chin the younger ones the black lace long scarf. In a box on the table are one for each of us only for church. the Lady go every morning at 6 A.M. as she is still in mourning the children and I hafter get up at 6.30 but Sunday when you are taking your first beauty nap poor me must get out of my warm bed at 6 A.M. so to sweep up the horse dung be ready for 7 A.M. mass. the Lady dont want me to be late so she call me. its good I was a good mass goer before I came here She think it is so nice the minute she call me I answer. Well I like new ways and changes. but I would like to have my Sunday morning sleep. The Girls love their home in S. America and often say to me we all are Americians.

the Girls are so very sweet they are taught never to sit down and ask you to bring them something but each one do for herself. they get up early to practice their musice before breakfast. the mother hear them through their reading lesson then they sit down to breakfast and are taught never to refuse anything and never leave anything on their plates not even a piece of bread then they play in the yard for a half hour then lessons and they nit and do fancy work after they work in their flower bed the yard are in terraces with seats and peigeons houses on one side each take care and plant their flowers they are loving sisters so all gardens look the same there is the chicken ducks and rabbit yard then the Vegetable garden orchard and garage. they have oranges figs and many almond trees.

After lunch they study again then they play with their dolls and make dresses. then they darn on under cloth and stockings. the mother are sweet but she never tell them anything twice they make their beds and tidy up their rooms every day excep one and thats the day I put the bedding in the sun but you never pick up not one thing after them and they are happy they are all taught to cook and each can go in the Kitchen make the charcoal fire and make an armlet and many other things. The Young Lady daughter are 20 and make all the dresses for the 3 small girls. She is such a lovely Girl and can cook and do everything. a few doors from us lives a mother and daughter they have a Dry good store the mother are 85 and very ill her daughter are in the store all day so the Senorite Elvia go every night to sleep and get up in the night with the mother and their house are very cold She is happy to do it and the mother say it is good for her to learn to serve others. they have a beautiful Sun Parlor to practic they have a big class room. they had all their classes at home with a teacher till this year then the 12 yr. Girl are in a Private School in Barcelona She hate to be away from the sisters next year the other two are going to the same school. and the mother will live in Barcelona most of the time.

The Srta. learned to speak English from an English governess but have forgot. The mother was glad to have me come that She may renew it. she is ashame to speak for fear I will laugh at Her. But Carmen the ten year and youngest is so cute and smart and so anxious to speak she get a paper and pencil ask me a sentices write it as it sound to her and learn so fast. they never want me to do any work that I dislike they have a woman that come and work every day.

The Mother said that everything I know and do it just perfect and if I stay all things she will give me and that it seem I have been here a year because she never tell me anything. I thought to myself thats about the nearest to a year I'll ever get. She is afraid to let me go to Barcelona for fear I wont come back every time I say I am going She will say we two will go to gather but I want to go by myself. because I want to tell the Lady at the employment office to get a place for me in a Hotel as maid to speak English and Spanish. but I'll try to stay here a month they have such good food and such a good bed. I had forgot much of my Spanish but are picking it up very fast.

the first Sunday afternoon the Girls took me around to the homes of all the Cousins all wishing that I may stay many years. I am planning to go in the City to-morrow so will fool my Lady and not say a word till 10 minutes before train time then I know She cant get dressed to go with me.

Nov. 17.
Molins del Rey near Barcelona

Working at the Beautiful Home of Senora Montserrat de Planas after being here since the second of the month I went into Barcelona yesterday and the City look so gay I'll give up my job just as soon as La Senora get another Girl. I went in to see the Lady in the El Rapido agencia about another place and she said La Senora had been in to see Her a few days before and thanked Her getting me and she will give me 14 duros instead of 12 and a nice present if I stayed. But I told the Lady I did not want to stay at The Windmills of the King as it was dull and Barcelona Gay. gay is to dull a name for Barcelona.

I went back on the last train 9 P.M. Walked to the house and decided I wouldnt go in as the next day will be Sunday and I will want my Sunday morning late sleep. so I went right pass the door to a Hotel 3 blocks up in the same narrow curving street the room was nice with white blankets on the bed but one of them had moths, after taking it off I had a wonderful night the next morning at 7 I thought I would dress an go as it was past mass hour then it started to rain so I just snug up in bed and clapped my hands for the Waiter he brought hot coffee bread which mean sausage and Cataluna are famous for. and it is good. then I went back to bed because I felt tird from my visit to Barcelona and it rained all day and I slep until 5 when I had dinner in bed. and went to the House at 7. They were glad to see me I said nothing about the Hotel and They never said a word but Molins is a Village and some women said She saw me going up the street when they came out of the movies the 3 Muskets were being showing. You can see how dull Molins is all these years and that film just reach here. I told La Senora it was to cold in Molins and very warm in Barcelona. so I wanted to go when She found another Maid. She made so many promises. go I must.

Nov. 20. The Maid came to talk with the Senora a pretty blonde girl of 20. Her mother with her and in her arms a 3 month old baby girl. The mother said the man did not want to marry the girl so the girl had to work and take care of the child. La Senora said she would take the Girl but the baby couldnt come. the Grandma said she wouldnt Trust that Baby with any body she loved it to much. She so young and pretty I felt so sorry for her. I went out and she was surprised to see me with a hat and gloves. She said I truly must be rich if not I would not ware a hat I told her in my country, France and England everybody wore hats but she couldnt see it. she said she like so much to ware a hat but she being a servent could not I told her if she wanted to ware a hat to ware it being a servent made no differents but she could not see that. she has a sister that work near she are keeping company with a very nice young man both of the girls are perfect little flappers in dress but never ware a hat. Molins del Rey 1929.

Barcelona Nov. 24.
Calle San Ramon

I left Molins del Rey this evening at 6. Senora tried very hard to get me to stay I said I was coming back in two weeks I didnt like to do it as I know I would be gone from Barcelona. She told me I was welcome to come to them any time. in the mountains around Molins are great for hunting rabbits. I enjoyed returning to the City with the Sunday crowd the train were packed each man had one or two dogs and a rabbit or more in his bag the women had flowers or bunches of sage. Its said that the Catalonias are not much for smiling that sure were a Smiling Crowd. I am always happy to be in Barcelona but I feel the cold very much I ware a velvet dress a sweter under it and my heavy coat. It is always sunny only a few clowdy days and then only for a few hours.

I went to my favorite Resturant To the Cabrat last night was a big Entertainment 5 young man put on several good sketches they keep us laughing all the while. the wife and two children of one of the young men sat next to my table when he finnish acting he would come and hold the baby and give it its bottle. To me a show was going on all the time. the Couple I always sit with were there with their little baby daughter so smart and a boy 3 yrs. half past one at night and sitting in the Cabret.

Nov. 27. I left this morning for the Sacred mountains of Montserrat with a heavy heart as it was cloudy and I was sure of having a misty day. It was very cold going up I got off to change cars and had a good breakfast and very Cheap while I was having it meet a Gentle-man that had spent a few years in Cuba and a few months in N.Y. the mist disapeared and the sun was so bright on the next train for Montserrat I meet a Ger-man Gentleman that was on a tour of Spain so had company all the way up. it was very beautiful each mountain have a different beauty. and you get a view of the snow caped Pyrenees which seem near but are so far away. at the only flag crossing are a boy about 14 years he has a dog dressed in overall and a cap and sit on a box and hold the red flag until the train passes it is very clever but the boy had an Idea of business the Passangers throw penneys out to him.

The German Gentleman was my company going down He ask me to go that night to see the Russian dancers but I didnt want to go to see the Russian dancers in

Spain. then we change for the Barcelona train and we went into a coche and who should step in to but the Friend that I had meet in the morning He knew a little English and he said, "Is that your friend?" I Laughed. "Well, yes," I said, and so are you my friend. we all talked togather then but I forgot all about the German and he got so restless it was funny. the Spanard made a date with me for the next evening at 5. then he got off at the next place. I was to meet the German at 9. but I layd down to rest and went to sleep woke up at 11 so that was the ending of the German.

Thursday I went up to the beautiful amusement Park at El Tibidabo Funicular it was so gay up there I could not think of coming down to Barcelona at 5 P.M. so that was the ending of the Spanard.

Sept. 28. I love the street musice here all the players are disabeld in some Way like the French they use very much the accodian and the gutia and Voilen and have real good voices I stand for hours on the Corner of some side street where ever they sing you can buy a sheet with 4 songs for half a cent.

> *Valencia Spain Dec. 13.*
> *Plaza de Collardo*
> *La Aragonesa Room 15*
> *3rd Piso.*

I left Barcelona stoped off at Tarragona and just as I arrived at the Arch Under the great old Roman Wall a

Shepard in his short black pleated Mother hubbard
Coat like they ware and in France he were driving a
number of black goats home through the Narrow
streets and we meet. I left on the afternoon train made
Friends and accepted food a Gentleman offored me because I was hungry. after I had eating enough. the
Gentleman proposed to me. He was a Valencian Bach-
elor showed me his papers and three other Friends said
he was a good man and If I liked going to Church as
he did he would make me very happy all the time I was
planning how to get rid of him before I reached Valencia. I always want to go into a new Town at midnight
by myself. I did get rid of him and walked out the station and in and out of so many little streets it did look
so Spanish every house is white and brightens up the
town. when I came to one street sitting in a Chair was
a blind man playing on his guetar and singing for fair.
I said "Oh, Senor do you know what time it is?" "No
Signorina." He didnt know it was midnight. only we
two in the street I was looking for the Cheaper Rooming houses so I ask the bell boy of a Hotel and he went
with me a few blocks away. the next morning I found
the big market the most beautiful than any country or
city I have Visited yet.

I got a lovely freshly painted room just a few doors
from the market and a maid do the Cleaning and I pay
a dollar a week. The very first thing I had to buy was
a black lace head dress as everybody ware it here and

you cannot enter a Church with other than one on. the first part of the day I had to ware my hat it was so funny the way the Valencians look at me and little boys would say my how alegant you are with your hat on. I was glad I had it on they made me laugh so.

the City are Pretty no old looking houses and no poor and beggards the young men stand under the Balcone and talk to their sweet heart. I got a job from the Paper and went to work It is very nice I wouldnt sleep in as I had planned to spend just two weeks here and I wanted to be free. they have 3 other Girls I only do the work I like to do the other do the rest. their hearts are in the right place but they dont always know just what to do. the Lady say I must not ware a hat but I did and she could not get over it.

The Street musice of Valencia all are disabled men and women in couples or an orquesta good musicians one sightless I saw reading the words of the Songs of raised letters. One couple I like so much to listen to I often spend an hour or more walking through narrow Streets looking for them. They are blind the man about 28 years and the Girl a pretty little flapper and have the cutest Bobed hair. Shes about 19 yrs. and have a lovely voice and sing beautiful Spanish Songs He play the Guetar they always get many Spanish 10 cents and when She has each of her pockets well filled She whisper to Him She is tird and He say then we will stop. He swing the Guetar on his back take the Chair under his arm the Girl on the other one. And they go through the many little curving streets togather Whispering Words of love. and alone as though they had owls eyes. and I always walk just a short distance behind for several blocks just to look at them because they are so happy.

She had a blind husband but he often Whipped Her. they had a little baby but he died very young then She wouldnt live with Him any longer. She and this Sweetheart are very happy together. All I have to say is She sure can sing and I love them both.

Dec. 16. I left at 6.40 A.M. and the Country became the very picture of the Country about the Holy Land. and I got off at the Town of Elche known to be the most fascinating Town of Spain. it is like Damascus with streams running along the side of the streets. I wanted to spend the night and next day so I took a room with a Widow of Rico. Bright and early in the Yard below my window a turkey started gobbling I didnt mind as it made me think of Xmas and I thought I would enjoy the gobbling it may be all I'll get of a Xmas turkey then the hens begain to sing. a stream run through the yard and the maids were washing and singing so I did not feel lonely. The Cuban Ladies say they dislike the Spanish servent because they sing to much.

The cafés with covers over the sidewalks to keep off the Sun and the many date trees make the town look much like Jaipur India.

I went to the date grove of the Priest the most beautiful one in the town and had my dinner of dates I
stoped at the bakery and bought a loaf of hot bread.
Elche have many flappers and all are Hollywood fans
and all the Picture House show the Calif. Films I am
proud I choosed Calif. for my home before I left as
every one know it.

I refuse to eat where I stay because they put the salad
in a large bowl and every one eat out of it. That dont
suit me as they dont use the tooth brush any to freely.
they have many ways of the East. they wake up at 5 in
the morning and begin to sing both men and women
all singing a different song the old way of singing is
much like the Japanese and Arbic. I watched the
women washing cloths and had great fun with them I
told the women and girls if I was married I would be
at home washing dirty cloths just as they are during.

For 2 cents You can get a large glass full of wine and
it have a kick from here to La Fayette Park.

Last night was not such pleasant sleeping a big fat
couple had the room next to me a large Window served
for the Two room half on their side and half on my
side. Yesterday they got up with such a long face said
that they were cold all the night. I told them I was alone
and not fat and how could two sleep in a small room
with the Window close. I promised not to open it last
night they said the Window had been open all day.
They had company last night so I spent the whole

evening in and had supper with them and a nice gentleman that spent 3 years in Penn. during the War a
Soldier then a Bull fighter now father of twins. he had
forgotten much of his English. I expect to leave at 6
for Granada then to Sevilla. On the way to the Station
at 6 A.M. I bought rolls and Tomatoes I always have
salt in my pockets When I got in the coach I begin
to eat it Two Ladies sat near me one said Look This
Senora have a stomach for Tomatoes at this hour of
the morning We laughed so hearty over it.

The Trains at least the Local ones travell along just like
a cog train and make the same noise the Spanish never
leave the train Without shaking hand with You and
wishing You a happy journey which make one forget
the old train and everything are very pleasant and they
never eat without offoring to the others sitting in the
same compartment it would be wrong to accept. But I
accepted just that once on my way from Tarragone to
Valencia because I was hungry. Three Young men got
on at Murcia. Two that had been away from Home 7
years and 5 of them spent in Pittsburg Penn. they sat
in my compartment and I spent a most pleasant 3 hours.
The best looking and very sportest was love sick for
his Girl that he had left in Penn the other one was
happy as he expected to see his Boyhood sweetheart.
I told the love sick one I was sure His Father had a
wife waiting and he would be married in Two months
and would never see Penn. again. He swore it couldnt

be The Train arrived and a horst were there to meet them the Old Parents had drove in a 4 hour ride from the Place to the station and such rejoicing all of them tryed to get to the Boys face and standing looking it seem that would murder Him everybody crying I thought what good Boys to return to such a forsaken place in the most barred part of Spain. here are still some obeiden Children.

Then the next station which was in half an hour ride another son and His Wife and a horst to meet them and the same durings. then the next another Son and I begain to love the old train and I was sure I was on the Train of the Prodigal Sons. At that last Station a Stout Lady fell on the Son sholders and fainted away they layed Her out in the waiting room and was working over her when the train left. next a Father and all the children were at the station to meet some one. it seem that all the home commers lived between Murcia and Zurgena several hours from Granada. Then I thought after all I like my life best I am so free and dont have to go to see any one. Most of the Country grow Olives it seems much like Palestine. also we traveled through many orange groves.

Granada Dec. 18.

I stayed in the coch until all the passangers had left as one Gentleman wanted to help me off with my suit-case which was kind but I never leave the train with anyone. then I passed the station masters office He being out I steped in and hide until all the Hotel Porters and drivers had disapeared then came out a Boy about 16 was walking by and I asked him to take me to a Boarding house near the Station I had on a Sweter suit and a heavy coat so the ice on the grown did not make me uncomfortable. He took me to a Family a Widow with 4 children 3 Girls 2 of marrage age but not engaged and a Son. They were sitting in the dinning room having coffee with 3 Friends I gave the Boy a peseta he was so pleased I displeased because I couldnt get it changed to give him half.

The Eldest daughter went up stairs to show the room. the Home nitted spred was so white But I knowing how close the Spanish live pull off all the bedding and put the sheets on the floor. all the while She was telling me they was clean I said yes but some one had slept on them and how did I know that they were ill. She very sweetly brought up fresh ones. I heard them laughing over it.

The next morning every Body were so kind and I had my choice of Two rooms on the grown floor it being warmer. I was out sightseeing I often ask a Spaniard the way because they enjoy showing the strangers the Way just like the Itialians. I was walking through a curving narrow street when I got my first View of the Snow covered mountains right over the City and on another hill just below lovely green plants and near that The hight of Alhambra.

This is the First Town where the High Spanish Combs
and Mantillas are worn and most of the men ware the
wide Spanish hats and black or blue broad cloth capes
with red or green velvet lining. the Alhambra are a
most Wonderful Place. it made me feel that I was back
in India only I did not see anything in Egypt or India
quite so beautiful as the race of today are not much
for beautifeing.

The Catedral is beautiful white and light which make
it Cheerful. at first it was a mosque. here are many
Gipsies. I stopped a man on the street and he took me
to just the place to eat well for a few pennies. I Went
home early it being cold and wanted to go to bed but
they wouldnt let me so ten of us sat around the table
where a large shallow pan of hot ashes are put under
it and then a yarnd table cover that reach to the floor
to keep in the heat of the pan. the doors are only shut
at bed time so there You sit with all Your coats and
sweters on with nice warm feet. It was very jolly of
course the Son thought as I was single why not marry
with him.

They are not much for clocks in this town but the
mother called me twice so I reached the Station at 7.30.
and I bought a good lunch of crisp fried fresh sardins
or minners as I know them and other things. The trip
to Sevilla were through olive groves and then oranges
the wine had gone up so high I had to pay 1 and a half
penny for the same as 1 cent for Alicanto wine but the

olives had come down which pleased me as they are more fattening. We got a good Shower on the subes of Sevilla so it was lovely and Warm and so delightful after Granada.

Sevilla Spain
Dec. 20, 1929.

Arrived at 5 P.M. I saw a boy with a Waiters White coat on and ask him the way to Cook's he was going that Way it was a good walk from the Station. at Barcelona Cook paid 6.65 for a dollar at Granada He paid 6.90 at Sevilla 7 peseta and 15 centimes most Banks pay less than Cook In Cook's They have the most kindest young men it is always a joy to go to them. Sevilla is more Spanish than any I have seen yet but the little Streets will make many's hair gray and the whole life is in those narrow streets. The Kind of room I want are not so easy found I had an address and stoped two men to tell me the way they went with me and from there to another and they did not want to leave me and its nothing I hate so much as having a man with me When I am looking for a room then they thought I could take one of their room and they would bunk togather for one night. But I thanked them and said good night.

I passed a Hotel and a fat Porter was in frount and he sent me to the home of a Friend that let a few rooms. the room wasnt clean to suite me so I cleaned it and the Husband told me to clean it all I wanted I told him to mine his on buisiness. But the Wife was sweet. but one side of me a Couple talked late and another room there were a Young Mother and her Mother and a crying baby the poor Grandma was up all night the daughter would tell her to take it out and sit in the dinning room they had many cannarees and when the bright light was turned on and the Baby begin to cry they started to sing so I got up early and started out to find a room. and found this Perfect home.

I was wishing for a place to cook my Xmas dinner and I have a lovely balconey a corner for a Kitchen with a charcoal stove with Two burners the sunny roof just a short flight of stairs up and a nice laundry and toilet all on this floor. and the Husband work in the Exposition and if I go with the little daughter can go in free.

The Yards of the houses are known for their beauty. living are cheap if You care to look for it. There are few beggards but quite a few Gipsie Women and Children beggards. The Exposition have its beauty but lack the gayety of the Barcelona. Along the streets are well shaped orange trees but they are bitter I ate one—thats why they are always on the tree. I have my Sunday dinner on now cooking in a nice pot it is a piece of nice beef hog ears celery onions maceroni and sweet potatoes and parsely.

57 Alvarez Quintero
Near the frount of the Tower of the Giralda.

I call my poch the sitting room I wonder to my self
how I can find such Places there are so many little
streets running every way.

A lovely newly married couple have the room next
me. She and I use the stove but we are never in each
others way she cook the Lunch and take it to a café
where her Husband Work and spend the rest of the
day with Him. they expect their first Baby in Feb. but
I am sure it will be in January While I am here and
will have to give it a present. for that reason I am useing her cooking things but I had to buy one pot and I
spent all yesterday afternoon looking for one at my
price and found a perfect fit for my chicken and
Turkey.

Turkeys are the one thing that make it like Christmas
to me droves of them in the streets men women and
boys carry them from door to door. I had a great time
shopping I bought a nice chicken a first and second
joint and part of the brest of a Turkey and everything
that go with a Xmas dinner and the Turkey is as tender
as a new born baby the Chicken the same it is stuffed
with the best dressen I have ever tasted. and just as
brown as though it were cooked in a big White Stove.
and are now floating in nice brown gravy. Then I have
another pot of noodles made with the wings neck and it
is already I wouldnt cook on Xmas day when I am

not getting paid for it. My chicken and turkey cost about 75 cents. and I have enough for three days or more. The Spanish keep it quite Sacred up until Xmas day when they eat like wolves. The Cathedral Bells are ringing for 5 o'clock mass I am going to say my prays and take a bottle to get 2 cents of good wine and buy a half pennies worth of olives then my dinner will be completed. I have celery nuts oranges apples and I may buy a cents worth of candy and cake.

I can beat any of the other ladies marketing they wanted to know if I was a Moor one man said that I sure knew how to buy. If I came to Sevilla just to do my marketing living is very cheap and the dollar high which pleases me still it isnt high enough to keep me so I'll be reading adds. in a few days. Instead of Santa Claus they have Kings and Christmas night they have a beautiful prade of the three Kings and their Courts in gay colours lantens and baloons. the Kings each have a coche With six horses and their Court ride horseback. The Black King were the most popular. He threw out more Carmel candy.

Jan. 1. 1930.

I had been looking all over Sevilla for an office to get a job and walking along the street on a corner I saw several Women standing around one seated on a stool and stop to see what it was and thats how I found the employment office of Sevilla. Maria her name was

written on the stool on the sidewalk and she had her
book with the places. She would write on a bit of card
boad or paper the Ladies pay but not the Girls when
the Ladies want a girl they stop on the corner and tell
her. she changes the Corners as the Sun shines.
She sent me to a place right away Dec. 31 at 5 P.M.
as up stairs girl they keep a cook 2 butlers laundress
the House was pretty but so cold and the many fat
Ladies with so many cloths on made them look like
bales of cotton setting in the chairs. I ask the maid
did they use a long handle mop on the floors she said
no I told her if I got down even on the boad that they
used I would take cold and also get my cloths soiled
and my knees I use only to pray on. the room for the
upstairs girl was so cold the bed to short and narrow
and the blankets even shorter so I was up and dressed
and ready to go New Years morning at 7.30 but the
maid would not unlock the frount door she wanted me
to waite until the Lady was up. She had been during
the upstairs work for Two days and wanted to be off
New Years day and I didnt want to stay that day as a
bull fight was on. I was very anxious to leave before
the Lady got up so said to the maid if I stayed I would
have to have coffee milk and rolls and then would only
talk to the Lady and go so she unlock the door for me.
I went back to Marie this noon and ask her to find another house but She would not send me again a young
Boy were there and he told me if I wanted another job

he knew two other Corners. There are so many people that cannot read the first thing they will ask you if you can read. it seem so strange a country so near the other European Countrys and all Spanish people. it seem to be like that more in and about Barcelona and Valencia that may be because it is larger but the most common question you hear is can you read.

Jan. 6.

I went to the Bull Ring School where most of the best fighters learn. it were on the out skirt of the City and seat about 500 being so small it brought you very close. they had an old men 4 piece brass band they had forgot how to play and it was funny to hear them trying to play the pouplor songs of the streets then they would clap and say dont stop that good musice. the 4 young fighters come in in their tight pants pink sash and short white coat and rose capes. the ring was a little slippy as we had just had one of Sevilla light showers. both the men and bulls had many slip up.

one of the Judges were standing and the bull got him in between his horns and he had a great struggle before he got to safety and then with many long slits in his pants. The boys must have scratches on their skin because the pants are skin tight. instead of the fine horses to drag the bull out they had two mules everything were so different from the big bull rings.

all the houses have pretty Patios and plants everywhere

on the roof also. but all the houses are cold as they
have tiling or brick floors and the roofs are useual open
over the balcon. after I get throu cooking which is only
once a day I put the coals and hot ashes in the wide
shallow copper pan that they put under the table for
their feet. I put it in my room and it keep my room
lovely and warm and I also heat my supper on it. a
most pleasant life.

Jan. 13. Alvarez Quentero.

Today are just like Spring. after having an all over
bath the first I have had in Sevilla you never take one
when it is cold most of the Family had a bath. I went
out to look for a job and meet Two young girls and an
old girl also looking for a job we had a jolly time
neither of us wanted to cook. The Girls said that I
couldnt be very poor because I had so much gold in my
mouth. I was frighten for fear I would get a job. This
is the first Place I have been to and went out for a job
all the time afraid I would have to take it. I just really
dont want to work. I like to be out in the sunshine—
in another place I can make up for it.

Last night was the first time I went to a night Club
there are Spanish and Gipsie dancing I like it because it
is gay with the girls in their ruffel dresses and bright
shawls yet respectful a plesant place to spend three or
four hours you order a glass of coffee and milk una
pesetar and have a table or a Chair at a table.

One of the Ladies I intervud for work was a Widow I saw 7 girls the eldest about 12 and all were in deep mourning that they wore at all times. I thought in a cold house with all those black cloths not me. I am making myself contented in my pleasant home for I am sure it is much cheaper not to work in one of Sevillas cold houses and take cold pay out more for medician than you earn 4 or 5 dollars as much as they get a month and how the Girl can sing on top of those small wages and hard work.

I was talking with a Lady that own a big store She ask if I could cook a German that cleark in the store and speak English laugh so when I said no. and I told her in English I wouldnt cook for the Spanish its always a host in one Family different from my country where you can cook for a Family of 2 or 3 and then I told her not to tell what I said. She did though, I passed there and the Lady didnt speak.

Jan. 18.

There is a pleasant couple where I live he make the minute Postal Cards on the strets they stay in a city for the Busy season and then go to another. I am teaching the Husband English and He gives me lesson on picture making I wished I had thought of that before I started on my trip I could have made so much money in many countries where they have not the minute Postal Cards and It cost so little and the manchine are not to large to carry. its no need of me learning it now as the countrys I'll Visit later have them.

I am also learning to knock the * Palillos for 75 cents you get a half an hour lesson everyday for a week. I like going to the Dancing Salon the master is a little short man quite and Plesant. Sevilla is a great place for learning everything thats Spanish. and one like the city better and better each day. but it is such a crazy laid out City worse than Rome. They have many beautiful houses hide in the norrow streets but the beautiful well kep Patios of each house make the streets light and gay.

Its only the rich can buy butter. to we Sevillans butter is to dear. its much cheaper in Barcelona. one day I wanted butter so bad and my neighbor she make toast and put red or white lard I thought I could never relish that now I cant get along without it they mix powdered red bell peppers with the fresh lard and it sure is good on toast.

I met a Gentleman that own a book store. Two or three times I have had coffee in his store in the afternoon. anything I want to ask he tell me. sometimes he get me a little better seat for the bull fight with my 2 or 3 pesetas.

Today for Dinner I had Fried eggs with red lard toast stewed navy beans with salt pork onions parsely turnip tops potatoes tomatoes and olive oil oranges. Supper

* Note: click the castanets.

navy bean stew fried fish roll and Sevilla pastrys. coal
for 3 days 35 cents.

Sabado 25 de Enero de 1930.

I have been buisy all the afternoon cooking a nice half
of turkey I wanted another good feed before it went
out of season so have been cutting down all the week.
altho it only cost 50 cents but that look like 5 dollars
to me.

I teased Josefa the Young Wife she bought rabbit I
said you have a husband so must eat rabbit I am single
so can have turkey. I wont have another dancing lesson
for 3 days because I spent the money for the turkey.

another thing they eat here are birds You see the notice
outside of a open air café or others Hoy paparitos fritos
4 Petas. Today little birds fried one do. for 4 petas.
I buy four for 70 cents at the market then boil them a
bit and use the water for rice bird soup it is very good
with celery then I fry the birds. I have very fatting
food.

I go to the highest Class dancing School in Sevilla and
it is so very interesting to see the masters teach the
beautiful Sevillan dancing. I ofen go at 5.30 to the
Childrens Class they are from four years up I am the
oldest pupil. All people send their Children to learn
the old dances for the Feria, the very latest and the very
oldest dances are taught. I thought it was a good idea
to put 6 or 7 pesetas in my dancing and meet all the

lovely people. I can knock the Palillos better than either of the 4 Spanish Girls in the house where I am staying. I keep them hanging on the head of my bed and the first thing I say a short prayer then begain to knock the Palillos.

Jan. 28.

I got up early and went for a walk around the Exposition I passed along the river side and a man that have a char coal stove and a table and sell to the men that work on the boats He and his cousin was just sitting down on two Jemmy jugs to eat and they ask me and I said no but he walked up and put a spoonful of beans to my mouth I was so hungry they turned another jug on the side for me. We had a good lunch of beans tomatoes and meat potatoes olives wine and oranges. He ask me my name and when I said Juanita he was so surprised he leaned back and the jug rolled from under him I ask him if he didnt like it he said of course it was the one name he did like.

They wore corderoy pants and red around their waists. one thing I notice he had a large piece of salt pork and the men would buy bread and a slice of raw pork and I see women and children eating it. another thing You can buy in the market and it is really good is chilled blood fried.

one of the things I enjoy as I go to each country is how the breakfast of the working people change Italy it is little crisp fried fishes. Bucharest Rumania little suckling pigs meat. Cairo red beans young green onions boiled eggs and olive oil Sevilla fried rings of bread browned rich and hot, stewed tripe with tomatoes parsely and wine five or 4 cents. a plate very good. You must go near the markets to learn such things. and thats why when I get off the train I ask the way to the market. Sometimes it is called different names so I ask where is the place that you buy fruit and vegetables.

Another thing they eat very much and I and several others sat for an hour last evening around the Kettle in the market until they were rended leaf lard cracklings very good with boiled rice cooked dry. I have enjoyed my cooking so much. I bought a beautiful aluminum pot for $3\frac{1}{2}$ pesetas. it is a wonderful pot I can fry eggs in it I can fry meat, it is wonderful for heating water Josefa and I have our pots on the balcone. I am thinking if I should give my pot to Josepha or Keep it in case I may have a place to cook in Madrid. She want it auful bad. I dont think that she'll get it.

I just spent 6 Pesetas for two loterie tickets for the 1st of Feb. just to try my luck it make only 7 Pesetas I have spent for them.

Feb. 3.

It is so nice and warm most of the time I hate to face the cold at Madrid but I have spent what I had planned to spend here. and expect to leave Sevilla for Madrid at 8.40 A.M. Feb. 6. Sevilla havent those cold winds

and if it blows here are so many narrow streets you can
turn in and away from the Wind. it must be dreadful
hot in Summer. I have been on the look out for a party
of tourist to go in the Palace so yesterday I thought I
would have to pay the 4 pesetas and I stood near the
Palace think of all the days I could eat of 4 pesetas
when 50 German turists arrived and I made 51. so I
earned 4 pesetas. the Palace are of the beautiful
Moorish style and the tapries are the clearest I have
seen on any Walls.

I stood at a news stand and read in a New York Herald
of Paris that it is freezing in Calif. and Fresno had their
first snow in 25 years. I didnt buy the paper it was 4
centimos just what I was going to pay for my supper
and was on the way to buy it fish fried fresh brown
and hot bread and oranges. I read a little on my way
and on my return finnished it. When I have a salad I
always get an orange for Vinegar.

I have not patience with married people as a rule they
make such a mess of their lives. But Josepha is nice
looking, modest quiet and only does light housekeeping
and her husband never go any place without her.

Feb. 6.

In route to Madrid we are at the Town of Cinco Casas
I have enjoyed the trip I had a good lunch of boiled
Chicken fried meat balls boiled eggs radishes french
rolls fried sweet potatoes cocanuts sweets cakes oranges

and a bottle of red wine. I sat in the compartment with four very pleasant young men. The fields are green and there are olive groves and many goats little Boy Shephards tending them.

Feb. 9.

I arrived in Madrid at 9.10 P.M. expected to find it cold and dressed as though I was going to get off at the North Pole and found it just as warm as Sevilla. I stoped and asked a man that had a two wheel cart with a oven that He baked irish potatoes he had sold out so went six blocks to show me the street to find a room. It look so funny to see the two of us in the middle of the street I forgot to take my hat off and so put it in my pocket and his cart made enough noise for dozen trucks the streets are of brick and uneven. then a night watchman went with me to find a boarding house. He kep saying "This is a bad buisness for a woman to be out this time of night. but I knew how to quiet him just say the People of Barcelona are kinder than they are in Madrid. he was old and sore because he was ready to go to bed. when I got tird of his talking I said, "Oh, I wish I was back in Sevilla, he answer "The people of Madrid is kind to but its a bad piece of buisness. we had to clap our hands for some time before a Watchman showed up to open the door. each watchman have a Key and candles to light up the stairs I spent the night in an apartment and they wanted me to

stay but the room didnt open on the street so I told the
lady I didnt like the room.

I got up early and asked a young man on the corner
what newspaper had the most adds. and he was buying one so bought another one for me. then I went in a
postal card store to write out the places to answer and
the Sales Lady showed me an add. in the Magazine
A.B.C. a daily paper for an English speaking nurse at
the Hotel Savoy.

It is a young couple from near New York with a dear
little Girl Joan 2½ years. I got the job they pay my
room rent. I come in the morning at 9.30 if it is nice
and 12.30 if raining. They pay me well. they do not
speak Spanish so are delighted to have me. it begin
to Snow so I went back to the Lady I told I did not like
the room and take it because it is not so high. This
morning the grown was covered with 5 or 6 inches of
snow but I am pleased with it all.

Feb. 11.

Little Joan and I spend much time on the Paseo del
Prado. I love Her She is just a little dear and we have
a good time. The Mother and Father are nice but I am
not sure yet if I like them. the Mother never tell me
any thing about the Baby. She can see that I know how
to nurse. I am getting about 5 times more than I would
with the Spanish. We have a beautiful View from their
Suite of rooms. look like Centeral Park in New York.

Feb. 15.

Mrs. B. are buying many pretty things for little Joan. I dont like it because Joan gets so tird trying on Cloths. But I get a lot of fun when we are on the Street the Spanish young men say so many loving words to Mrs. B. and she doesnt understand a word. and when I tell Her She is so surprise. She has Beautiful blue eyes and wear beautiful jewlry.

When Mrs. B. took Joan out because she didnt have a nurse and the People stared They were wondering why She did not have a nurse The Spanish have 5 or 6 children and have a nurse for each one. Joan are uster wareing legging and over shoes and they look at Her so hard and tell Her she will sure keep warm. They say she is a Poor Little Darling and ask me if anything is the matter with her feet.

I am teaching Mrs. B. how to say words also how to knock the Palillos so I'll be here in Madrid until I am ready to go to Germany.

Savoy Hotel
Madrid Mar. 1.

I stoped working for Two days we had a little falling out then I came back and got more money and more time so we are very happy and I am some lucky dog. if I stay until June I can take a trip to Northern Europe in July and Aug. Here are many Americans Familys their Husbands are here with the Telephone company. tomorrow the Carnaval begin.

Mar. 14.

I like the Carnaval here better than Cuba because they have less autos in the Parads and the wide avenue Rosales are crowded with masqurades on foot and they sing and dance along the avenue. a big Bull fight will be on Sunday and the American Bull fighter will be in the ring they say He is brave but not being a Spanard do not have the nock of teasing the Bull like a good Spanish fighter has. If Mr. and Mrs. B. dont go of course I'll be there.

They are very much pleased with me the first week we had a falling out because I refused to give the Baby anemener and quit as I didnt think she needed it and it would make her cry to much.

But I am very anxious to leave about the 10th of April to return to Sevilla for Easter. I love Sevilla and want another look at it. and this will be a good time to have the last Visit.

I rec'd a letter from My Lady of London a few days ago and she would like for me to come and stay with Her for good. but that cant be done. not in all that Fog.

Saturday was a great Saint day and in two blocks of the Hotel are a small shrine called Jesus of Nazareth. the line begin at 3 A.M. and the People were in it until 12 P.M. each Person passed and kissed the feet and ask for three things. I am very shriney myself so I went early in the morning the only Person that didnt have to get in line were King Alfonso I happen to pass the Chapel just as his auto arrived and saw Him go in.

Joan is just as dear as ever and we have a lovely time in the many big Parks. She are troubled with pin Worms and taking some very good Spanish Powders and are much better. we went in to High Mass at San Jeromino del Prado also saw a little Baby Baptised Joan very good in church but like to sing when they sings.

I went to The Plaza de Toros de Madrid at quarter to 4. the cheapest seats was 3. pesetas 25 centimos and I had only 2 Pesetas and stood around with a heavy heart because I could not get a dollar exchanged for Pesetas. Then after all the People had cleared away I laid my 2 Pesetas at one of the ticket Window before the ticket seller and He gave me a good seat. I saw several Bull fights at Barcelona and Sevilla. But today was the worse and most thrilling I have seen. Three Bull Fighters and Six wild and long sharp horned Bulls.

Jose Rays were gored by the bull and stagared and fainted and would have fell but the men caught Him and carried Him out. Noain a very Famous fighter took His place and kill the Bull Then the American Bull fighter of Brooklyn came in in less than 2 minutes He were gored by the Bull and carried out dangerious ill it happen just in frount of where I was sitting on the second floor. the same Bull hooked the horse and threw the rider and injured Him the horse had to be stabed in the ring. I had just ask the man at my left to tell me when Franklin come in and He said that was Him they had just carried out. Jaime Noain the Hero of the afternoon had to kill the six bulls and He did it so Wonderful that altho I felt nevious over all the excitement I felt happy over the Cleverness of His fighting. He could turn his back right in the bulls face and He always drove the soward in the sholder up to the handle at the first trial. after He had killed the sixth bull the Ring was filled with hats caps and coats and a crowd ran and took Him up on their sholders and carried Him about the Ring. and altho a Fan. after all the excitement when I left I felt weak in the Knees. In a block of the Bull Ring are a Resturant where they serve hot broiled lamb chops potatoe chips rolls wine or beer I wanted a chop but did not have a Peseta.

Mar. 17.

I told Mr. and Mrs. B. all about the Bull fight and she got so excited. He want Mrs. B. to go with Lady Friends and she wont go without Him she says that She know she will faint and She want Him to be there to take care of Her. The morning paper said the American fighter are very ill. He have been in the ring for 5 years and said to have made much money. Monday 18. I heard that Franklin are not expected to live. Tuesday 19. Today Franklin are out of danger. March 20. A Baby Girl were born on my floor to the couple that have a little girl. I gave it a dollar.

Mar. 20th.

Little Joan B. gave a party all americans June 2 and a half years born here and speak only Spanish She is the dearest of all the children Alice American Born in Habana she speak Spanish English and French and dance the Spanish Dance graceful. But are a swift little lier. The Childrens mothers came. We had Two table one for the mothers and the other for the Children served coco jelly sandwichs cheese and ham toste strawberrie jam and tea. We had a delightful time. Joan looked like a little pink rose in a pink silk dress.

Mar. 21.

Today I had to do the thing I so much dislike I had to go to a French shop to talk for the Lady I am with. They are to cheap to be true Americans. Its a shame any one so pretty and young and yet so stingy. Well She ordered a dress to be made they made it then she did not want it and I had to do so much sweetly talking and they were so nice and keep the one she ordered and sold Her another. Then there was another She wanted and all the talking I had to do we were there from 4.30 to a quarter to 6 P.M. and Little Joan did not get any outing as we had to come home she has her Bath at 5.30 and supper at 6 and sit on the stool at 7. and go to bed at 7.30. If Joan hadnt been so sweet I would not have stayed with them one week. I try hard to like them.

Mar. 25.

I room on the ancient old street Toledo in a few doors of the Old Palaza Mayor I love this part of Madrid because it is the oldest part of the City. from my room Window I can see the Beautiful old Church dome with the stature of 12 Apostals around it. called the Great Catedral of San Francisco. just a few blocks up Calle Toledo are the big Market and I have a Resturant where there are always a great crowd and all are great eaters and that make me eat much more the wine are thick and good with the rich food a good size glass for 1 and a half cents.

In the morning Joan and I Visited the first floor of the Museo del Prado One a Painting of King Philip IV and His Queen and Two children are the only one in the room the window are half open so that the light fall on the canvas the only light in the room on the wall are a large mirrow one can see it in it. and make it very real.

I just love the way I am living on a job at the Hotel Savoy in the morden part of the City and through the day with American English French and Spanish. then at night I am over on my ancient old street with all Spanish. Where I have my room each floor have a kitchen with a Charcoal burner for each room I have to clean the kitchen every 8th day. when you get through cooking you never leave anything in the kitchen but put everything in your room. It is always free

of everything only a basket for papers and the ash tin
this is why they are like a big Family.

Mar. 31.

Joan and I went with Mrs. B. to exchange a pair of
gray snake skin slippers that she and Mr. B. bought
Saturday and which wasnt right. and the Same with
everything. I have the hardest work getting it exchanged and have so much talking to do. This is the
first time She have been out of America and expect to
find the same make here as there yet they have nice and
good things in Spain. It would be a pleasure if She
wasnt so cheap. I am just holding my breath to see if
they will be big hearted enough to give me something
extra when I leave. the French maid and the Spanish
boy are ever so sore at them All the guests pay 10
percent and they never give them a peseta anyway I
managed to save good out of what I got and I enjoyed
being with them but I wont cry about leaving them.
Mrs. B. say she dislike it here because the Wives are so
little with their Husbands. She said they have got so
they dont miss each others company. the Wives go to
the shows at 6.30 and the Husbands play pool all get
home about 10 P.M. for dinner. all the Women does
is give teas. and eat to many sweets.
I dont know much but I'll always know how to get a
job I dont care about what country I am in. it is so
healthy here for Children. The Americans can well

take lessons from the Spanish Mothers how to dress their Children.

I promised to stay until they could get the English Girl they had in Brussells. Mr. B. is a nice Husband and Father. He did not go with the other American Husbands to the Lido. one of the best dancing Hall where are Spanish Girls to dance with the men. he is a quiet Quake Young Husband and do not dance. I often go just to see what go on and are often the only woman except the hired Girls.

April 3.

The English nurse arrive last night so I am off my job. it is good to be a lofer again now that the Sun are nice and warm. I wanted a few days for sightseeing before taking my trip to Sevilla. I went to the Royal Palace to see the Changing of the Guards. they in their beautiful uniforms and prancing horses good musice and always a Crowd altho it take place every day.

I went to the Theatre to a musical Comedia mostly morden dancing I hate morden dancing in Spain. Here I like only the very Spanish plays. I had a quart of cocoa and milk 3 fresh eggs fried with salt Pork. and nice fresh groun steak such a lot for 7 cents I didnt want to buy an onion so I walked through the onion part of the Bazaar and found a nice one in a basket.

Sunday I took the Subway to a Town Tetuan to a Bull fight I lacked 25 centimos and the ticket seller would not give me a ticket but a Policeman that saw him refuse paid the rest. The Bullfight was great my Favorite Jaime Noain. The Brave. killed the Bull but I did not like to see my heroe teased so long by the bull. it sure is a great sport You need four eyes. Bull fighting and ice cream are the two best things on earth. The reason I like the Spanish bull fight is they are the only one cant dope the bull. I lost all faith in the grey hound racing I like a sport for the sporting part of it. I thought I wanted to leave Spain now I dont feel like I want to leave the bull fighting.

April 9.

I left Madrid last night on a local train and had a nice compartment only a Policeman Officer in it He left at 6 A.M. then I had scrambled eggs with butter and Cataluna Sausage on my meter which I like better than canned heat. Arrived in Sevilla in the afternoon. It was good to see the snug bright streets again. on my way to my same home I stoped in the Catedral to finnish my last prayer for one month that I had not missed a day going to a church to pray.

April 10 Sevilla
Calle Alvarez Quintero.

There is such a difference in the Sevillians and the Madrilenos. Here the People are so gentle lovely and truthful, even though They may loose a sale. They will not lie. the people of Madrid will tell a lie to make 10 cents and loose a customer that may spend hundreds of pesetars. Still I owe thanks to Madrid because the secon day there I got a good place and good pay and keep it until the day I wanted to leave.

Today I choosed this month for my Thanksgiven month and will go to Church every day and give Thanks for the happy three years I have spent roving about the world at this moment I feel as fresh and rested and the 3 years have been like 3 weeks.

The Sevilla houses have a fancy iron gate that are locked and when one ring the bell they ask who is it and press a button. always when I came I gave a hoop and they all think I say Coucoo. So when I came to my old Home I gave my hoop and I heard every voice in the house say thats Juanita and such pushing back chairs and saying hurry when I steped in the Patio and looked up I knew just how many were in the house because every head were looking down from one or other balconey. it was just like coming home not that I have ever had a home to return to but it must be something like it I was glad when they told me that my own cozy room were all ready for me. The same little Couple are here and our little cozy balconey for cooking. with a beautiful new Baby. When I left in Feb. the trees was thick with oranges now all are gone and the air are so sweet with the perfume from the orange blossoms and the hanging bright flowers from the windows. One thing about the Spanish Catalanicos they pray with a full stomach not like the others that have meatless days and fasting. they have fish every day and also meat twice a day and a lot of it. ✕

Good Friday.

I went to Church this morning and on my way to the market right at a man's foot I found a duro a Spanish dollar.

I am lucky that I arrived before today as the Hotel and Rooming houses are packed. the streets are filled with Chairs. they are getting ready the Wonderful floats and Imagenes and in the Jewelry shops on display are Wonderful necklaces that will be on some of the Imagenes. everybody are buying dresses shoes it is a time when every one come out in their best.

Palm Sunday
April 13.
Domingo de Ramos

The grand old Catedral sure had on a grand and gay look the great columns draped with those long red and gold plush hangers the alters covered with purple good musice the men heavy voices and the boys sweet ones. it was much more beautiful than in St. Peter's at Rome. Then that night the first grand Procession all the Imagenes are very life like and the robes and Capes made like a cort train of gold and blue velvet. another green and gold.

Lunes Santa
Holy Monday

I had a good place on the wall of the pretty square and could see the Procession. each Church own 12 or more Imagenes and in front of each are their Priest Choir one of the Imagenes its whole brest from the neck to the Waist were covered with dimond broches I counted 25 and on the floats were pure silver plates with the scene of the life of Cristo. and candles and fresh Carnations flowers in the hundred of silver vases. on the float.

Semana Santa
April 15.

King Alfonso XIII Queen Ena and the Royal Corte arrived this morning I fell in line with the Procession and found a place up a lamp post in Plaza San Fernando above those that stood on chairs. I was just in front of the Royal Box. 50 or more pieces in the Procession and Andalusian Singers they compose the words themselves all about the suffering of Jesu Cristo and the Virgen.

I followed along side the float with the Imagene of the Virgen with tears from the eyes this evening and its

when you get in the small streets and the People sing
with a free will and not paid are when you get the
real joy. A Handsome young Boy on a balconey sang
wonderful He said I can see the suffering in Your Holy
face then when he stop another young man across the
street sang. he ask the Virgen for her prayers to protec his young Sister. Yet no one were ever sad always a
jolly gentle crowd It turned in the street that I took a
place to work and left it so quick I felt guilty when I
looked up and saw the Lady and Husband on the Balconey. 2 A.M. I can hear the drums and it make me
think of the Hindu Temple of India.

Sevilla is just like a bee hive. even the wine is running
short. I ask for a glass of white or red wine at 1 A.M.
it was all sold. you get auful hungry and thirsty fol-
lowing behind the Imagenes and there are always wine
and olives for 2 or 3 pennies nice fresh fried fish hot
for 2 to 5 cents and oranges tables on the side walk and
in the middle of the streets to sit and eat and laugh
talk and rest and listen to a song.

Another interesting thing are the men under the floats
it get quite warm under there and they have a blanket
in a roll on their neck where the pole rest so they rest
often and when they stop all call for water at once a
waterman with a big cooler come up. some of the men
wives walk along and have coffee or wine and bread.
Sometimes a man will come out and stand before the
Imagene and sing as good any of the Paid Singers.

April 17
Jueves Santo
Thursday Holy.

Today are one of the greatest holy days. I had my good place where I could climb up and look my fill on the Royal Party in Frount of the Municipal Library it were bright with red silk hangars and red carpet. The King wore a light blue and red Military with white feather in His Cap and Queen in black high comb and Mantillo Prince Alfonso Pio Christino Eduardo tall and pail in a dark suit and just back of the Queen the Princesses wore grey dresses high combs black mantillos and beautiful gray fur coats. When Princess Beatrice wanted to put her Coat on the gentleman just behind her got up to hold her coat and the poor fellow made such a mess of it her mantillo got caught inside of the coat and she laugh and got it untangeld. the King left early. But the Queen always remain maybe thats why they like Her so much She is a good sitter. each Imagenes were turned round to face the Royalty.

Nothing are shabby I have gone around to all the different Churches in the day time and had a close look at the robes capes and the Imagenes and nothing patch. the candle holders are washed in hot water and polished each morning and the Imagenes look so graceful in the Wonderful gold Crowns and the long gorgious Cloaks. It is truly worth coming to Sevilla to spend Easter. Through this month the Spanish never say good by as they does at other times if you are in a store or market when you leave they always say go and may God be with You. Some cut it short and say Go with God.

April 18.

Today was the last day for the Holy Week Procession and the longest and most gelourious. I was parked up on the little square in Plaza Duque I took my supper along six Children were near with Grandma mother and aunt they brought their supper and bottles of water I also had a bottle of water. The King walked in the last or just ahead of his guards with the Bishop. Two Girls that sang from the Balconey ask the Virgen to protec and guide the King.

Sevilla April 19.

Everybody have a move on them. Today is the chance for the shop keepers. where the streets are so thick with the drippings from the Candles they are sprinkling Sand because it is slippy and the floor of the old Catedral are thick with it. The Society Girls are out in bright gay costums pinning flowers on the men for the Hospitals I walked up and down Calle Sierpes and watched them they would let a dozen men pass looking for a handsome one and when they see one would just fall at him the best looking had many where the homely ones had only one or none.

Easter Sunday.

I went into the Catedral to say my prayers and saw the red carpet and knew that the King and Queen were coming to mass. I found a snug place on one of the colums many were wondering how I could stick up there but I felt comfortable and could look right down and see everything. In a few minutes the Royal Court arrived. They came in the side door that are open only for the biggest bugs. The Palace Guards in their light blue red and gold coats and white pants and a bunch of white feathers on their silver helment were lined from the curb to the Catedral door. then from the door to the alter gate were policemen in their dark blue with red and brass buttons. a Canop of red velvet and two red plush Chairs for the King and Queen. They arrived in big shinny autos. the King in a uniform of dark blue and red and red pants. His face is nice and body but he has little skinny legs. The Queen is "quapa" it mean in slang some baby or how beautiful. The musice was sweet loud and beautiful the Prest with gorgious robe Preach a quick snappy seremon. The King always sat down before the Queen He would drop in his chair so quick then the Queen would sit doun with such a slow and graceful way. She is the right higth for a Queen and just stought enough with slender line fire like golden hair and fair nice skin dark or sky blue eyes. but her nose are a little to large. She wore a black silk dress with small red flowers a very high comb and the

Holy Week long black lace Mantillo. The Princesses dressed in light broun and black Mantillos. Both tall Beatrice the Spanish dark and pretty with a ready to smile expression Christine light and like the Queen not so good looking as her Mother but the same nose and reserved english expression. When the Sun shines on the windows up at the sceling of the Catedral and doun below are in shodow. it is very beautiful.

Sunday 3 P.M.

The Bull ring were filled I was there when the door open I went to see the Ladies and not the Bullfighter nor the bulls. It was just the beautiful sight I had pictured in a Sevillian Bull Ring. pretty Girls come in partys of 8 and 10 dressed in light blue pink green red cream. high combs white lace long mantillos. all wore the silk shawls and spreaded them out on the banster in frount of their seats. then the Crowd talking such laughable things and the Water sellers, the Candy loteria and other sellers one could enjoy that kind of noise forever any way if you understand what are being said. Then the Royal Party arrived. The King was not there. Princess Beatrice got a big kick out of the fight laughed and Clapped while Princess Christine sat very english. a Big man were in the Royal Box they called Him President of what I cant say. He had a little present for each Bull fighter and when He would throw doun the box with the gift the Crowd would yell out not to give it because he did not deserve it. The ring got a little slippy after a shower Manuel Bienvenida took off his little Black pumps and fought in his pink stocking feet. Many came in the two seated surry with two slick fat mules with red and yellow hornses and sleigh bells the driver on a high seat dressed in the Spanish tight fitted suit of eton jacket and Wide hat. I climbed over and crossed the ring after the fight got there in time to walk out at the heels of the Royal Party.

Then I felt hungry one always does if he be a fan. I went to a fish shop where I buy delecious cod fish in thick batter to a rich crisp brown on the outside and enside the fish so soft and free of salt.

April 26.

This noon I went to a big bull fight. The Queen looked well in a Alice blue suit. just below me sat two young Handsome American Couples and it was their first fight. the eldest Girl about 25 the other one a perfect little Flapper about 18. all chewing gum it looked very funny to see them chewing but I got a kick out of it being so home like. It was a good fight Fortuna a very clever and Handsome Fighter and Kills his bulls in such a dainty way. I wished for another pair of eyes my two was so busy. My four Countrymens were in a high pitch making about 50 chews to every second when Fortuna did such clever teasing in front of the bull then the Picador came up to spear the bull, the bull got

his horns under the horses's belly threw the man he
fell on the bulls back rolled under his feet. The Picador threw his bright Cape over the full length of the
other Picador as he layed still while the bull was standing over him they atracted the bull away then the Picador got up without a scratch but the horse was being
led out with everything hanging from his belley. the
little Flapper cried and the Young men had proped up
their chins with their hand and giving a chew once
every 2 or 3 seconds. then they all had a smoke to quite
their nerves You never see a Spanish Woman smoke.
well they looked like four wet chickens the little Flapper
She would never look again excep when a handsome
brave Young Fighter would tease the bull so Clever.
so of the 4 I liked the little Flapper best am sure she
could be a real Fan like myself.
The Horses are blindfolded and when they walk out of
the ring they are Killed but when a human get wounded
they must suffer for months and thats Why I never feel
sad. The Picadors work very hard to save their horses
but it cant be helped any way it is the best sport and
no gambeling but honest beautiful brave and clever.
there in the house they tease me and say I should marry
a bull fighter I say if I did I wouldnt want him to fight
any longer.

April 29.

The Feria is at the other end of the Exposition growns
with colored lights and lantens and on each side of the

Boulvard pretty bright tents. I arrived at the entrence
of the Feria just as the Royal Party were coming up the
Bo'Lv'd the Queen in a well fitted gray riding habit red
sash and wide gray hat the Queen sure can knock them
dead she is beautiful look like a sister to the Daughters.
They enjoy the Sevillia Feria they can be so free as they
are seen so often the people dont trouble them. They
stoped in front of the Tent of the "E.R.77" a seclect
Club and a pretty Girl dressed in the Andaluz dress
brought out wine. They all talked and laughed. One
of the minute postal men wanted to make Her picture
when she took the glass from her lips. Of course a
Queen would not like to have any body taken her picture drinking wine even at the Feria. Well She saw him
and You should have see that look She gave him. I got
so tickled she turned the horses around I liked her much
better because I could see from that look She had pep
enough. The Princess that look like her mother when
there is something to laugh at she can just bend double.
Princess Beatrice she laugh often but not so hearty. the
Prince wore auful soiled white riding breches maybe he
didnt have any clean ones. I havent time to write about
him he look to sleepy.

Sevilla May 6.

Its not so easy to leave little Cozy Sevilla and the Ador-
able Sevillianos. But I now are all packed to leave for
my trip north. Sunday will be another big day here

but I'll not stay if so something else may be on for the
next and I'll never leave.

I went to the exposicion groun to the building of
Oviedo in Asturia where they were demestration churns
I ask the young Lady if she had any butter milk She
gave me all I could drink. the first I have had in nearly
three years. sure was good.

The Royalty left Sat. night we didnt have any Royalty
in our house but we at least had staying here the man
that look after the corns and bunouns of the Royal
Family's feet.

I went to a bull farm to see the bulls that were to be in
the ring Sunday it is a beautiful place garden laid out
and refreshment places. Yesterday I went to my last
Bull fight here I wanted to see Little "Pepe" Bienvenida he look like a little fat round face 12 year old
girl. Not being tall it was hard for him to run his
soward in and when he had killed his first bull felt so
tird he sat down and they had to remind him that he
had not made his bow before the President party.

When I went to the market Monday morning. In front
of one of the only meat stall that sell the fighting bull
meat it were a line of cooks and house wives in a line
a half a block long it sells for about 40 cents a pond
being the highest meat in Sevilla. I wouldnt eat that
mad meat for anything.

I went for lunch to a place where they serve the best
snales I like them cooked with rice. but had never got

up enough courage to eat them plain for the first course they served a plate of snales and a glass of white wine.

El Escorial Spain
May 8.

I only spent the night in Madrid and did not have time to call at the Savoy Hotel to see Little Joan. The weather are bright but the mountains are white with snow and one need warm cloths.

The Escorial is a wonderful great big building. I got acquainted with a family that has lived here all their life. and own such a quaint house the Kitchen are in the frount. La Senora are the mother of 14 Children seven are alive and all beautiful. I told them all about the Feria then one of the boys began to play the Guetar and I began to dance. one of the sons Jose was a wonderful dancer. he said Caramba and jumped up and danced with me. the mother came in with a great bowl of milk and the father came in with manure on his hoes. They ask me am I argentina but I said no American del Norte. they own 5 fine Holstin milk cows I drank two large glasses of the rich mailk with the good spanish bread and I always have a bottle under my arm when on a journey so they filled it and I'll have it for my midnight supper. I am at the station will take the 11.30 train for Burgos.

San Sebastian Spain
May 12.
La Pena Calle del Principe

I did not get off at Burgos the town looked so sleepy and cold we passed through many snow capped mountains. San Sebastian is a beautiful City there are many bridges across the wide river of clear blue water that run through the City and are very noisy. it is a most beautiful picture the way the two mountains extend into the sea and make the small beach look like a blue pool. the day I arrived was a wonderful Summer day and the beach were crowded. Some fresh little boys came along and woke me up so I called them down in their own Sweet Spanish. it was a bit to hot but I sleep all afternoon and have a baked face. one can always get work as a sardine packer if you can get over the smell. they ware blue hospon aprons and wooden shoes. The resturant food here are not so well cooked as in other parts of Spain I found it cheaper and better to cook in my room. no two towns have and bake the same bread just as each town have their style aprons. the children nurses look funny in their red blue or brown dresses with dainty Cap on the back of their head. white stockings black slippers white gloves and long ear rings.

I must have a will of my own otherwise I would have become a Catolic. I am always meeting ones that try hard to get me in Yesterday Una Senora had me corned off in in this house for hours. I agreed with her that the

Protestants lacked a lot she said she didnt believe they ever went to confesion I told her that some of them confest Sometimes but only the good things. I had a hard time getting away from some Indian-Portugise Friends at Bombay they went so far as to get a job for me in a convent where I could spend a while and study. I go to Santa Mary's one of the oldest Church it have a shrine to La Virgen del Cora a black Virgen with a black infant in its arms it has a beautiful white satan and gold vestment a jeweld crown and a long gold cord with gold letters at each end and we kiss each and ask for Her proctions. This Church also have a big black cat that strutts about during mass like a Priest.
The men doesnt make love to the ladies on the street like in Madrid. Its getting a little Frenchy here sometimes I meet a Frenchman and they want to speak French I tell them I know Spanish very well. as if I am in a hurry To speak French. I am all packed to leave in the morning for the French Frontera.

Biarritz France
May 14

It is a beautiful ride along the ridge above the ocean Biarritz are very pretty but I like San Sebastian much better. I have a nice red room with hot and cold water and a good big bed in a very quaint hotel on a very quaint street and little houses with blinds. I will leave tomorrow and make a stop at Bordeaux and other places on the way to Paris. where I will look for a job. I am out of the Land of Royalty and Bull fighting.

May 15.

a red room with cream curtains are pretty but when I awoke this morning looked like I was in a great blaze no more red rooms.

Bordeaux France
Rue Bauffard Hotel Londes

I left Biarritz on the electricly train at 3 P.M. arrived here at 7 P.M. The City looked a little glumy after so many bright spots but I knew there were beauty to be seen. and in a few minutes I arrived at the Cathedral St. Andre where Richard II of England were baptised and Girls were singing during the 8 P.M. Mass. It was nice because in Spain it had been more the men singing.

I thought altho. I had forgot much of my French I still felt proud of knowing how to read I passed several resturants reading the menue I wanted so much a good boiled dinner having had eggs every style in my rooms for 3 days cooked on my meta. I gave the Waitress my order I wouldnt trust my speaking I pointed it out to her and sat anxiously for boiled beef and cabbages. and what I had pointed out was two eggs baked in a little pan. I had to eat it.

I have a complet change in my food France have good

fresh butter and many kinds of cream cheese good milk
and very cheap so I dont use olive oil now I dont like
the french olives nor the French wine. the Spanish wine
are better and sweeter and you need wine with the
Spanish food. but I find the living much dearer than
Spain. I like the City an the very wide River Garonne
I choosed a room in the oldest part of the City a nice
cheerful little room the wall paper are blue Vases filled
with white roses and look so real I feel a fear of knocking them over. the streets are wide and many trees the
gayest part in a street near the museum.

Tours France
May 17. rue Jules Favre.
Hotel l'Alhambra Top floor.

I arrive at Tours at 5 A.M. the first thing I saw in
frount of the Station in big letters. Ringens Bro's
Greatest American Circus. In a second I knew that it
was a lovely place I walked along and enjoyed Counting the houses that some one sleep with the window
open not many open altho. it was a pleasant night.
then I found the Beautiful old light gray slender built
Catedral both doors stood wide open and it smelt so
fresh and looked so light. I was the only one in for a
while. The tombe of the two small children of Charles
VIII were interesting. I then went to the beautiful very
very wide River Loire. it reminded me of Paris with

the swiming bath boats along the banks. many bridges cross. the other side are residently I enjoyed looking around over there the small cottages are always name Castel or Chateau. the People were crossing the bridges going to market so I did not have to look for it. they have everything good to eat I had a good bowl of coffee and milk with bread. Then found a pretty Park and had a nap.

a big Fair are going on the City are ever so gay I sure have luck for arriving at the gayest time.

I went up this evening to look over the U.S.A. Circuis. I enjoyed the outside peeping through the crack in the dressing room of the clowns teasing them in English several French Girls also peeped and got a kick out of me talking to them altho. they did not understand.

This noon I had lunch at the big market in a corner are a resturant while taking coffee this a.m. I saw the chicken lives boiled beef hog heads ready to be cook so fresh and clean then I said this will be where I dine today. I returned at 12.30 they had four long tables down two isles of the market with white paper on it. I think that every farmer and his family dressed up and spent the day in town and had dinner there many of the women in the pretty fine caps. the tables seated about 3 hundred or more. Everthing was cooked so good and bread they bake it by the yards and hundreds of yards went I put away about a yard. I had chicken

lives and potatoes soup then went out for ice cream.
I have such a pleasant home. A lovely couple have this
small house I had to pay 15 f. so many Visitors in the
city it was hard to find a room for less than 20 F.
my room is so nice with lovely furnishing pretty little
orments on the mantel lace curtins a large palm a nice
couch red tiling floor. the bed I need a chair to get in it.
the house are antique looking but smell fresh the enside
are freshly painted my room have a new paper of small
green flowers. the top border with little birds in pairs
sitting close togather. in just a few minutes after arriving in a place I feel that I have been there all my life
I feel just like that everywhere.
I went aroun to all the auto turing companys also to
the station to plan my trips to the Castels. Today have
been very warm the brick street were so hot to my feet
I had to buy a pair of the crape rubber sole work
sandles.

May 19.

The Castels are fore apart and the trip through forest
and Valley crossing many lovely streams make it so
delightful. There were Two French Gentlemen and
four French Ladies. We visited the castel and Dongeon
at Loches had lunch in the Pretty Village with a River
running through and a mill built across it the houses
are built on the river and give it a Venice look.

May 21.
Quimper Brittany.
Hotel du Cheval noir.

The maids ware tight fitted black basses full black skirts and a steeple shape white hand made lace cap starched stiff. the beds are good and high. the hall and stairs are scrubbed and are as white as a bread boad. Everything as clean as the caps that they ware.

I went to the market it sure was a sight worth seeing. Their caps and aprons are like the Hindu cast marks You know what Villiage each are from by the cap. some high some with blue or pink ribbon streamers some the shape of a tea cup with long white streammers. but both old and young in black dresses felt slippers and when on the street put on the wooden shoes. To here a crowd of children running one would think a Thousand horses were coming.

the Town have a Cannal it is clear and shallow they catch eals there. the men ware black or wide yellow straw hats with a large buckle and black velvet streamers. I am so pleased that I came up. but the best time is July or August those are the great Feast months.

A Circuis arrived this noon I watched them stretch the tents it open tomorrow I wish it had open today I may not be here tomorrow.

There are Auto bus trips but I dont care to see the Country its the People I want to be with. I dont believe

there are one in the whole Town that speak English I
am geting my French back rapidley.

The men are not so bad looking but most of the Women
are homely. I want to laugh when I look at them they
look so much like Hooling of the funny paper. all are
nice and rosy cheeked. They never stair at You and
never ask You your buisniess its a nice change after
Spain. where they are more Family like.

Douarnenez Finistere
May 22.

A great fishing place and the uglar old fishmen in their
tamosham caps and red over all suits look interesting.
the caps are different and more becoming to the women
than the Quimper style. I hiked along the Bay 9 miles
to the Shrine of Sainte-Anne-La Palue and got a peep in
several farm houses asking the way. An old Lady in a
Two Wheel high milk cart were coming behind me
after I had been on the way for an hour I said to her
will she have a Christian heart and ask me to ride at
her side she stoped the nice light brown fat mare ask
me where I was going I said to the Shrine of Santa
Anna. She said will You ride with me English not
being sweet enough I said in Spanish yes Madame with
Your permission. it was just room enough to put my
feet as the floor of the Cart was filled with Yard long
loafs of bread. She were nice and fat rosy cheeks a
white cap. She ask me if I was going to ask something

of the Saint I said oui Madame and Oui Madame to everything. They speak very plain and I understood much that She asked. but she did not ask very much maybe it was because she know what the answer would be. am sure I said yes many times when it should have been no.

I liked sitting beside her and behind such a pretty fat horse and every villiage we came to I felt sorry thinking we must part. She told me the Chapel would be closed. in about two miles of St-Anne she told me the way I shook her fat red hand and climed down. the Chapel is just above the Bay. I walked around to the side door tried the latch and to my delight it open. Its a very large Chapel gray with age but beautiful and light. I had been there about an hour when a man came and went up to the roof. He were working and that was why I had the luck in finding the door open. on the side of the altor was the postal card albums and the price of them I put the 2 and a half francs on the altor. I felt just a little tird when I reached the Town.

On the train at the Station 7 P.M.

Two beautiful Girls got on blonds Cheeks like red apples their costums are perfect wide pleated collars blue ribbon streamers and a large bow of white tule pined at the left bust. The People have bright clear fetures but different from others. sitting on the train the elderly ones knit stockings. a Young man sitting opposite me offored me a nice banana I wanted it so much but like the Spanish I refused. He saw me in Douarnenez.

Paris France
May 24.
Hotel du Reims

I am near Tour St. Jacques half a block to Des Halles the Central Market and just across the river to Norte Dame. the Hotel are nice but in the mornings we cannot get out on the side walk for the market people and Vegetables. I went to the Herald Office and put an Add in cost 18 Francs. when I am roveing I feel sad when I think I must get back to Paris and on a job then when I arrive I feel sad for staying away so long. May 27. I rec'd two answers from my add. one I knew the writing but couldnt remember from whone. but when I reached the Arc de Triunfe new that it were the Same Lady that answered my add. Two years ago.

I refused the Place then but I guess I'll go in the morning to let the maid show me and work for Her just to get Her off my hand But I am sure She is a set Lady Devil.

Paris seem much quiter than two years ago or if may be myself after going around to the gayest places for such a long time it seem quite. I went to see Mrs. M. the first one I work for in Paris. she said my travellers should be put into a Book. just as I have written them misteakes and all. I said that if the mistekes are left out there'll be only blank.

June 3rd.
Ave. Foch Paris
Top Floor.

Tonight I am back in my room after being locked out
Sat. and Sun. I told the Madame at noon I would leave
Sat. and went up to get my things and She had gone up
and did something so I could not get the Key into the
Key hole. I got a locksmith to open it now I take my
suite case out every morning and back at night. When
I started in work here I thought things looked quire.

June 6.

I wanted so much to leave today. so I packed cleaned
the room hid my suite case in the kitchen so I could just
step out at 2 P.M. I asked her for the first weeks pay
willing to let her keep this week I said I wanted to buy
medican for my cold really I had to laugh at her she
said no that was just an excuse she wasnt going to give
me any money she said to Mary the English woman that
clean now Mary you watch her and dont let her go out.
Then She sent the Chaffer back to see If I was here.
We get many good laughs but we need it.
its the Ladies that should give me their references. I
dont need any to get a job I like written references more
to go with my collection for if they are written nicely
and kind they give joy. and the memories of the writer
are sweet.
I told the Lady I only wanted to work with Americans

She said she were born in Indiana. Monsieur is a pleasant little Cuban Gentleman He plays golf 3 mornings a week and are very active. He is 80 and Madame is a Short stout Lady of 72 or so with a healthy head of long red hair little fat feet look like Chinese feet. they married 50 years ago and have lived in this house 40 yrs. it is on the swellest street in Paris and once keep 10 servents now the 18 rooms that are filled with treasures that once glittered are covered with covers and newspapers. all the walls are covered with fine sating. She is very neat and a good dresser have wonderful Jewelers and fur Coats the hardest tast that I have each morning at 10 is helping her in her rubber corset to keep the fat presed down.

She is of Russian American Parents are worth millions. She never eat meat He have it only for lunch nothing stylish about their meals they never have company at home nor callers. the Choffer has been with them 2 years and She like him because he is always 10 minutes early he is a Russian refugee Prince of a very large family all were shot excep he he is truly very Prince like.

Madame goes to the dress makers milliners and beauty parlors and meet Friends for tea so from 2 P.M. to 5.30 we can do what we pleases. She locked up the domino sugar and Cheese and the napkins I washed and ironed now I have to keep the two they are useing washed and the rooms are filled with treasures we could take a trunkful out and all her handsome furs never locked up.

the gentleman told me she had been ill and did not know what She were during and to stay on until Bertha the maid she uster to have return and He would give me 25 Francs extra each week.

There are thousands of people in the mad house far more sane than She. I have great respect for her husband he are good to her and When she is ill in bed He does all the Waiting on her. if you go each morning and ask for 15 or 20 francs for the food which is only 80 cents she goes to pieces but she like to write a check for several thousands.

June 10.

This is my seventeenth day and I am just beginning to understand how to get along with her but it is not a pleasure to be with her altho. the pay is good and the work is light. one thing She doesnt go about the house nagging you but its when you go in to her dressing room. it have a large mirrow and while You are helping her to dress She stands in frount of it looking at You in the mirrow and calling You such auful things I run out many times she call me right back. One thing she like as She have travelled is to hear of my travelling and think its wonderful when I am so poor. but she often gets my got. so I say things to her it seems to help.

June 16.

Bertha returned yesterday. I fell in Her arms I was so glad to see her. I had told Madame I had an interview and wanted to leave at 9.30 I wanted to get out before it was time to help her with her corset. She got up early and paid me all except 26 frs. when I asked her for it she said She never pay all. But I saw the Gentleman before I left and he gave me 60 frans extra. Bertha's brother cook in a big house near here and bring much of what she is supposed to buy. so she is making a lot of money off of them and that is why she have stayed.

June 22.

I feel I am out in an open country so with the freeness of a bird I will walk 4 or 6 blocks out of the way just to go through a tree line ave. or Park in This beautiful City. and now and then a good natured Frenchman to throw a mushy love making word at me. but being a swift mover it dont stick I like best to tease with the handsome blue caped policeman. because when I have heard enough I can step away from his beat which he can not leave.

I went up to light a candle at the Shrine of St. Genevieve the Parisienes Patron Saint also mine. While there one of the 3 best sports that I like took place a funnel 1st. then a wedding 2nd and a bull fight 3rd are my full joy.

I am getting a real kick out of the interviews from my add. But I am afraid I will find a place I like and the fun will end.

June 23. Hotel Passy-Centre
Rue des Belles Feuilles.

This is the street of the beautiful flowers but without one. I have a lovely room and moved out of the hotel I was in this afternoon because last night when I was ready for bed I went to the Window to open it and a woman lifeless form laid at my window where she had fell from the six floor Window she had on orange colored pajymas and I couldnt get them out of my mind and I pass such a misiable night I felt just as I did when I came out of the Czechoslovakia train reck.

June 24th. I sleep like a Sleeping Beauty last night but at 5.30 such a chopping under my room and I looked and there are two very nice butcher shops anyway I have something to Wake me of mornings.

I met a French man with a real English accent. He is part French part English and part Indian. He said to me, "I've lived here for many years I am in buisiness I am a chiropodist." I said, "Oh, you have a lazy business." He asked if he could make an appointment to meet me but I was looking for a place and didnt want him on my hands.

I answered an add in the Paris Herald Waitress in an American resturant away up in the heart of the Latin Quarter. I love it up there. The Manager a nice American Gentleman was very anxious for me to take the job but it looked to much like real work he paid 600 frs a month he wanted me by the day. nothing during.

June 30. I feel as home like in this house as tho. I was in Seville. Its as clean as a peacock and quite as a corps and I sleep like Rip Van. I was coming out of the American Express and I met my friend the Frenchman I guess he had ben hanging round the Ex. like a Spanard he'll find you. He is a nice looking man he wear wonderful cloths a beautiful felt hat in the morning always a derby in the afternoon shiny shoes and striped trowsers. He invited me to come to his buisiness place I didnt want to go but the minute he invited me to see it thats prove enough to me he has one. It's just as easy to choose a man who has something than one who hasnt. He respecs what he has so he'll respect you. A man is auful glad to respec a woman. We meet in the Park. He has traveled a great deal and I am refreshing my German with him.

July 6th.

I answer an add for a Captain and His Wife Mrs. C. of the American Army. he have charge of work conected with the Golden Star Mothers. she had a French maid but did not like her. French maids are not as good as they are wrote up to be. and I like my job fine. The first few days I was ready to quit at any minute the Lady and I was spitting at each other all the time yet she didnt want me to go. Now we understand each other and get along just fine. Capt. does the Marketing every Sunday morning. I hate marketing for other people and He doesnt mint it at all. I get a big

kick out of it its just like a visit to the States another
American couple are just across the Hall. I am taking
German and Russian lessons from my most interesting
English Indian friend. He is very English and auful
Frenchy.

July 10.

I went to one of the Biggest races at Longchamp the
last of June. the track are not dirt but a nice green
lawn and in a beautiful setting. I paid 5 francs to go
in and had planned to bet 10 after my long walk
through the Bois de Boulogne Park to get there I spent
most of it for lemonade mint ade and sandwichs I dont
ever want another mint ade. two other Ladies were sitting near me then a fourth came up and pushed the
smallest out of her place and she pounded her on the
back with her little fist but the Woman keep the place
it sure were an interesting scrap and lasted about an
hour. they tried to get me in as a witness but I couldnt
remember how to say what I wanted to. and so I only
looked on the Elderly Policeman were in just a few
steps but he pretended not to see and when they called
him would not hear. I wouldnt give one Bull Fight for
all the Grand prix de Paris.

July 13.

Yesterday was the beginning of the French greatest
holiday dancing on the sidewalks and in many streets.
Paris are very American looking with the Mothers ar-

riving the building enside and out are draped with
French and American Flags. It was Steamer Day so the
Express Office was like walking on Broadway In Los
Angeles. I rec'd a letter from a friend at Colombo Ceylon and they had such a bad flood and so many home-
less. another Friend at Rangoon wrote about the bad
earthquake and another about the fighting in India and
this time last year while I were at each place everything
so peaceful Yet I knew that the People all the way to
Burmer are displeased and want home rule.

July 26.

I went to the Station to see the colored mothers it was a
beautiful Sunny noon. The Leader of a noted colored
Jazz ban that are engaged at one of Paris leading high
class Resturant asked if they could welcome the mothers
with their band. It was very nice Mrs. C. gave me
money to go down in a taxi but we are only a few
dozen blocks from the station a tram car werent in sight
so I was running for life down Ave. Presedent Wilson
When Major and Mrs. B. our neibors stoped their car
and I got in I told Her not to tell that I was running
down. The taxie money I wanted to by a ticket for the
Opera "Werther" that was to be sung that night at the
Opera Comique. I went and it was beautiful. I like
my job ever so much. If we had a big scrap when I was
ready to go home in the evening the Lady gave me 10
francs to by icecream if it was a little scrap I got only

5 francs. Now we are happy and I massage her head some mornings and get the francs just the same. Capt. gives me a hundred francs extra a month for pressing his suites so I am really making a good bit.

August 7. Paris.

Sunday the Grand Fountain at Versailles Played an at night it played and had beautiful lights of all colores and the most gorgius fire works a band on each side of the Fountain played during the time when the Fountains were playing and 6 musician with the French Horns that they played in Josephine's Time. It alone is worth a trip across the Atlantic it lasted about an hour you feel you are truly in Fairy-Land it is all open air and it was a perfect day. The seats was from 5 franc to 30 frs. I had a 5 and that was on the thick grass right on the edge of the water. it was great fun the Frenchmen can always think of something to keep every body happy.

Aug. 29.

I told Mrs. C. I would like to Visit the Passion Play. Now they are afraid I wont come back to them and so am I. I am proud to have Kind People to Want me to be with them so I made a promise to come back in two weeks like the promise I made to Mrs. M. but I dont think it will be two years. But qu'n sabe (Spanish) Captain have work that will keep him buisy for the Gold Star Mothers they have had Wonderful luck with the

Mothers altho. many are unfit for the trips several have been in the Hospital but all excep one that came over have visit the graves the Doctors did not think it wise to let Her go and she were pleased they made large pictures and gave Her She arrived back home safe. The 55 colored were all nice fat Mamas one thin and She am sure could stand more than any of the stought ones.

Sept. 1. Today found me at my best yesterday I got off the job I wanted to give it up a week ago but they offored me some useful presents so I had to stay to get them. I always get a job when I go out to get one but never feel any to glad no matter how good it is. Its when I am ready to give it up that I have the grand feeling. because I save all while I am making it then spend it afterwards. I am leaving in rout to Oberammergau I want to see the Passion Play for myself and for all of my Friends that cannot be there.

Paris is a Beautiful and delightful City always something to see and everybody pleasant. The French are called the Sweetheart Nation because they kiss and hugh right on the buisy streets. Yet they are perfectly harmless in the house.

I visited the Flea market a street market where you can buy everything from a dimond to a dill pickle. I feel sorry for the many tourist that come to Paris and rush around for a day or two. and I feel more sorry for those that cant do even that much.

Sept. 2 in route
to Strasbourg from Verdun.

I feel I am lucky dog because I keep my job until last Friday it got hot. We laughed about how lucky I was to get off the job just as it got hot.

The one special monument I wanted to see more than any of the Battlefield were the Trench of the Baionettes. I read about it in Cuba during the War If I am not wrong I think that the avator that were flying above and saw it when it happen were an American. I was so sadly surprised to over hear a fine looking Frenchman about 30 years say to his wife when we were walking in the touring party around the trench he did not understand the meaning of the Baionnettes sticking up. Much of the Battlefield have not been cleared up of the shells and have danger signs on them it was a gelourious day. I got to Verdun and left for Metz.

7.30 P.M. well just now we arrived at Sarrebourg the place to change for Strasbourg and I had to grab up everything in my arms papers mapes cross under grown over to this track I ask how many minutes the conductor said no minute so I just cought it. it begain to get German now most of the train men are Germans it pleases me because I like German men. lucky I had a big lunch I had only a large piece of bread and sugar for supper I havent had time to get any food.

I may stop at Baden-Baden Germany's leading health resort. A nice looking German told me where to change

and wishing me a pleasant journey ask me if I would
pull the train bell if he should kiss me good by. I tole
him that I wouldnt I just pick him up and pitch him
out the window. he was still laughing when I last saw
his face. /

> Baden-Baden Sept. 6.
> 3rd floor with a Grand
> View. Butten and Baldrest
> Streets. Hotel Kulmbacker.

I thought I would get off at Baden-Baden so to have a
few minerauil baths. But I went to sleep and woke up
at the next stop after B. B. 3 A.M. I had great fun putting the blame on the conductor the ticket man had a
heart he charged me just the fare back to B. B. I did
not have any marks so he took francs just when we had
arranged it a nice German American came up out of no
where ask me if I was short of money a train left in 10
minutes we had a pleasant time when he tryed to make
a date for B. B. I was to foxie. there will be plenty of
Germans where I am going. so I was changing cars
from 5 P.M. until 5 A.M. but it was pleasant and the
joy was I did not pay that nights room rent.
It was a beautiful dewy morning just getting light I
walked along the gay little brick bottom river with its
many little water falls it runs through the heart of the
City. it was cold but the air was sweet and Brisky. /
while roveing about the Streets Two night watchmen
and a Policeman with a police dog came to me and

while they were coming I made up my mind to get arrested just to see the jail and maybe a hot cup of coffee. they ask me what Hotel I was stoping at I said no hotel. if I had no money I said yes. they ask me to show it I said I would not. if I had a passport I wouldnt answer yes or no. I was speaking all the time in English French and Spanish and they were trying to understand what I was saying. after all my durings they didnt make any move like taking me to jail so I took out my passport and let them see it and we parted the best of friends. The Girls were coming in from the Country with their fruit veg. and flowers in push carts I followed them up to the high terrace in front of a beautiful Church where I went in to say my prayes and nodded until 7.30. then went out to get money exchanged. the Town are gay plenty of musice mornings and afternoon bright hanging flowers from balconys and window make me lonely for Sevilla.

I had a bath at the Augusta bath house next to it under grown are remains of the Roman Bath. first I undress and put on a night dress cut low trimed with red braid then go into a room very white and the girl put a red cap on me. then into a room and stretch out on a wooden couch and a maid scrub with soap then you get under a Shower and go into the big dome on the second floor only arches sepreates each pool so you can see all of the four pools the first are just warm enough the next are not so warm you sit flat on the bottom

which are black sand the water reach to your neck then
the next are the large one for swimming and cold. it is
white stone with steps and tiled peacocks and paridice
birds and the 11 coloms are life size the molden are
gold birds and the top of the dome are pretty colored
glass. I stay long in the swimming the last are like a
deep well and just like a tum of ice am only to glad to
come out. a nice looking maid wrap you in a large
towel and rub the life out of you. Then you go to your
locker to dress and the last but not the least leave a tip
on the dresser. I feel like a 2 year old race horse when
I come out.

When I have swimed long and feel tird I have what I
want to eat sent to my room in the hotel. I am the real
lady now. I worked 3 months so now I must enjoy it
in a beautiful way then I will be willing to work again.
When walking along the little Oos on the Lichten tale
Allee it seem I have never been in a more beautiful
place as Baden-Baden. I had a glass of grape juice in
the glass covered terrace next the Casino not for the
juice but for the place that are decerated with artifical
grapes and vines the Girls have two long braids and
dressed in one of the German natinal dress.

Market day I went butter are not so good as the French
butter they have so many good sausages and fruit and
vegetables are very cheap and I bought food for two
days I can get meals so easy in my Room and eat many
times for the same money that I spend in the res-

turants. I like the German people they never get impatient when you are marketing.

Sept. 8. I went to a large German Protestant Church I like the way they drop their voices and hold their notes long. in the musice. I went in the bus to the Village of Oetigheim for the Festival. A muzzled gong sounded to call the people in. Three trompet sounders dressed in the Swiss coustoms of black and orange strips. then from the main building in the Yard came on the steps Napoleon and His Soldiers and then to my delight a heavy shower. they looked so funny standing there in the rain going on with the play. the most natural acting I could ever wish to see. then the Sun came out. "Andreas Hofer" the play was staged right in with the horses and chickens.

You could never tell who was the actor or actress a little bare footed boy leading a goat or a Girl leading a milk cow or the Blacksmith would stop shoeing a horse and step out and be the actor for a few minutes. a white pullit and a black hen when ever there were space enough were in the yard or stage scratching then a big yellow hen with 20 chickens got mixed up and such chirping until they got togather it was to amuseing all so wonderful played it truly must be a smart head that handle so many people. then the men went off to war the battle took place upon the Hills the young girls became strech barriers then Victory and the feast with 3 may polls the girls danced graceful and all the

time the goats sheep cows horses made it so natural.
one thing I miss was a dog. but I didnt miss it until I
got home and was in bed think how wonderful it was.
then I thought of the dog. /

Oberammergau. Sept. 10.

When I got here there were no one in the Village but
the Home people an American Couple and myself. but
today it is filled up the band came out everybody locked
arm in arm marched from one end of the town to the
Stations thats the way we celebrate for the new arrivals.
When I arrived I saw standing in the street Two little
fellows with long hair. I ask them about ein Zimmer.
I always feel a little Boy can help a stranger more than
anybody else I have found it so in many places. But a
woman or a Girl I never expect anything they never
know. so I found a beautiful room with bright new
rag rugs curtains are dainty and a nice painting of the
Village on the light blue walls.
1 A.M. I just returned from The Cabaret where they
have a delightful Troup Working people come in I
enjoyed being there what the Passion Play lack the
Bavarian's caberet players will make up. /
Just as I got to the gate our pretty little maid were
coming up the lane with her Sweetheart so unlocked the
door for me.
I will be up at six go to mass so to see the Passion Play
actors they go to six o'clock mass every morning dur-

ing the Play season. I am sorry that I'll be in the
Theatre tomorrow and cannot attend the Funnerl that
will be at 10 A.M. the man dug the grave Today and I
stop by several times and each time he were digging up
bones and skulls. I went in the Church yard at 7.30 to
say my evening prayes and a bunch of little girls started
in one saw the pill of durt and she told them what
was under it and such running away.

The Theatre were crowded I feel sorry for those that
rush in to Oberammergau see the Play and rush away
the next morning I have enjoyed so much the Village
and the People. The Play are wonderfully Played but I
am very much dissipointed in the stage I like the Hollywood Passion Theatre a thousand times better. and
Knowing the streets of Jerusalem. I did not like the
stage one bit. after seeing that play last Sunday out
doors I expected so much of this Play. The Two out-
standing Points of the play is the acting and the Vow
which make them live in a way to put their heart and
soul in it. for me it is not real enough. not that I know
enough to be a judge but I know that I miss much.
Where Christ ascents cannot come up to Hollywood
at all. Here he stand in a little dark tomb a scren
slide back he stands with a gold ray in the back and
step aside just like a sliding lantern picture. its no
good.

The People wait outside the stage door for hours and
He goes out another door I think it is rude of Him I

laughed so when Two Americans told me they had
waited all afternoon at the stage door and about his
house and didnt get to see Him. I told them I had just
passed Him I see Him every day but I never look for
Him. He has a permanent Wave right on top of his
head Sholders a bit round. He has bushy redish brown
hair a nice Voice tall Slender and not such a pleasant
face. not another man in the Villiage that look like
Him. /

Wed. 7 A.M. Today when I saw Him on a side street
with another man I was the only one in the street I had
looked at Him all I wanted before he saw me then He
looked at me and I just turned my head so proudly. I
sat between Two Women at the Theatre. one came in
late and droped the money I being the smallest had to
get under the seat and find it she had a bad cold and
when she begin to cry such blowing. Then She took
out a paper bag and anoyed all by taking food out and
such smacking. Thursday I spent the whole afternoon
sitting on a terrace near the dressing room and saw all
the actors and actress as they came off and went on I
enjoyed it just as much as being enside.

I expect to leave Oberammergau for Bonn tomorrow. I
meet a German Girl and stoped in to see her. Her room
was next to the frount and the cow dung pen next to
it you had to pass it to get in I told her she would
make a good Hindu. am glad somebody have cows I
have enjoyed so much the pure milk and butter.

I had to send so many cards to many people about the world that have been kind to me which is a small bit to do. but it have amounted to dollars with stamps I wanted to stop at Heidelberg but cut it out so to have it for postage.

> *Bonn Germany Home of*
> *Beethoven*
> *Hotel König Sept. 16.*

I fell in love with Bonn am just around the corner from Beethoven's Birthplace. the narrow streets are much like Sevilla. grapes are so cheap I am taking the grape cure by eating a bunch every morning. I went up to mount Kreuzberg Two men walked down with me a long walk from the Chapel are lined with English Walnut trees. on reaching one a man was up in it knocking the nuts down for his self they told him I was a stranger and when he saw me picking them up he begain to beat them down like rain. he may have said if she can pick them up under that let her have them. I would like to have 5 cents for every time a person stop me to ask the way. but it is great fun and I often make a pleasant friend.

> *Cologne Germany.*
> *Sept. 21.*

I got a room near the Y. this is a city like Rome often You see part of the Roman Walls it make it seem ancient also the streets are running everyways. Friday night I went to the Opera Der Postillon von Long-jumeau was to be played and I found some one to tell me the play. then it turned out different so I ask a girl in the cloak room that spoke English. She said it was Madame Favert they could not play the other because the leading man was sick. It sure was a gay Opera. The Cologne's fair are on I went across the river to see the growns but did not go in as I am tird of fairs. I went on to the Zoo the Bears when you stop each do a trick and put their paw out for something. last night I went to a toping caberat. Day-Willis an American colord four they were dressed O.K. But they dancing was just fair.

I shall leave for Brussels in the morning and would go through Holland but it is to late I hope to visit there next Summer.

Bruxelles Belgium.
Sept. 23. 1930.

Belgium was freeded from Holland on Sept. 23 1830 so they are celebrating their one hundred Birthday. I finished my buisy day of sightseeing at a nice Caberat the Belguims are fond of dancing and You have no need to sit out a dance Six nice looking men ask me to dance not one over thirty. Everywhere are musice its a real gay feast I am getting such a kick out of it as it's a surprise to me.

I went to the Centeral market they riffel off Chickens and such things the best looking poultry and such good butter milk. I visited the Famous Painter Wiertz's Musee the most and best of his pictures are such horrod thoughts. While painting he must have had the devil in him as big as a horse. as he was surposed to have been some what of a distempered man.

I like the Royal Palace better than any Palace of all the other Countrys it have a pretty laid out Sunking garden and look so grand and homelike.

Sept. 29.

I went by train half hour ride to Malines. the Chimes was well worth the trip. the Cathedral a grand one. it was much damged by shells. The big old Notre Dame Church have a famous painting by Rubens. "Maraculous Droaught of Fishes" The head of the Angel are said to be that of his second wife if so she was a real knockout.

The Cathedral chimes and beautiful old Town hall and Palace all fit in well but what toped it off was the clean Kitchen on wheels that sold hot fried potatoes I have never like fried potatoes as I always felt they lacked something and its the Flemish People that put the touch on. mustard pickels.

Sat. night was a pretty illumination Procession through the streets. I was just going to sleep about 4 A.M. a young man came and could not get in and I had the room that his Friend George had before I came. he stood there calling Georgie my window was open and

he threw a rock in I closed the window he still called
then a lamp lighter passed and he asked him to reach
up and knock on my window I threw it open and attird
in a tan night dress and a all wool red sport sweeter
speaking english. I have laughed so over how they
stood stiff looking up at me. Sunday was the biggest
and last day a Pageant wound its way through the City
it was of diffent centereys Charles V and His Queen.
I went up to the foot of the Cathedrel as I knew it
would be more fitted and beautiful to see it coming
from there. the lovely sounding old bell tolled until all
was around the corner.

many english people live here and the Girls Friendly
Society will get you a job any time but I dont care to
stay. the winter will soon be here.

Because of the unsettled condition in China Juanita de-
termined not to complete her journey around the world
at this time but returned to the south of France where
she remained until May 1934.

Jan. 10, 1934.
Chemin de la Garoupe
Cap d'Antibes

I still have the joy of making this dear little Villa my
home that belong to the nice English couple. They have
taken a Villa for 2 years at Mallorca and they say when
this Villa is Vacent it is my home. I havent had a house

all by myself and when I can have it I do not mean to let it stand empty.

I worked about 4 months the pass year have just spent the time in the sun eating sleeping going to amusements and have just as many Francs as the year before as I can see. I have a place at Antibes near Juan-les-P. that I can go whenever I feel that I had better hold up a week or two on my francs. but it will be time enough when I no longer have this sweet home. for then I will have to pay room rent so must take a place. I have put aside to spend on my last half of my world tour. The last year have been the happest of my whole life how long this happiness will be mine I do not know but it cannot last for ever.

It was interesting to me watching the Alpes take off their white winter robe by July they were complety nud and now I have enjoyed so much watching them put them on again it is more beautiful with the Sky blue sea than their brown bodys. the Pin trees seem to be much greener and they grow leaning the sea breez blowing on them all the time. for 3 days I have been hoeing out the garden and pruning the plants. Mr. and Mrs. Rose are now in England Visiting her Parents at Cornwall but I do not know if they'll stop here on their way back to Mallorca. There are a very few English and American Sunning this winter as in the pass. Well what was bad for them was good for me. An American wife 64 her French husband 32 live in a swell villa near here. She is very rich she have a young girls shape nice silver bob gray hair dresses nice I spend much time looking at them. He doesnt work I wouldnt expect him to when he hafter put up with those 64 years he is tall and Handsome. But the youth in her face are gone forever. she stands on their poch and watches for him if he be a little late for supper I can see that she are scolding him when he does come.

> *June 20. 1934. Paris*
> *39 Rue de la Bucherie be-*
> *tween Saint Julien Le Pauvre*
> *and Place du Petit Pont*

I am enjoying my new home. each home have a new beauty and a different comfort so I never long for one of the pass. already I have forgoton that my wonderful Villars on the Cap d'Antibes ezisted. As soon as my permit to visit Russia come I'll leave here.

At 4.30 in the morning I am dress and are out its the only time that I enjoy Paris and the air are so pure. I walk over to Les Halles and bring for two days all I can eat. fruit salad vegetables the peaches and mellons are just the best ever. its so fresh and easy to get and all free. no wonder around there are so many bums. They open the baskets and on the top if some have been mashed they just put it inside I am the only one that touch them after the packers. so you can see that Paris feed their Bums well. I am back have a good soap cold bath and gone to bed until 8 A.M. Here in my room are a crate basket of large fine tomatoes they found some mashed and didnt trouble to lift the next paper. I have a cute black hat one night I was strolling along in front of Du Point on Bd. St Michel a man picked it up and I being near gave it to me new and a perfect fit. I really aught to love Paris but these high heel shoes hats night and day and black cloths damp my feeling. the Scripture Say ask and it shall be given. I am in much need of a warm skirt for my coming travels so I have written a note to Mrs. Morris asking if she have one she do not really need. I can get one for 30 francs but ned the 30 frs. for travelling. Am going to leave her some tomatoes just to see what I say are true, I am the only one that have tuch them. They have lived here a long time yet may not know the life of Les Halles Bums.

Yours truly Juanita.

July 27, 1934.
Middelburg, Holland

The train from Paris up here are nicer in the W. C. as they have plenty of soap clean towels but the seats for sleeping are not so nice and soft. a nice Belguin Girl and a youngman Dutch were in the same compartment. They gave me nice oranges and it was just the thing at 5 A.M. at Rosedale the Frontier Town he were much amused to see me handle my two suite cases with so

much ease that are all from those 100 of Sun baths at
Juan-les-Pins. the Sea and the Pins are the thing. On
the train coming to Middelburg were a nice traveling
Saleman years ago He spent 5 years in Boston playing
on the stage and He was so gay sing the love songs of
20 years ago. But I knew each one. he told me many
helpful things for my trip.

there were 4 other young men in the compartment they
earn their living going to different places on market day
as each place are always many Tourist and they have
their Pictures made with the Dutch in their Native
cloths. they like myself like wholsome food and a clean
bed so between the 4 I learned everything needed. They
buy a ticket by the month for about ½ the straight fare
so that told me if I were going to be here to get one for
8 days. then they begain to eat their breakfast of fresh
nice brown fish and told me I must eat fish as it was
always well cooked fresh and cheap. They were pleased
when I told them it was just what I liked and told me
to go to Rotterdam by boat it was cheaper and more
beautiful. the men were ever so kind about helping me
to get off.

I checked my cases and went out to join the crowd. the
whole Town turn out on Thursday street musicans were
about and every hour the Chimes of the 16 Centery
Gotheic Beautiful Town Hall. the market Place were
a gay and interesting sight. but I was glad I didnt take
a room with the Family my young men told me but

went to the one the Porter of the Grand Hotel told me
about as I was in need of a good nights rest and it was
up the other side of Town so I didnt here the Chimes
until 5 A.M. I got this nice room for only one guilder
and the bed of feathers are just ideal.

The strong dogs draw the vegetable carts the children
are in red yellow and blue wool socks they play about
in wooden shoes. Every window are glitting they are so
clean and all curtains white pot plants in the windows.
there are no Balcons but They could not enjoy one as
the tempture changes to often. the French would feel
unhappy here with the bread. the husband of a store
didnt want to sell one franc worth of butter so I was
eating a whole loaf outside and a bottle of milk and
the little fat Pink wife came out and saw me and she
get fussy just like a little hen and said I must have butter
and winked at me and butted every slice of bread she
must have put about 3 francs worth on the bread. in
the afternoon when I was passing she was at the door
and waved at me across the street. So you can see the
Dutch women are the bosses.

Then I felt tird and sleepy but didnt have a room as I
gave it up so walk around to the cannel and right on
the bank I took off my sandles and laid down on the
clean grass the sun was warm just enough breez and I
was sleeping wonderful but They are so Kind I was
disturbed several times. first a man said I must not
turn over into the Cannel and not until I told him I

could swim did he go. Next women would pass and
say sleep well and smile. when walking through the
streets a curtain will be pulled back and two or more
faces will look at you.

I took a bottle from in front of a store and hid it on one
of the bridges and while I was moving my suite cases
down to the Boat the bridge open and my bottle went
into the Cannel but I got one from another door with
a rubber cork. I saw a milk wagon and rand after it got
a quart of buttermilk. I sat down on a low step at the
edge of the Cannel and had an enjoyable meal I still
had several slices of that butted bread. then washed
and returned the bottle.

one minute it is very hot during noon times but even
then it changes in a second and the winds are quite
strong. How they do eat rost beef in Holland you can
have it hot cold well done raw before and after
the Theatre smoked els. pickeled herrings They
stand on the corners and eat them like an Italian eat
Spagetti.

On Boad the Koningin Wilhelmina.
The Boat a tug like carry fraight left at 8 sharp. a
beautiful bright morning but the skies are never without clouds. on each side of the wide Cannel the three
lines of trees and the grass look like a lawn. after
going through the locks at Veere we are now on the
Sea or I do not know just how to say it as Holland are

the Sea itself. While the men were conquring the Sea
they also made the parts that they conqued beautiful so
nelected the style of their women or their costuoms. At
Zype the 3rd stop they took on a few of their light
brown fat horses that you see graving on the grassey
spots with the hundreds of Holsten cows. although we
are on the deep sea are always in sight of lines as well
set out trees and raised lawns. Sea guels are flying
about a few wind mills turning.

We get to Rotterdame about 3 P.M. the train are one
Guilder more I think that is about 70 cents and this is
a more delightful trip. where a Dutch go also his Bike.
This is like rowing down a driveway line with trees
and green turfs no wonder the milk and butter are pure
the Cows enhale the pure air. all day. Of all the things
Mrs. M. gave me in Paris the black tights are the most
useful. I have spent the whole day on deck and not
another woman and it was all to the tights what a life
this is some times it hangs on a pair of cast off tights.

Helsingor Denmark
Aug. 7, 34.

I loved Holland the Dutch are more Romanstaice than
the Latin countries when you say Holland You say
water. it sure have plenty and they sure have smiles
and like to have their feet comfortable. I spent 9 days
in Holland Traveling most of the time from Town to
City water and rail twice to Amsterdam, Den Haag

and Alkmaar always had a nice place to sleep and good food to eat. Then by water to Hamburg one day there. ate good. Had a delightful trip to Marken, Volendam and Edam. at Marken are many Sparrows and at the back door of many of the cute little cottages are a little house much like their own nailed upon the wall for the Sparrows. At Edam young men sat along the cannels fishing and going in and under Their legs was cats from the neighbors house and when they caught a small fish always gave it to a cat. At Volendam Had lunch with a couple and their 7 children all beautiful and healthy and how They can eat I ate so much I felt uncomfortable. From Holland all the Way up to Trondhjen are the land of white tennis shoes and bright red socks, green and yellow and pajams in every shade and in every city and way side place.

I planned not to like Denmark nor the People and said I would stay one day and Here I am more in love with Them Than any Countrie I have been souppose I hadnt come I would have miss all the charming and good Friends that I have meet.

I was to leave tomorrow but I meet a refine gentleman that lost His sight in the War and are very anxious that I stay a while. He traveled most of the worlds now He has the beautiful memories. The eve of our meeting from 7 to 11 P.M. I had to tell Him how I looked and it made me think of a Spanish Play I saw wher the fine rich young blind man fell in love with The Poor homly

Girl and he pictured her to be very beautiful and she said yes that she looked just as He pictured Her.

I had a wonderful day going to Snekkersten a fishing Villiage Bathed in the Sound. Walked up to Helsingor along the sea visited the Castel then took the Ferry to Hälsingborg Sweden didnt have my Passport. He wanted to know what I had in the bundle as I went through the costum and must have a passport when I undid the blue beach hankerchief and had only a red bathing Suit He were so shocked let me through. I went in bathing being a hot day. and came back to see the Beautiful Helsingor Revew at 7 P.M.

Kopenhagen 1 A.M.
Aug. 8.

I can get nearly a ½ roast spring chicken here for what a stamp cost. This is the Place for good food one can get anything they want at any hour hot or cold the People eat light but so often the chicken are deliciously cook brown gravy. A Friend where I buy my roast chicken spent 1½ years in Chicago and are ever so kind to me. he always give me 5 nice boiled potatoes hot I never think of cooking. ice cream and chicken are my daily diet.

I just left a place after I had a large glass of milk bowl of fresh fruit jelly with a pitcher of fresh cream Then I meet so many pretty looking girls and handsome men going in to eat and the musice nice I went back and had a large cup of hot chocolate the jelly and cream was 6 cents and the chocolate 6.

The maid here are so nice to me I promised to give her something out of my case. she is one of 7 children the mother died so I shall leave one of my cases with her I'd like to have the cloths but some Madame will give me some more but I wont be giving up those darling tights. my charming Friend were a bit peeved with me this evening because I agreed with the Danish in eating and He doesnt like it He say they live only to eat but you just cant help it its all in the windows I walk along and watch the People the Windows where cloths are never any one the crowd are always at the windows where the food is. The air are fresh and the streets wide so in a few blocks of the last place you are ready to eat again. all the men have very much room in their pants for a large stomach.

Tonight after I left my Friend at 10.30 I spent one hour looking for a street where I get long crisp slices of bacon cut thick for 2½ cents a slice I walk along the street eating it and pickled Vegetable morrow.

I stayed here because my Friend would have been sad not to see me again and altho. I didnt promised to see him. He were waiting for me. and also I would have stayed anyway just to get a few more Chickens as I didnt have chicken to often in France. and such Wonderful apple Pie.

Aug. 20. I came by steamer to Oslo spent 4 delightful

days and left on a seven day Tour encluded traveling by train boat Horse and Cart and auto from Oslo to Trondheim. the Norwegians are so soft spoken you just do not be a stranger. I stayed in Private homes the other Turists went to Hotels but I would go through the Town and choose a house and go in and They never turned me away and They were as Kind to me as if I had been an old Friend I learned so much and a Hotel would have cost many times more.

Aug. 21. I like the Swedish People already. am staying four days in Sweden. have a grand time here at the swell caberets and resturants. There are no end to my Friends. I have no time to do any writing.

Aug. 28. I bought a ticket to Finland after I learned I could go another way more interesting and cheaper so I went back to get the money and the man he did not think They would change the ticket. but I said to Him now you just go in There and Tell the Boss and dont be to proud to say its a poor lonely Woman. They changed it and had a good hearty laugh. Rajajoki the Frontier stayed in a lovely Fennish Family. It was a beautiful home they had a sun parlor a nursey for the Children. the Son 17 played the swell Paino I had a nice piece of French musice. You would have thought I was an old dear friend. the Madame had cooked many wonderful and good things and I sure did feast. Then had a nice lunch box. They are refine Fennish and I felt that I had just arrived home.

Sept. 1. a plesant three days trip to Leningrad. At a stop before we reached the City were meet by a most Plesant Guide and we had nothing more to do with our baggage.

Leningrad Russia
Hotel Europe Sept. 2.

I thought the world were small until I arrived here Leningrad is a world in its self I wouldnt give it for all the 25 or 30 countries and city that I have seen. I knew it before I came but am overjoyed to find it so much to my liking. I could fill a hundred sheets with what I have seen and enjoyed since 2 P.M. yesterday.

This is a swell Hotel it is run by Inturist a special Organization for Traid with Foriegners with everything that go with a first class Hotel wonderful service in every way I do not know how They can manage to give us so much for so little when the franc and dollar are so much lower than this money. We have nothing to do with the Exchange we pay just as though we paid francs. they accept all Foriegn money but not Russian in the Hotel they give us change in our own money. I am the only one here that have a cheap Tour yet I have the swellest seat in the fine cars that take us ever where. I went out and marched in line yesterday with different groups of young men and Girls that were geting ready for the Great Yuths Day. then I met a Funal Procession went to a big white Holy Church with a big blue dome and 4 smaller blue domes and the Funal with a

Preast was one of the most impressive I have been to. after the Body were buried a young Lady of the Family passed around a large bowl of boiled rice with sugar in it and several spoons each made the signe of the cross and took a spoon full and so did I. I had crossed the length of the City with them and on the way seen many things I wanted to get back and stop in.

Today have been just wonderful I have looked on fine beautiful healthy clean living young men and women during the finest exercise. I visited at the workers apts. and the nursey for their children and the regester office of marrage and saw a marrage. They do not really need to go through it nor regester it is just as leagler if a man and woman love each other and decide to live togather and their children have just as honest a name. In Russia is not one child that are living under a false name each have the name of Their Father is There another country can say that. not one. and if the man lies when he takes another woman as a wife before every thing have been settle with the last one he will get 3 years of hard labor in jail. where is a country like that. every father support his children or help the mother until the children are 18 years.

I meet a young man a Studient from Washington D. C. a pure American come here in June as a Tourist he couldnt get a job in Washington but He went to work today in a School in Moscow. and he know less Russian than I do. Here are no unemployed people thats if They want to work what other Country can say that.

the Saying of Mr. Lenin Learn, then learn some more then learn learn That's Their motto and are in big red letters on many buildings. its good to see it while its in the making. Here are no cast, and class no who's who. Here you are more free to do what you want to than any other country thats if its clean and honest.

There are a grand bunch in the Hotel all full of Pep and we have some snappy words while sight seeing the 3 hours. after we are free to go and do as we please I was everywhere in line and cross line and every where singing and dancing and not one unpleasant thing the Young men and Soldiers were as gentle as mothers with their babies. I cut across many places and the Police blu his whistle I didnt even look back I would like to have had 5 months here before it got cold but I Promised my body that I would never spend another year where it felt the cold. I turned down a swell job as I must get down where there are always Spring.

Sept. 4.
Moscow.

I left Leningrad at 10 P.M. had a sleeping compartment with a Honeymoon couple from Monteral and a very fine Jewish man from Grater New York he snowed a little I turned about all night. But the Honey moonsers sleep like a buck. it was 3rd class but very nice and clean as could be. They were no curtains but I had myself beautiful and Private that yard and ½ of black satin with the gold work I all ways have it ready for any need. well I pined it up on my bed the others had no private That showed the Wise and the Foolish.

This is a fine Hotel and I have a private bath and Toilet and everything its very beautiful and the room are much nicer than the one at Leningrad but that Hotel are a much finner than this one. I am now looking out on the beautiful Kremil and the River. The food are much better at Leningrad and we had a good full orchestery there. I felt like Kissing every one good bye when we left even to the plain old gray cat that Sit in our Dinner room.

But its here that the people like best and stay longer. I am the wonder of all the turists as I am the only one that are going to Siberia. its much warmer here do not need a coat. I was up early this A.M. stoped in a a box like little Chapel just across the bridge from the Hotel to say my morning pray and I felt like the thing in a peep show. There were another and the man look after the chapel the door ajar and the People stand and peep in. Some Churches are used for a Machein shop some a Police Station but I Found enough to pray in. Then I went to the big market you buy your milk there and tast it first to see if you like the tast or if its sweet. for 20 Kopeks I got one nice apple that is over 18 cents high in our money. Plenty of food in the markets and

plenty of People buying. and plenty of work its the one
reason I would not care to stay its to much work every
where building going up and they are building the subway and have a night and day shift. it is very gay here
not at all like Leningard the people dress much better.
but I like Leningard.

I met a Fine Swedish Lady when I was walking along
Prospect 25ro street she said look how the Girls are
looking in the windows at the silk under ware am sure
they wish for it. I said but they are Happier without it
as it is so much more trouble to wash than the little
cotton flannel that they ware. as They all ware the
same no one are grudgful. I hope in a few years this
will be a country after God's and the Young's heart 40
and 50 years olds have nothing to do with the making
of the Present Russia. A learned man said to me yesterday, Yes the the Youths are Happy but what about
the old I told Him They have had Their day. He said
but you do not speak Russian as well as I can so how do
you know that they are Happy I told Him that He had
just arrived and He had not romped and skiped along
the streets arm in arm with them of course I did only
for 1½ days but I felt their hearts. We do not have
names for any day only every 6 day we rest. Today we
are resting and Thousunds of workers young men and
women with the best guide on art goes to the art gallers.
when I step up to get the ticket being in the mist of the
workers and looking more like one the guard say step

in line so I steped in and stuck. My Visa from Russia to Asia would have cost 20 dollars but at the Hotel They got it free for me I being a poor lonely woman of course that lonely look helps me a great deal but there never were one less lonely than I am.

October 2, 1934.
Kobe, Japan.

I had a wonderful 8 day Trip from Moscow To Manchuria in comfort good Friends and good food and every minute was so full of interest the 8 days passed like 8 hours. I traveled 3rd Class for 80 dollars that was with a berth and the coches were just like little well kept Cottages good matthews soft and clean white blankets four pillows nice green curtains at the windows in the isles as well as the comparts a nice table with a green shade lamp and a porter swept and dusted ever 10 minutes and at each Station when the engin took water a woman in unform came in and washed up the floors with very Hot water and washed the Windows. there is a nice bath room with large tub and shower plenty of hot water.

In my Coche every Body were clean most of Them bought food at each Station there were always plenty of fresh milk in bottles fresh butter roasted chickens muton Pork sausage boiled eggs tomatoes mellons sour cream Cottage cheese The Chickens were 10 and 15 Rupees an Admirer wanted to buy a chicken for me but

I only accepted from Those I could give a silk dress to. I had in my suite case many silk dresses blouse scarfs silk coats all given to me at Antibes and Paris and I exchanged them with my Friends for food and saved about 15 dollars as I didnt need to buy. silk are very expensive in Russia so it was not only a help to me but a pleasure as well and it were a fair deal. I gave a garment according to the food if it was a nice piece of roast Pork or chicken then I would stick my hand in my case and give a dress to one of the Young Ladies. the minute I gave it she would combe her beautiful bob hair powder and dress up to show the others.

It was spring Summer and snow and at one place the Lake and mountains like Switzerland. the women didnt get nasty over my fine looking refine Admirer. the last of my Friends left me at Chita Siberia I had only a night alone and arrived at Manchuria in the A.M.

It being Sunday I was just in time to go to the lovely Russian Church with a full good Chour then to the market and left it with a blue cotton handkerchief well filled looking like a perfect Manchurain cook. I visited the Trenches and meet a very nice Manchuria Gentleman the Money Changer. He went to Harbin in the same Train and made it nice for me. He pointed out all the Bandit fested spots in Manchukuo There were a small regement in the worst spot to proct the Passanger Train. I had a berth in the nice 3rd Class coche of the Inturist. all the Russian Train men at Manchuria junction the Russian Frontier left and a new crew came on. many gay little station Chinese Mangolies Russian and Japanese in the bright kimonos and Soldiers at every Station and a Soldiers band playing. I feasted on perfect rosted spring chicken They were sold at most of the Stations between Manchuria and Harbin for 20 or 25 American cents. they do not cut the head off nor the feet so the juice cannot escape and such good white bread it was a surprise to me to find it in Manchuria. Never in all my Travels have I had so much rich food. My friend wanted to take me to the Theatre that evening but I believe in having the way clear so I can be looked after by a Gentleman of the Town I arrive in so I thanked Him and said good Bye.

At Harbin never have I been so careful looked after I felt like a Vauleable Pearl wrapped in a shaby cloth as I didnt show a sign of chic. from there I bought my 3rd class ticket to Kobe.

The trip from Harbin Through Chasen Korea were most gay we had a stop at Mukden a very lively place the Towns People and cloths and my new Friends. as often as one left me another got on and getting off at every stop for the food made me the most buisyest Person on the Train. I understood all the languages and again the 4 days went before I was ready for them to go.

Fusan is French a Beautiful Port The Steamer left Sept. 20 and we got the begining of the Typhoon that took so many lives next day at Osaka and the 8 hour crossing over to Shimonoseki were over or under the jolly Waves. they broke open the doubled doors and stair case of our floor. And we were saved by the quick work of puting wide planks and canvas sheets so when another big one came it was close. Never have I laughed so much. it were Japanese matting floors we sat or stretched out as we liked and when the waves tosted the Ship on the side about 300 Bright Kimonos women and children Babies men suite cases Tea Trays all went to one side nothing to hold on to. we was as helpless as though we had neither hands or feet it was just like you would sweep up a long row of bright apples in a trough then turn it upside down again. the sliding was play to the children and They laughed to almost fits with me. a Young Boy played a snappy Japanese air on a mouth organ. its great to be a good sailor. When the ship Landed they was looking for the lone American and didnt know when they saw me. when They did see the Passport He said you are traveling 2 class I said I had to travel 3rd as they had no 4th. and where are your baggage I said I left it in Los Angeles 7 years ago and one suite case is one to many. and he stop to speak to a gentleman and I was gone. all this were going on at Shimonseki and all the clouds were turned up and the rain was fall out.

We left at 10 P.M. I had one hour eating Ice cream and looking at the bright Kimonos we traveled all night in the Tail of the coming Typhoon never have I seen it rain so and wind but I steped off at every station which was brightly lighted but often the wind put them out and then They telephoned down for the train to stop as the tracks were damage and we arrived at Kobe 4 hours late.

There are always a full House in the Third Class thats why I like it and I being the only stray Bird I amuse as well as being amused. The real shock is when They learn from my Passport that I am an American. Then they think so little of it They forget and begain with me as though I am a Countrymen of Theirs. One said to me I do not like that dress pulling my dress You must get a Kimona. its good to be in Asia. I have been longing to reach just this spot and I have found everything more beautiful and jolly than I expected thats why I always get it.

> Y.W.C.A.
> Kobe Japan
> Oct. 4.

I came here to the Y. after looking at some of the Hotels I counted my money and felt happy that I still had $6.30 in travels checks and enough yens to keep me for 3 days until I got to the Express. on the Steamer I saw the Japan Chronical the daily English Paper and felt happy as I was sure of earning my daily bread.

Tuesday I put an add. in the Chronicle and Tomorrow my add. in Japan will be in the Kobe Shinbron. 3 yens without publishing my name with it and 250 if I had my name published. it was very amuseing Visiting the Office and every one were very polite.

I love here in the Y. They do not keep largors but let me stay in the cottage that is used for English classes sewing and cooking classes. it is a sweet and pleasant home and every one are kind and gentle to me I am glad that I didnt keep them waiting any longer for me to come from the Cap d'Antibes. The mountains are just in two minutes back of this nice Cottage and I like the Scenerey more than the Cap d'Antibes. Each morning at 10 the class begain and as many as 25 or 30 young Japanese Ladies come in and the only way I know They are in the Kitchen is by 30 pairs of wooden slippers propped up side the front door and 30 bright pasoils in the rack never a sound and the same in the sewing room one step across me in the Hall there are 15 or more young girls speaking so softly and yet I can sleep right on as I never here a sound. and I am a light sleeper.

The same way in the Theatre the actors and actress sing and speak very softly. I enjoy very much going to what I call a nude reseption The Public Baths at night with about 100 women I the only stray one They are much interested in my little silk draws and more in the little silk pink brazzier my Paris friends gave me one can never tell what little gift will become Famous as they do not ware them. 3 times the black tights have held the first place that outfit make me the most famous one in the bath. and I am much interested in the number of things that I see. I notice They do not take a cold water bath after the hot one as I do. my cold bath is shocking to them and every piece I put on over my head. They go out in the Wind and that account for them always having a cold and have the bad habit of spitting anywhere. yet their babys are keep so clean. /

Kobe Oct. 6.
116 Yamamoto Dori Chomez
Y.W.C.A.

I was to stay only 5 days in this Cottage But they say to me I am a very good person and as I give no trouble I can stay as long as I wish. the Y. are in the swellest part of the City At my bath room window I have the mountains frount windows large weeping willos on the Poch two large plum grannes Trees that are bright with fruit and from my bay window I have the sea so I do not miss Cap d'Antibes. I sleep eat and read spend many happy days here in my room. Thursay afternoon and eve. are the Floral Class and that day I go to the Theatre because they use my room and bath. the day classes are pay the night free The managers are all Japanese Ladies and very kind.

Last night I brought in a large pot of chicken gizzard wings and I made a grand feed celery onions tomatoes cabbage carrots and noodles food is cheap it cost about

15 cents and there are 5 gas stoves here so I can cook as
often as I like.   I pay 6 yens a week for my home here
that a little less than $2.00

I had an offer of a nice place here with a little girl only
afternoons but it was not enough to pay my Room Rent
and I was living so cheap and will be so buisy going
about the Islands to Festivals I wont have time to work.
I arrived here just in time for the big autum Festival the
Moon Viewing Festival and the Bazaar and women in
bright Kimonos made it a beautiful sight.   The good
things to eat are sold hot for a Penny a stick as most
things are sold on a stick keep me very busy eating.
they have fine tall apt. stores and all have beautiful roof
gardens. the resturants are good and cheap.   I went up
the Mountains with some of the Y. Ladies to a grand
picnic we had fresh sardines in batter and sweet potatoes fried over a fire we cooked down by a stream and
at Sun set went up to the high jig zag road to a Tea
house had Tea wonderful scenery many thousand feet
above the City among water falls Shrines and Temples
and came down at twilight perfectly wonderful. The
weather are delightful.

The Exchange are about the same as the franc 3 yens
are 33 cents but you get better valure here. My living I
spend just about what I spend in Paris when I get my
market free there. Thats about $1.40 for 3 days room
and my meals.

Kyoto Oct. 24.

I come to Kyoto just to see the "Jidai-Matsuri" Historical Pageant. It take Place Oct. 22. The Bath cost 1 cent here in Kobe its less as the living are cheaper there. It is so funny to see more than 100 women with the high head dress and slit eyes enjoy me as much as I enjoy them. Like the Baths at Kobe my outfit of pink silk brazzier and teddies make me the most famous one in the bath. As I have only one out fit is why I must change bath houses.

My favorite Temple are the Kiyomizu-Dera and the next are the Chionin Temple. Today it is raining so I will enjoy the day at the best Theatre to me its a waiste of Sens to go to a Theatre on a fine day or night I get a biger show on the streets looking at the brightly dressed people.

I stoped at Osaka for 3 days to enjoy the High Class Japanese Theatre and never have I enjoyed a Theatre so much. I stay 6 hours a different play last about an hour. You get all the Amusement in the Building even to a perfect Ice Skating Palace.

I am having a nice Kimono made and will ware a bright silk sash as I do not like the obi. it make one look old the sash give youth altho. you are not so swell dress up as with the obi.

Kobe. Nov. 10.

To Mrs. Rose,
Villa Des Verveines
Chemin de la Garoupe
Cap d'Antibes.
Dear Mrs. Rose

I hope that you are enjoying life as much as I am for then I know that you are happy. Soon I shall end my two months of delightful traveling in this beautitui country with The Kind and Gentle People I have lived with Them as a Countryman and not as a Tourist. but realy I am not very Japanese when it come to sleeping on the floor. I feel the need of a real bed. /

I have traveled up and down the Island from Shimono-seki up to Tokyo stoping always to enjoy a Festival. The French cannot touch them for Fetes. At Tokyo I enjoyed the Geishas Dancers and took a room right near the Geisha neighborhood so that I would be sure and see the Festival at its best.

I leave on the 20th Nov. for Shanghai so will become Chinese on the 21. Of all nations the Japanese women are only worth being called Mother. Children are the happest of all the rest of the world because Father and Mother are proud of them they are treat as their own not like Orphants. I wouldnt give One Japanese mother for the American ones and I would exchange just two Japanese mothers for all the French. The Japanese have it on us because their eyes are slit Far and They can see front and back.

I am useing the warm clock coat and fur you gave me.

I am truly yours,

Juanita.

Shanghai China
Dec. 8, 1934.
Belthesda International Mission
Broadway.

To Mrs. Felix Morris
Rue du Cardinal Lemoine,
Paris, France.

Dear Mrs. Morris:

You are the only American mother that I like and you are so wise and kind to give me those life saving black clinging tights they have been use at some time in every country and now every day when they need a bath that day I stay in bed and my bed are so soft and warm. This is a lovely home to stay in its used for Service Chinese German and Russian all very nice looking People.

I enjoy so much the Chinese the women are so Fasinating and They dress with the Tandalizing slit on each side from the ankles up to the knee You would be surprise to see so many big handsome men and They are so charming I am still enjoying many adventures and they are so clean minded so much nicer than Europeans American or Englishmen.

I enjoy going to The Sincere Department store Roof Garden, "Great World" as it is called and its a world for its there you see the Pretty Girls. I had a Visit to the beautiful City of Hang Chow and Then to Nanking and rushed back to get a Chinese Coast Steamer that were to sail for Canton but the sea being very rough it will not arrive until tomorrow. I would stay longer in China but I do not like to get up of mornings because its cold and I will not waiste my time staying in bed. So after Canton will get down where the tights may have rest.

I want to stretch my cash to take me to Singapore Java and Baile then back to Honolulu.

I am writing this at the Russian Chinese International Resturant on Range Road. good wholesome and cheap food. its a nice crowd Chinese Russian English and Americans all good to look at. I am eating here as on the steamer for 5 or 6 days I'll be eating Chinese food and be all dressed up just like a coolies wife. Here I buy nice hot sweet Baked potatoes on the street corner and always draw a great crowd as I am the only European that are seen buying them. So it gives me two pleasures as I get a nice size one for less than a French sou.

When I think of the good things I can get to eat for what the stamp cost I just stick these letters in my case.

Truly yours Juanita.

Some Ladys at Church ask me if I were a 7 Day mem-

ber I said I was a member of every Church that believed
in God and that I was nothing but a glob trotter that
had faith only in Prayer.

S.S. *Hai Shang.*

When I got to the Pier this noon the Steamer was just
coming up to the warf. I was looking about for some
one that spoke English to ask when the Steamer left. I
saw a fine rich looking Gentleman standing on a bail
of cotton as the Jetty was crowded with bails of cotton
packed willow baskets big boxes several Chinese coffens
with Remains to be Shiped to their homes somewhere
along the Coast. He told me the Steamer would sail at
noon tomorrow. and said to speak to Mr. Shang up on
deck. I had been admiring Mr. Shang He was so nicely
dressed He seem to be so buisy geting His Ship docked
but He were not so buisy that He hadnt notice me so
when I started away he called down to the Gentleman
in Chinese to know what I wanted. I was to much
dressed up to speak to Mr. Shang. I'll just wait until tomorrow when I am in my Coolie cloths as I want to get
to Canton for 10 Chinese dollars about 4 American
dollars. Thats 3rd Class and its 4 or 5 days with several stops. The English and all the other European companys make a rule to let no European woman Travel
3rd and often there are only 1st class and its 95 dollars.
I told them I wouldnt waist my money traveling with
other Europeans. Well I prefer a Chinese or Japanese

Boat as I want some interest. I expect a Royal treatment tomorrow on Mr. Shangs none to Handsome steamer. I am packed and have the little extra things such as bread butter condensed milk and a tin of powded milk coffee. so I expect to have a pleasant trip.

I went to several Dance Halls and two caberets just stayed long enough to look all over and left before I had to pay. One were all Chinese Girls beautiful dressed some in silk Chinese dresses with short sleves and others in long low neck cut Europen dresses looked swell. another were a mixture of Chinese Japanese and Russian all in the long latest dresses. When I got back to the Mission I was locked out. and I was trying to squeze through the iron gate to reach the bell but couldnt just then a rickshaw man stop to help me he had a long rod that reached the bell and woke up the old Chineman that look after the down stairs. There's always a friend.

Swatow China Dec. 14.

We arrived Here last night and will have two days before the boat leave. when I went on boad I told them I wanted the cheapest and they gave me a place under a Tent on deck I got all fixed as though I ment to stay had a mat spread between two nice neat old Chinese men. and also near a family of four. They made me welcome. after it started they called for the foreigns

and I got a cabin on the best side uper deck cost only
4 dollars American You pay as much as you can. I can
see everything and entertain my Friends from the Port-
hole.

next Cabin to me are a Theatre Troup 3 Sing Song Girls
a mother and the Young man they are acting Partners.
There are 3 nice Russians one serve me hot water and
hot rice and I keep His best suite of cloths with his
money in the pockets as he sleep on deck.

This is a real Chinese City so warm Banars trees grow-
ing everywhere. Girls in their light flowered silk
trousers and a bright slip over skirt hair braided. Little
boys have one ring in the left ear and many queer kind
of hair cuts. I look so much Chinese am not at all out
of Place. So every old Place is Home.

Dec. 15. Swaton. I have been on the go day and night
the streets and buildings were like a Christmas tree it
being a Fete. In the street stalls they sell fat worm that
we call grub found under the fresh soil they take the
enside out and the worm with the little feet are fried
so nice and crisp I came near buying some after looking
at them being relished with so much gusto. theres not
so much difference in Human Biens once you mix Them
up. The boat leave in just a few minutes and I am glad
so I can rest. The Chinese Women are very Friendly
unlike the Japanese the Japs and Swedes are the most reserved of all People Of course I do not mean that they
were reserve to me.

Well in the Park here I was as buisy chatting like a perfect Chinese of all the bound feet its here they have the smallest the feet are just the size of your two fingers togather and they have little wooden sandles with high heels and walk only on the round heels and some have nice slender ankles not broken and they walk without a limp. Some are tall well built women. I visited many of the Cafes and Police Court altho. a guard made me get out but I had been in some time so didnt mind. also Visited the American and French Consuel a mission school Chinese boys school Japanese School the stores market and did my marketing. as useual had one of my large blue cotton handkerchiefs full of oranges bannas bread butter lime drops and a large bunch of celery and carrots hanging out just like a real cook and I Paid less than a Chinese and had so much fun and They enjoyed it even more than I because of the crowd I would draw. it amused the crowd to see that I got so much and paid so little They expected it to be just the other way. But before I buy had been to several places. They are very honest but like all the world will soak you.

Its the money you must watch there are so much copper 20 cents pieces made in place of the real silver pieces everybody are sure to get some then you must sell it for half the Valure. its amuseing to see every one looking it well over before taking it.

I have a nice beef steak fried in plenty of onions and

several slices of good boiled ham and 3 eggs to take on boad. The cook at the Asia Resturant fixed it for me. It may be 2 days before we reach Hong Kong this is a big cargo steamer and well loaded.

I have some Friends on boad a mother Father Girl 12 and two younger boys they sleep under the Tent on deck she have bound feet I like to measure mine with hers. Her legs are very small as I had large legs she thought its well that my feet are large.

When I returned I found a nice looking German Lady in my Cabin going to Canton she about 42 but fat speak a little English am glad she doesnt like the upper berth as I like to be up over everyone.

The only food they give us in This Class are twice a day plenty of well cooked dry rice that is why we must have other food. but we can buy 1st Class Chinese or European food or 2nd class Chinese but it cost very much So I am always well supplied. I'll go out and look at the farewell as we are leaving now.

HongKong Dec. 16.

It was just one day trip but I am glad I bought plenty of food as I'll not go ashore I didnt want to get a Transit Vise as I must come back To HongKong to take a steamer and the Transit admit you only once. cost $1.50.

Well my companion are alright but she came on with only a pot of jam and two rolls and tea she said she are often sick and never ate but she werent sick and how she long for some of my Ham. As I have just enough to last until I reach Canton she gave the Russia men money to buy bread milk and eggs.

The water are so soft on boad I Shampooed my hair we have plenty of hot water then I had a bath in the cabain scrubed the cabin floor washed my cloths dryed on a line in the beautiful Sun had a good lunch then had a real amuseing time calling to the women and Chilren on the Hundreds of house boats near. I also go across to a big Patiguise Steamer to visit.

Dec. 18.
Canton Y.W.C.A.
Fung Ning Lo Street.

I am staying at the Y. just to see the place and the Girls but as I'll be here a week or two must be in a more private place so I can sleep and eat in bed when I get tird of looking at the People. The buildings are new with a California apearance 3 nice buildings for classes and one very large for lardgers both members and none members. that attend schools. the Girls are refine many are studing musice a few speak English. I am sharing a room with a High Class Chinese Girl Mrs. Fan her name mean Square. She has very small feet not bound her Father a Christian but not her mother. She is a designer and was first educated in a Mission School She live very much like a Christian as

her 17 Children are all Christians She married at 15.
had bound feet but her Husband forbid her to bind
them now they are the natal size. We pay $1.50 a day
Canton money 50 cents American which of course for
me are dear. for the Students its cheaper as there are
7 or 8 beds in the very large rooms.

I like the arrangement about the food if you wish to
have breakfast or dinner you tell the matron 20c or 30c
lunch and she lets the cook know. its Chinese food and
suit the Europeans better than the Japanese food. Its
said the People of Canton and the French are the best
cooks in the World. They are geting ready for their
Xmas Plays so I'll be much at home.

Dec. 27. Yut Kun
Hotel Canton

I went with Mrs. Fan and two refine Chinese Gentlemen buisness men of Canton to the "White Cloud"
Resturant for a high class lunch where the wealthy
men go for their light lunch one of them Spoke Perfect
English and I enjoyed the food of many delicious
Chinese dishes it was only a tast in each dish I could
have ate 10 times that much more it being a high class
the cost are very high.

After I went to see about my passage and learn the
next steamer for Manila sailed Jan. 4. I moved to this
nice Hotel on the Bund for $1 Chinese a day and at the
Y. paid $1.50 and roomed with another.

Dec. 21.

I went to Langnan University had lunch at the Chinese Resturant in the Small Settlement of the Campous. Then visited the lovely well built buildings and at 3 P.M. saw the Xmas play and went to the Garden Party on the Campous. and Took the University motor Boat down the River to Canton at Sun Set.

Dec. 22. Canton.

My room have been freshly painted and one side are 4 large glass shutters freshly Painted Pea Green. the celing are very high and no room have walls up to the celing. everything are for coolness. the Two young men keep everything as clean as a Swiss House Wife. Up-stairs are just one small room where the charcoal burner are always kept hot with hot water for baths and a Kettle of boiling water for tea. The Chinese beds are without Springs in place of them are a boad then a straw well made mattrews a sheet a heavy comforter covered on one side with a sheet the top side red silk. the beds have a canop musketo net and looks very en-viting but hard I sleep on the lovely large sofa.

Dec. 2.

I took a little painted House Boat of an old Chinese mother Her daughter and child the little Baby had a lease under his arms so it couldnt fall in. the cat had a lease so a neighbor couldnt get it to cook. the chickens had a lease on the foot so not to be drownd. They rowed me up the river to Langnan University at twilight. it was delightful She accepted 10 cents but I gave Them 10 coppies extra which pleased them it cost 20 cents on the moto Launch so I helped Them and my self. I went up to the Christmas dinner and Student Party which took place in the newly built Girls Dortomidy. First we made bright paper caps to ware at dinner. The young men were the best at making them and many were quite artistic but they had a weakness for long streamers. I had a bright red French cap chic cocked on one side my head and wore two purple and two yellow hearts being the only one with hearts gave me a high place in the eyes of the Charming Chinese Studients.

We went down to the dinning Room about 75 in all there were more men than Girls. The men wore dark coats and white flannel trousers. the Girls wore pretty silk Chinese dresses with the slip up each side Some of them when They sat down I could see far above Their Knees the lace on their rather tight leg short draws.

I sat at a table with a couple from Los Angeles Both Teachers and a Chinese Girl of New York and the most beautiful of all the Girls. and two young men students one Mr. U. Beng Young we fell for each other I for his name He for me no doubt because I said I perfered riding 4th Class in China than 3rd in Japan.

THE DINNER. first a large dish of brown mushroom with gravy boiled rice in large copper Kettles on the side table. a meat fruit salad a dish of lettuce leaves. next a dish of fish and a green cabbage like vegetable then the most delicated and delicious in a metal dish stewed cat from the look of its neck it must have been a tom cat. That American Prof. and his Wife got much of my share of that Stewed Cat. I didn't get half enough but made up on other delicious dishes. Then Bird Chop Suez with the birds skined heads and feet for garnishing it was very good a bread dressing like ground up with the bones and altho. the bones were small I would have liked it better without them. Then the very good Canton Fruit. After we went up to the large reseption Hall where they gave a very short but comical Chinese sketch. My Mr. E. Beng Young were always at my Service and threw peanuts at another studient that sat and Talked with me.

Then we enjoyed several games I always keep near the thickest Boy group. thats where I am at home as they like myself are natunal at all times.

at 10.30 we left and walked the long pleasant distance to the Pier where two moto Larnches took us down to Canton by the light of a full moon and the thousands of House Boats of all sizes made a wonderful Christmas eve night. Many of us took the Pretty Red Rickshaws with their clean white red piped cushion covers. we arrived just in time for the beginning of High Mass

the Cathedral was decerated in Fresh yellow and white
Cythankers and flags of all nations. the Chinese Preasts
looked noble in the Rich cloth of gold and crimson the
Shing musice of Violins sounded well with the setting
it were a beautiful Gathering. At the close of the mass
from a large pole in the Yard were strung thousands of
fire crackers which they lit. I stayed until 2 A.M. the
end.

I went in the yard just back of the Cathedrel and got
some shrubs and made my Xmas tree and out of pretty
colored papers hearts and stars & crowns while making
the tree just across a narrow street I heard a big brown
dog morning for life. They had hung him and after
he died scraped him clean then scaled it cut it open and
cleaned everything from the enside then cut it in half
and a man were there to buy it. I was looking forward
to smelling it cooking.

The Few People that have a cat or dog for a pet guard
over it as a great treasure and it are always on a lease
even at home if not it would be stolen. They have cats
in baskets in the markets to sell just like chickens also
little puppies. Well the next day the 26 being my
birthday and I do not love it I took a good dose of
calmnl. and spent the day in bed and talking across
the way to a Chinese Family. I knocked the Spanish
Paillos for the 3 children and then one of the little
girls sang to me.

Jan. 21.
Taihoku Formosa.
Tropic of Cancer.

I have been in this Beautiful City since Jan. 9. was to Leave on the 11th for Manila But I went to a Circus and it was so interesting I miss the steamer. and am glad as I have had a jolly time here with the Gentle people. Now I have only 5 days more as the Carnival begain in Manila Jan. 27. After Canton I went by steamer eight hour trip to the Potiguese Port Macro and what a great treat to arrive in that Spanish admerfer after Canton. you have to stay on the Bund to know what it mean. I just thanked God for given us both.

Then I went to Hongkong to get a Japanese steamer to here when we arrived at Keelung as I had come through Russia they took me for a spy so to my relief and enjoyment kept my suite case so I hope They have as enjoyable time with it as I have had without it. I had only the dress I had on so I bought goods and such fun here when I went to the dress making shop which is open on the street and young Chinese men do the making I had it made Chinese style which are pretty and will be useful when I get the stiff collor cut off in Manila. There was a crowd of about 200 watched and I danced about holding the skirt. Total cost goods making and all 75 American cents. Here in Formosa the food are much to Americans Tast. more so than the

Japanese food. There are so many delicious dishes the
Chinese make in the smaller resturants but you havent
the courage to eat it its so many to work over it. But
it never have a disagreable odor.

The Chinese make and cook on a oven carried about on
poles and they cook more perfect than in a gas gange.
the cabbage is very delicated the way they cook it and
a wholesome dish is Cabbage curry. They put a small
piece of pork cut in inch strips in a pan and fry it with
onion not to brown. then they cut the cabbage in small
strips add curry salt and water to keep it cover with
liquire and cook slowly. Thats what I had for my
lunch.

You can go in a good Resturant at the Window in a
wire cage are a number of different kind of long snakes
You can choose the one you like and in a few minutes
serve to you à la King.

I am staying with a lovely Family here I like so much
the Patio with the green and fresh plants. about 10.30
they go to bed but at 6 A.M. ever one are on the stir then
at 9 A.M. the house work are over and every thing are
quiet until 5 P.M. I am writing this sitting on my Japanese bed which we call Palate. I washed my bloomers
and little sweter last night so must wait until the Sun
rise in the Paito to finnish drying them. I have a clean
little Choal burner to heat the room Put sweet potatoes
in the ashes eggs in the Kettle. The maids laugh when
They come to put coal in and water.

I enjoy the Service of the Girl Maids in Their bright Kimonos and the food served in the many little bowls on a table 4 inches high. I just ly on my Palate and dine. They think I am ill and the Husband wife and two maids with the medican and good things to eat came in. I kept the good food and told them if I was ill I wouldnt be in bed its only when I am well and enjoy my food and service I stay in bed.

The woman here have the smallest feet of any that I have seen and I have three gifts of little shoes by Chinese Ladies one pair 4 inches one 3 and a half and a pair three taken off their feet to give to me and the fun I had in geting these shoes I went to each Home and how much They enjoyed it that make me feel so proud of the shoes. and They are proud when admired. The most interesting thing here after the small feet are the Funnels. After a rest of several months in the Philippines I hope to visit 5 other Countries. By that time I wont have any more Boat fare. But the way I feel now I would hate to just stop in one place for a whole year or more. life wouldnt be worth while looking at the same faces day after day. I trust I'll never endue such a sad life as that.

Mar. 15.

This is the 12th day on this cargo steamer around the Southern Cross I have made it a trip of enjoyment and also an anjoyment to Both the Officers and Crew. my

Best companions came on Board at Jolo Moroland in the Sulu Seas Thousands of Chickens Ducks and Proud White Parrots. No other woman are up here on the Top deck of the 3rd Class. there is a Window at one end that look doun on the big cook stove where all 1st and 2nd & 3rd class meals are cooked and I get on my knees and Touch one of the Philipines cooks and tell him what to pass up to me some times its of the most simples and again the choucis. just how I feel and They are so delighted to serve me it is a free for all fight.

I spent a delightful month in Manila before I left for this Southern Cross Cruise. but I wouldnt care to live there. I admire the women for their modisty they are the nicest that you can find in any Part of the World and their education are Foriegn with other nations govering. the Black wool tights are hanging from a rope on one of the life Boats I shall keep them until I am in the land of Eternal Shin.

.   .   .   .   .   .

April 19.
S.S. President Lincoln.

We are just half way between Japan and Honolulu my geting off place. I made up my mind to get to Japan to see the cherry blossoms so I left the Philipines on April 6 it being a little late for the Cherry Blossom I just bought a ticket through to China and return to

Honolulu. we had two days at Hong Kong not being a lover of Hong Kong I spent the time around the horbor jumping from one Chinese home tug boat to another I made it ever so interesting for the Chinese Familys. There were a Big French Steamer came in and I went aboad to visit and a Big Dutch steamer so I was a buisy one.

At night when Hong Kong are so pretty with the light on the high mountain side I went to my favorite Roof Garden to enjoy the tea the Chinese people and the lights of the City. We had a four day run up to Shanghai and I had a pleasant round of all my favorite Places one the Sincer Roof Garden where I enjoy the many Pretty Chinese Girls and Handsome men Me with a snapy eye for flirting.

I enjoyed the day at Kobe but the hard rain had destroyed most of the cherry Blossoms but the streets were gay with streamers and all the Tea rooms filled with Cherry trees planted in large tubs. But it was Tokyo that I had my mind on as I knew just where to go and I lost no time taking the train for Uneo Park the Blossoms was still beautiful and I was in hopes I might miss the Boat it was all so enjoyable. the arches lights and Cherry Trees made everything well worth a visit.

But I am glad I have my through ticket to Honolulu as I'll have some money left when I get there. I didnt go to Java and Siam because They sell only 1st Class to European women and there were no oriental line. On the High Sea are like on land this Steamer is a perfect home to me. So many delightful things passes each day. I put on a full short skirt and sweter my little black cloth Chinese slippers and a silk handkerchief to tie down my hair then I skip all over the deck like a sea guele. and The Sailors sure does enjoy looking at me and each one like to get a word with me. They are so big and young and so many funny things happen. The Chinese help are not any to kind to the Philipines so to my greatest pleasure I fight their battles. Every one seem to enjoy it and even the Irish Steward come into my Cabin to see what happen to me if I dont come out. On a very rough day when the Philippine Boys were sea sick I did the cooking and they all laugh to see me in the big Kitchen with all the Chinese not saying a word but cuting up the chicken fixing the vegetables the chief cook would say give her what she like and them that couldnt get into the kitchen peeped in the door or port-holes. I had a big pot of wonderful stewed chicken with onions celery tomatoes and mushrooms. I had on my bright Pink apron and a large bright red silk Hand-kerchief on my hair and the cooks was captured with these colors. Sun. and Thurs. are the chicken days.

April 23.

Well Wed April 24 will end my Plannes of 10 years ago and They have been far more beautiful and ples-anter than I had any thought of. How well we can carry out our plannes if its just yourself. I'll have to go out to get a job though against my will as I have not much left of my savings but I do not need to save for cold days and I need only to eat and a shelter. So a half time place will pay for that. Perhaps with what I have left I can begin paying on a little future nest in Hawaii and it will be a pleasure to look forward just as it have been a pleasure traveling. I hope it will come as easy as my traveling have but if it gives me any drudgery or displeasure then I do not want a nest.

May 9, 1935

I just awoke from a nap here on Waikiki Beach its very delightful to watch the rows of surf and the numbous of riders I had a wonderful time the first 5 days I went to a real Hawaiian Picnice before noon we had Hulu dancing by the best singers and dancers then a Hawaiian feed Barbecure pigs steamed sweet potatoes cup cakes and punch. afternoon Baseball then a great time with singing contest we laughed so head had to stretch out on the grass.

I found the room rent and food very high and par bon so went out to get a job although against my will. When I went to the American Y.W.C.A. the Lady in charge of the Employment said why did you come here. I advise you to go back as the white People here want only Japanese help Well when I got through talking to her She thought very different as if any nation can keep me

from getting a job and the Kind and Place and price
I want. I found a place just beyound Dimond Head as
much like Cap d'Antibes if it had been made to order
it was the one thing I was more anxious to get so that
I wouldn't feel lonely for the beautiful soroundings
that I had left in France.

I am with an American Lieut. and his wife He is on a
Submarine and left yesterday for 3 weeks of war just
as though they were out after enimes. They will be
under water 6 days at a time the Entire Fleet are on its
way to the Hawaiian waters and They must Scout them
the best they can as They know not where They will
arrive. and its all because They expect war some day
not to far off.

The Lieut. wife are more than glad to have me and
many of Her Friends enver Her. This is a perfect job
for me as They do not have company more than twice
a month and I have an understanding with the Lady
when they have more than 4 in She would have some
one to do the cooking and she said the important part
is that I take care of Them so beautiful and the House.

July 9.

This house are one of the 3 that are the highest upon the
frount of Dimond Head and for that reason have 5 diffrent Terraces on 3 sides all with a delightful View. I
enjoy all the Terraces both by day and night often I
sleep part of the night on which ever one that suite my

fancy. I have one of the large navy gray blankets in my room and roll up in it with a white pillow under my head. As the tempture changes every minute or 2 cool warm and cold I must through off or pull up the blanket but it is so clean in this country and nothing to crall over you only a little water bug if you are near water.

My bed room are very neatly furnished with a most refreshing view of bright flowers trees of bright flowers and a pipia fruit tree banna tree and another fruit tree that have a fruit that are much liked in Cuba as a drink The Mr. and Mrs. didnt know what it was and let it rot until I came. now they cannot get enough.

I painted the floor a dark green and sometime when I come in from the lawn I forget to remove my Japanese shoes. Every A.M. I go out and gather Hibiscus of several shades for the beautiful house before the Sun get over the creator. the Sun rises over Cocoanut Head mts. and shines right in my window.

I am right in the Playgrowns of Waikiki in 3 blocks of the Sea and two of the Picnice Growns Polo Growns Tennis Court & Band Park. Every Friday evening I go to one of the high class Hula Schools to see the studient dance its free and just beyound a large open air pavillion for dancing and that is the only thing I miss from old Antibes for here its only the couples dancing instead of a Family gatheren of Grandma and all dancing. And going from one café to the other meeting friends having a little glass of wine but more to be with friends and have fun dancing. But I have many other thing to take its place the Change of going to Chinese gatherns, Japanese, then Hawaiians and when I feel Spanish There are the Potegeise all ways on Saint Days They have some kind of Fête. This is the most wonderful part of the World and now that I have about finnish my travellers I feel very happy to have choosed this lovely part of the World.

I can swim and have the sand and large brown rocks and the long stretch of cocoanuts trees. as I write this my mind travelle to Zeurich Switzerlan Zufolo Iseral Philistine Sweden and Madras, Ceylon and Smiling faces stands out before me.

I say good morning and eat a nice Pineapple the sweetest that grown The Birds are awaken I'll soon have to dress.

EPILOGUE

NOW

That cheque from the Atlantic Monthly for my article gave joy. I got it on a Sat. and gave up my weekly job. This is what I am during with the money as I want to enjoy every penny. I had a Tent made to order of course This was my plannes before I left Cap D'Antibes so they have been carried out perfect.

Then I went around Waikiki looking for a privat Yard to Put my Tent So that I could be in a privat Place yet free good and cheap. I asked several just to see no one Knew of any place but I was only Testing that alway give encouragement. I choosed the best from several right here at Waikiki in the front Lot of a nice Japanese Family They have a Cottage in the rear and the Show bath and W.C. are in the Yard and I am right at the front gate so do not trouble any one freedom is my main point.

My grown for my Tent cost $2.50 a month and am in the best neighbor hood in frount is the Beautiful perfect Hawaiain St. Augustine Church with its large yard. Trees bright flouers. all the time I alway long to live in the Showad of a Catholic Church not a Protstant that

315

look alway like a Jail as They open it only on Sundays. At night Waikiki is more gay and beautiful than in the City and in a half block is a nice resturant with my Kind of Wholesome food fresh daily meals from 15 cents to 35. and there are two places Where I get the best ice cream. just back of me are the Beautiful Hawaiain Village so I get plenty Hula musice and dancing free. when there is a Ball in the Garden of the Royal Hawaiain Hotel facing the Sea we swim or wade and look right on the dancers and all the other things of Pleasure right near where I set up my Tent.

At six A.M. every morning I put on my red bathing suite rap a black flouerd Satan piece around my hips and have a swim take my soap and Towls and have my bath right there under the Show on the Beach. so I didnt need to remain at Cap D'Antibes to have a happy Home.

I meet a sweetheart just as I steped off the Pres. Lincoln and a nice sort. He have seen me just twice since because I move so fast and never trouble to tell and each time He have just by accident seen me going along with a bundle on my head at the time I make a move and so it happen when I was moving from my room to my Tent and He moved me in His car I had planed that Tent to be Taboo but the first minute in it I had to let Him Kiss me.

I had the Tent put up two days before I was ready to go in so that the Children in the neighborhood could

go in and out and enjoy it so They would watch after
it for me and They do. It was great fun there was about
25 Children the man said When you get through having your House Warming we'll finnish puting it up.
Now They never Trouble me. I had a 7 x 7 orange
Tent made just as I wanted it I had it that size so I can
take up my house and walk at any time without any
help or experinces. A fat German where I got it was
so Kind and let the Chinese Girls that Sew for him do
all the little extra work.

It have Two windows at one end and one at the other
and one pocket to stick my flouer vase it open at each
end the same way like what are used on sport shirts
instead of laped over or laced up and on Each wall
which are 4 feet are a pocket for my cloths and a strip
over the pocket for to hang a pretty bright Curtain.

I found a boy that made me a floor for a dollar but use
His Father's lumber. he lives on my street. the floor is
good but light so I can carry it on my head when I want
to move. I have a green linolien on the floor with two
small rugs I have a good army cot and a fine mattrews
made to order. a beautiful bright Chinese blanket a
good pilla bright ticken and two Sheets and one pilla
case made of outen flannel bright print. It is furnished
nothing like a home never any cloths hanging about.
it looks like a poch.

Well never in all my life have I slept so wonderful as
in my Tent the 4 holes in each of the windows where

the ropes drow up the Shade make 12 holes and when the light is out and the door and Windows closed the lights of the street shine through the holes and on to the Top of my Tent and it look just like the Stars.

I'll get a serfe boad and Take a few Hula lessons just to add gayness to that list of things the check bought. I want alway to be where wealth health youth beauty and gayness are altho I need very little for myself I just want to be in the midst of it. I have reversed the saying of Troubles are like Babies the more you nurse them the bigger They grow so I have nursed the joys. Well you have bring out your moth ball smelling cloths and no doubt feel very pleased with the world to be in a caged up Building looking out on others more caged up. I have gone through the same and how greatful I am to myself.

This is my first and only Home. Villa Petit Peep are The name of my Tent as I let my callers sit on a seat in the yard and Peep in so I gave it this True name.

after the Civil War. I told him of an old servant who had belonged to my grandfather, and who, after the emancipation, had drifted to Texas to live, but who made the long journey back to Virginia every few years to see her people, as she called my grandmother and my father. I remember our distress at learning, through a Texas paper, of her death by accidental drowning. A few months after reading of her death, she appeared, hale and hearty, wearing, as usual, her red bandanna. My father said: "Why, Aunt Silvey, we heard you were drowned." She curtsied and said: "Law, Marse William, I heerd that, too, but soon as I heerd it I knowed it wasn't so!"